CHICHESTER

A Documentary History

CHICHESTER
A Documentary History

ROY R. MORGAN

Phillimore

1992

Published by
PHILLIMORE & CO. LTD.
Shopwyke Hall, Chichester, Sussex

ISBN 0 85033 851 4

Printed in Great Britain by
CHICHESTER PRESS

This book is dedicated to
my wife, Sheila, who should
be its co-author

and to

Alec Down

LIST OF SUBSCRIBERS

CONTENTS

Page

List of maps, drawings and photographs   viii

Introduction and acknowledgements   xii

1   Topography, geology and land   1
2   Population and wealth   11
3   Health   22
4   Communications   34
5   Trade and industry up to 1700   41
6   Trade and industry from 1700 onwards   55
7   Buildings   61
8   West Street   70
9   North Street   77
10   East Street   89
11   South Street   102
12   North west quadrant   114
13   North east quadrant   128
14   South east quadrant   142
15   South west quadrant   157
16   Eastern suburbs   165
17   Outside the South gate   177
18   Western suburbs   182
19   Outside the North gate   190

Sources, notes and additional information   197
Index of names   216
General index   220

LIST OF MAPS, DRAWINGS AND PHOTOGRAPHS

Fig.		Page
1-1	Chichester – the historical setting (map)	2
1-2	The geology at Fishbourne and South Street (map) ...	3
1-3	The main property owners in 1750 (map)...	4
1-4	Land usage in 1750 (map)	5
1-5	Portfield and Guildenfield before enclosure (map) ...	6
1-6	Development outside Eastgate in the late 19th century (map)	7
1-7	Parish boundaries...	8
1-8	City Boundary changes (map)...	9
2-1	Population (graph)	11
2-2	1755 Rate – levels of assessment (map)	15
2-3	Alms and poor houses (map)	17
3-1	Market, East Street, mid 19th century	24
3-2	Remedy for cholera (pamphlet)...	25
3-3	Non-drainers (pamphlet)...	28
3-4	Cases of Fever 1896/8 (maps)	31
3-5	Burial grounds (map)	32
4-1	Roman roads (map)	34
4-2	Turnpikes and tollgates (map)	35
4-3	Canal route (map)	36
4-4	Railways (map) ... ... ··	38
4-5	Selsey Tram, a cartoon by Cynicus...	39
5-1	Malthouse	43
5-2	Location of merchants exporting malt in 1662 (map)	44
5-3	Destination of cargoes in 1614/5 and 1661/2 (maps)	45
5-4	Trades in 17th century (map)	49
5-5	Location of inns in 1604 (map)	53
5-6	Location of inns in 1670/1700 (map)	54
6-1	Location of malthouses in 1755 (map)...	56
6-2	Chichester tobacco pipe	57
7-1	Dean and Chapter properties in 1533 (map)	62
7-2	Timber framed house – constituent parts	63
7-3	Building types (map)...	69
8-1	West Street and Westgate (map)...	71
8-2	Townscape in West Street, north side	71
8-3	John Edes house	72
8-4	Townscape in West Street, south side	74
8-5	Cathedral Bell Tower...	75
8-6	Cathedral frontage, early properties (map)	76

9-1	North Street routes (map)	77
9-2	North Street, early 20th-century view	78
9-3	Central Market House before 1731	79
9-4	Prosperity in North Street	80
9-5	Dean and Chapter properties by the Cross (map) ...	81
9-6	Old houses at corner of Crane Street and North Street	82
9-7	St Peter the less Church, about 1850	84
9-8	Wheatsheaf Inn	86
9-9	St Olav's church, about 1850	87
9-10	Butter Market in 1830	88
10-1	East Street showing the Swan Inn and the conduit house in the 18th century	90
10-2	Bank plaque in East Street	90
10-3	East Street, Edney's fire in 1897	91
10-4	St Andrews in the Oxmarket church about 1850	92
10-5	2 houses East Street/Little London (plan)	93
10-6	Shippam's corner before expansion	94
10-7	Shippam's – previous use of site (map)	95
10-8	View through East Gate 1782, by Grimm	96
10-9	Eastgate Police Station	97
10-10	Corn Exchange, East Street, in mid 19th century	98
10-11	East Street, Old Punch House	100
11-1	Dean and Chapter properties in South Street, near the Cross (plan)	103
11-2	Vicars' Hall	105
11-3	Undercroft	105
11-4	Canon gate	106
11-5	Dean and Chapter properties South Street, west side (plan)	107
11-6	Townscape – theatre, bank and Regnum Club	109
11-7	Theatre site (plan)	109
11-8	King's Head public house	110
11-9	White Horse Inn, South Street	111
11-10	13th century shops (map)	113
12-1	North west quadrant (map)	115
12-2	Tower Street, the Grange – 19th century	119
12-3	Cottages at north end of Tower Street	119
12-4	Woolstaplers' site (plans)	120
12-5	Tower Street, school and Priors woolstore 1960s	121
12-6	Tower Street archaeological excavations 1970s	121
12-7	Central Girls' school (plans)	123

12-8	Slaughterhouse site, 1838 (plan)	124
12-9	Old print: from Tower Street looking south	127
12-10	Cottages, North Walls	127
13-1	North east quadrant (map)	128
13-2	Shamble Alley before demolition	129
13-3	3 St Martin's Square	131
13-4	Greyfriars, Priory Park (Guildhall)	132
13-5	Friary house of Hutchins Williams...	133
13-6	Development of St Mary's site (map)	134
13-7	St Mary's Hospital	135
13-8	St Mary's Hospital (plan)...	135
13-9	St Martin's church about 1850	136
13-10	Marks & Spencer site (map)...	137
13-11	Prince Arthur public house	140
14-1	South east quadrant development (maps)...	142
14-2	South east quadrant (map)	144
14-3	All Saints Parsonage House and White Horse Inn ...	145
14-4	All Saints' church about 1850......	146
14-5	Bottle seal	147
14-6	No. 7 North Pallant (plan)	148
14-7	9 North Pallant	149
14-8	Baffins Hall	150
14-9	East Pallant House before use as offices	151
14-10	East Pallant townscape	152
14-11	South Pallant Cottage	153
14-12	New Town – Lots offered for sale (map)	155
15-1	Cathedral in 1790...	157
15-2	South west quadrant (map)...	159
15-3	Old Treasury	161
15-4	Canon Gate and Bin Room, from Canon Lane	162
15-5	Bishop's Palace gateway...	162
16-1	Eastern suburbs (map)	166
16-2	Candlestick found in excavations	167
16-3	St Pancras Church about 1850	169
16-4	Victoria Inn, St Pancras	170
16-5	Red Lion at St James' (plan)...	171
16-6	Site of St James' Hospital......	172
16-7	Portfield Windmill	173
16-8	Farr's Court, St Pancras, 19th century	175
17-1	Plaque – Bassett 1698...	177

17-2   South suburbs (map)...   178
17-3   Railway Station before modernisation   179
17-4   Old Police Station, Southgate......   180
18-1   West suburbs (map)   183
18-2   Round church (old St Bartholomew's)...   184
18-3   Site to west of St Bartholomew's Church, 1846 (plan)   185
18-4   ”   ”   ”   ”   ”   ”   1874 (plan)   185
18-5   Brewery site 1846 (plan)...   187
18-6   Waggon and Lamb, Westgate   188
19-1   North suburbs (map)...   190
19-2   Development outside Northgate (map)...   192
19-3   Octagon Cottage   193
19-4   North Lodge   193
19-5   Infirmary   194
19-6   Cawley's Almshouses (workhouse)...   195
19-7   Cottage, College Road   196

Fig. 3-2 by courtesy of Avon County Library
Figs. 8-2, 8-4, 8-5, 9-3, 9-8, 10-9, 11-2, 11-3, 11-6, 14-10, 14-11
are by Alex Bunn.
Figs. 8-3, 9-10, 10-6, 11-8, 11-9, 13-3, 13-4, 14-8 are by Gerald Kirrage.
The drawings of Churches were made by Adelaide B. Tracey in
1846-1857 (WSRO PD 2011).
Fig. 14-5 was originally published in Chichester Excavations Vol. 2
(drawing by David S. Neal) and is reproduced by permission
of Alec Down.
Figs. 1-3 and 1-4 were originally drawn by John Piper from material
provided by the author, and appeared in Chichester Excavations Vol. 3.

1   Aerial view of Chichester, 1975   Frontispiece

2   The Market Cross at Chichester, painted by
            Henry Pether, 19th century   Dust jacket

Photographs 1, Fig. 12-7 and Fig. 16-4 are reproduced by courtesy of
The News, Portsmouth; 2 by kind permission of Sotheby's; Fig. 10-1
by Beaver Photographic and Fig. 3-1, Fig. 10-3, Fig. 10-11, Fig. 12-3,
Fig. 13-2, Fig. 14-3, Fig. 14-7, Fig. 15-4, Fig. 16-6, Fig. 18-6, Fig. 9-2 and
Fig. 14-9 with the permission of the County Archivist, West Sussex. Nos.
Fig. 9-6, Fig. 12-2 and Fig. 17-3 appeared in the Chichester Papers series.

INTRODUCTION

All local history builds upon the work of previous researchers. Chichester has been fortunate in receiving the attention of dedicated students who have translated, interpreted and catalogued chartularies and other original source material, and published it. These pioneers included W.D. Peckham, Francis Steer, W.H. Godfrey, Lindsay Fleming, A. Ballard and John E. Ray.

Each stage of work produces a new plateau. Students such as myself have been able to draw on this early work, to combine it with unpublished material and to further interpret it so as to provide a new plateau.

The West Sussex Record Office, firstly under Francis Steer and latterly Patricia Gill, has been responsible for harnessing present day amateur effort, whilst continuing advanced professional research. Modern amateurs working on Chichester material have included W. Thumwood, M. Cutten, Brig. Viner, B. Vick, N. Pilbeam and C. Searle.

The early pioneers and the more recent tillers of the soil have had little time to collate their work into topographical order. Thus when the intensive archaeological excavations commenced in the city in 1968 there was no cohesive organisation of reference material on the medieval and post-medieval layers which excavators would inevitably expose, peel off and destroy on their way down to the Roman levels. It is to the eternal credit of the then Director of Excavations, Alec Down, FSA, that he quickly set up the Chichester Documentary Research Group in 1969, with advice from Martin Biddle and Derek Keen of the Winchester Archaeological Unit. The Group started work with a dozen members; over the first five years these dwindled to six, and for the last ten years my wife Sheila and I have been the main regular researchers.

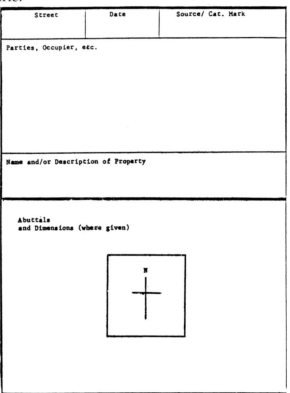

The front and back of an index card actual size 6" x 4" (15cm x 10.5cm).

Our task has been to study every source relating to property, land and trade - leases, rentals, minutes, tax lists, maps, conveyances, wills, inventories, port books and printed material. Index cards (see illustration) have been used to record all source material and 24,000 have been used. The cards have been sorted into streets and ultimately individual plots or sites. This simple statement covers 20 years of handling a three-dimensional jig-saw, involving ever-changing ownership, occupation, trades, buildings and land usage.

Only recently has it been possible to develop the mass of material on trades and occupations and this has now led to a separate card index of 2,000 names for 17th-century trades.

So now we have been able to trace, topographically, the history of sites, streets and development and trade patterns, to put the flesh on the bones.

Chichester is well endowed with property records for ecclesiastically owned sites. As abuttals are often identified, a significant part of the city can be filled in using these sites as 'markers'. The freehold sites which remain are more sketchy in their provenance. Interested firms of solicitors, notably Rapers, Arnold, Cooper and Tomkins, and Blaker and Peters, have deposited a vast collection of early material which has been examined. For the rest of the blank spaces official records have had to be used intensively – tax records, censuses, maps, depositions, also trade directories and newspapers. Many freehold deeds may still be in private and legal hands: many have been destroyed or made into lampshades. Thus some sites, in the chapters which follow, have not been as fully described as their antiquity may seem to commend.

Generally when owners have been approached for a sight of their deeds they have been very helpful and I would like to mention in this context: Marks & Spencer, Woolworths, Army & Navy, W.H.Smiths, Shippams, Co-op, Millers (Guildhall Street), Christopher Purchase, Ind Coop and Friary Meux, Victoria Wine Co., Waitrose, Post Office, Thomas Eggar & Son, West Sussex County Council, Chichester City and District Councils, Mrs. R. Purchase, Stanley Roth, A. Benn, Canon Parkes, M.H. Pigott, P. Coombes, Ernest Shippam, Mr. and Miss Allen, Louis Smith, Paul and Mary Simmons and R.G. Davis-Poynter.

Gaps filled after this book has been published will be added to the card index which will eventually be deposited in the West Sussex Record Office.

It is a chastening thought that of the thousands of people who have walked across the Chichester stage only a relative few have left a mark, because they owned, leased or rented property, had trades, became wealthy or committed crimes. The rest might never have been.

Acknowledgements:

The Bishop and the Dean for permission to use all sources relating to diocesan property; Canon Catchpole.

The County Archivist, Patricia Gill, for her enthusiasm and constant support; and all her staff, who have been magnificent. I must single out Alison and Tim McCann who were appointed to be the Documentary Research Group mentors and have given unflagging support, guidance and friendship.

The Public Record Office for permission to use their records for publication and for assistance with research.

The early members of the Documentary Research Group – B. Bird, J. Corah, R.D. France, Mr. and Mrs. Durrell, Janet Blackman, Pat Lee, Mrs. E.L. Palmer and Mr. D.A. Langdon.

Alec Down, Director of Excavations until 1985, for his encouragement and loyalty and for his use of the researches which made it worth while. He above all has dominated the historical study of Chichester for 30 years.

Noel Osborne, Editorial Director of Phillimores, who has given guidance from the earliest stages.

My daughter, Patricia, for her assistance with captions, photography and source material; my friends Alex Bunn and Gerald Kirrage for help with drawings.

For help in many ways: Kathleen Stanford, Rob Harmer, Mervyn Cutten, Norma Pilbeam, Emlyn Thomas, Peter Wilkinson, Alan Readman, Michael Moore, Peter Taylor, Marjorie Hallam and Leslie Holden.

And above all my wife Sheila, who has been involved throughout; has done half the research, all the typing, and has kept my feet where they belong – on the ground.

The following organisations have contributed financially and made the publication of this book possible:

Marks & Spencer plc
West Sussex County Council
Thomas Eggar Verrall Bowles
Stride & Son

CHAPTER 1

TOPOGRAPHY, GEOLOGY AND LAND

Why was Chichester established where it is? Why, indeed, is any town where it is?

Close examination invariably shows that it is a matter of defence, water supply, communications, food supply, climate and building materials. Which elements predominate depend on the date of foundation.

Chichester is of Roman origin, on a flat plain near the sea, with a good food-growing hinterland. Communications by sea were easy, and the Romans were good road builders. There never was a problem over water; the chalk Downs are a great sponge which never dries up.

The Romans had little difficulty finding building materials. They used dressed stone, brick, flint, tile, chalk and timber.

Defence turned out not to be an issue for the Romans, but the defensibility of the first settlement would have loomed large when its position was chosen.

As the Dark Ages became less dark there was still the sufficient nucleus of a town to ensure that Chichester could survive, although for 600 years its road communications did not match those of the Romans. There was abundant timber to compensate for the eclipsed art of brick-making.

Then the Cathedral moved from Selsey and progress to dominant town status was irresistible.

As will be seen later, Chichester, as a market town, could provide the facilities for marketing of grain and cattle and for excesses to be exported through its port: this compensated for, and possibly perpetuated the indifferent roads.

Agriculture and Soils

To the north is the chalk and the Downs. The town is on sand and gravel, with clay beneath. This has produced the best of worlds – good grazing for sheep, south facing slopes and heavy soils for crops, and sunshine for market gardening.

Earthquakes[1]

These have been recorded in Chichester on many dates: 1553, 1638 (great damage), 1707, 1734 (two), 1750 (four), 1811, 1814, 1821, 1824, 1833 (three), 1834 (two), 1835 (two), 1865.

One fault runs from Guildford to a point just east of Chichester, and the other through South Street to the Isle of Wight. Faults were created 35 million years ago when the chalk Downs were formed.

1

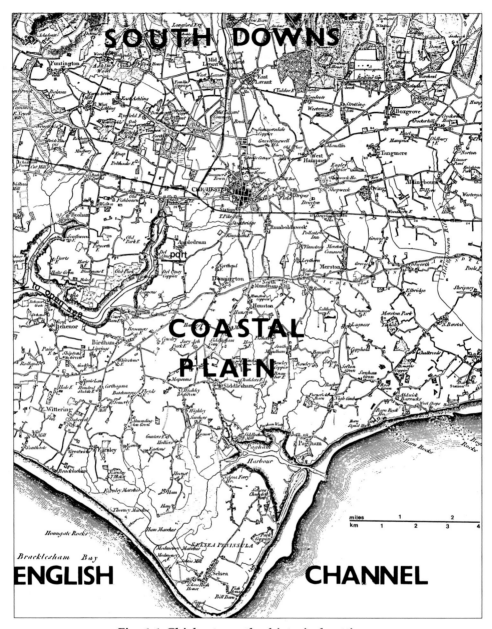

Fig. 1-1 Chichester – the historical setting

This map is based on the first one-inch Ordnance Survey. It shows the city in its relationship to the sea, the harbour, the Downs and countryside.

Land Ownership

The people of Chichester owe a great deal to Henry VIII. In or around 1550, he, and his successors dissolved the Black and Grey Friars, the Chantries

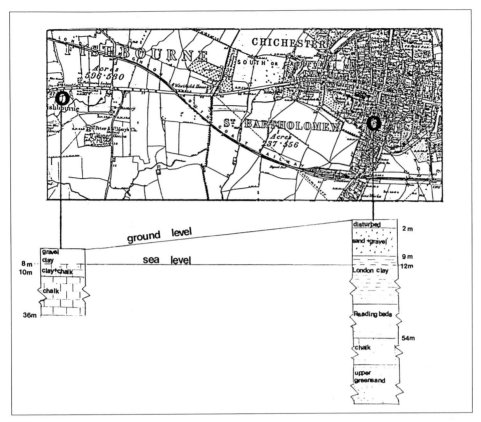

Fig. l-2 The Geology at Fishbourne[2] and South Street[3]

and the Guild of St George, and in so doing freed the large areas of the city held by them into more open ownership. The property involved was:[4]

Blackfriars:

the area now known as St John's Street and New Town.

Greyfriars:

now Priory Park

Guild of St George:

2 properties in St Martin's, 6 in North Street, 1 in Chapel Street, 1 in East Street, 4 in West Street, 1 outside Eastgate, 4 outside Southgate and lands outside Northgate (Penny Acre, Horse-down) and in Portfield and Guildenfield – in all over 30 individual properties of which about half were within the walls.

Chantries in the Cathedral (Mortimer, John Arundel, Earl of Arundel, William Close, Ralph Randall): lands outside Westgate and tenements in North Street, South Street, West Street and elsewhere.

These lands and properties had been amassed in the previous 300 years or so. In the case of the Friars and the Chantries much of the land had come via legacies from devout and apprehensive lay people who sought a way to the salvation of their souls. The donors were often men who had acquired wealth through hard business dealings; many of the bequests were tied to the saying of obits and the singing of masses for the souls of the departed, and were to cease if the service ceased.

The Guild of St George had been empowered to acquire lands for the maintenance of a chaplain within the Cathedral.

In addition the Cathedral and Churches were also taking up space. The Cathedral, started in the 11th century, soon had, as its endowment, the whole of the south-west quadrant. The other churches within the walls were all built by the 13th century:

South east quadrant -

St Mary in Foro, All Saints and St Andrew in the Pallant.

North east quadrant -

St Olav, St Martin's, St Peter the Less, St Peter Sub Castro, and St Andrew Oxmarket.

The Blackfriars acquired their site in several parcels in the 13th century; the Greyfriars moved from St Martin's Lane to the Castle site also in that century, but St Mary's Hospital moved in to fill the vacuum and has remained there ever since.

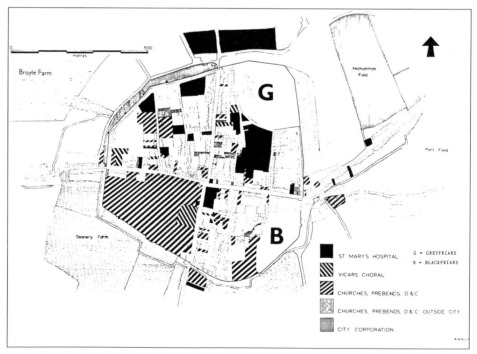

Fig. 1-3 Map showing main property owners in 1750

Fig. 1-3 shows the ownership position in 1750. Before the Dissolution nearly 60% of the land within the walls was in religious ownership.

Like the Friars, the Dean and Chapter and St Mary's had acquired many of their scattered holdings from legacies. The Bishop owned a large estate to the north and west, and also valuable lands in London's Chancery Lane (where a lane called 'Chichester Rents' can still be seen near the Public Record Office). The Dean and Prebends held large areas of land to the south, west and east of the city.

Ownership of land by the lay population and commerce was confined mainly to main street frontages, half the north east quadrant and the Pallant.

With the dissolution of the monasteries a slow process of change in ownership began.

The Court of Augmentations[4] had allowed the City to acquire the considerable properties of the Guild of St George for £100. The valuable Blackfriars site went into private ownership[4] and a mansion house was built on its East Street frontage; it remained so until 1809 when the site was sold for building plots,[5] the street pattern in so-called 'New Town' emerged, and another new church (St John's) was built. The Greyfriars site also went into private ownership and a house was built on the land; eventually the land was given to the City by the Duke of Richmond in 1918.

St Mary's retained their land as it was endowed for a specific purpose of maintaining the poor of the Hospital and not for religious purposes.

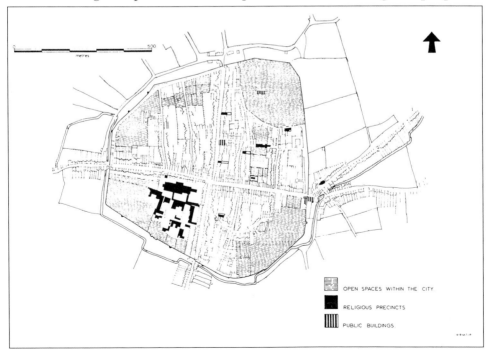

Fig. 1-4 Land usage in 1750

The Hospital held its scattered holdings intact until the late 19th century when some were sold.

The City held much of its land until recently but has been much more flexible in its buying and selling policies than the other bodies.

In the south west quadrant the frontages of West and South Streets were leased out by the Dean and Chapter and Vicars' Choral.

By 1750 land in public and religious ownership within the walls was below 50%.

Land Usage

Fig. 1-4 shows land usage in 1750. In the medieval period the north west quadrant had been the empty quarter, mainly gardens and barns.

Outside the city walls it is helpful to look at areas in relation to the four gates.

1. North Gate.

This was the last area to be developed. It was originally woodland – the Broyle – land which belonged to the King, and subsequently much of it was used as large farming units. In Chapter 19 two maps (Figs. 19-1 and 2) show the fields and the 19th-century development.

2. West Gate.

The suburb was developed from the 13th century and partly destroyed

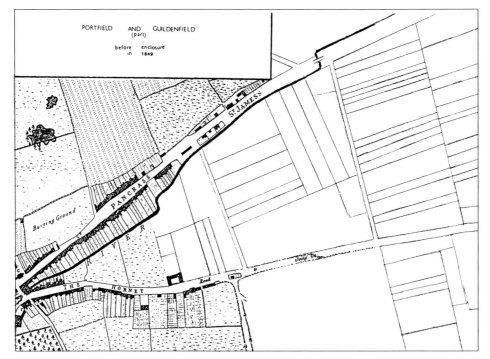

Fig. l-5 This is based on the Gardner Map of 1769 and shows some of the pre-enclosure field strips

in the Civil War. The Orchard Street area and around what is now Avenue de Chartres was used for farming until the 19th century. This is shown in the map, Fig. 18-1.
3. South Gate.

This area was almost entirely used for farming, except for some ribbon development just outside the gate, until the last two centuries when it was

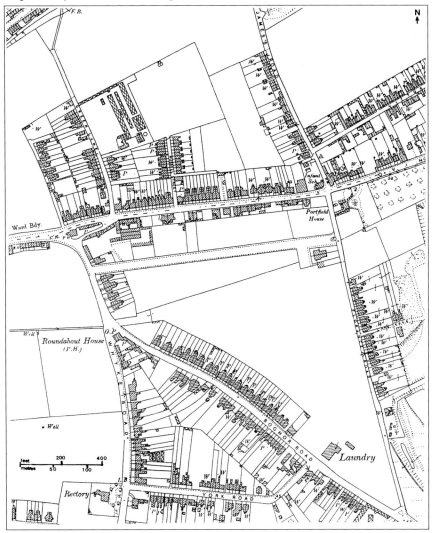

Fig. l-6 The 1877 Ordnance Survey Map showing the building development which had taken place after the enclosures by the late l9th century

the focus of transportation changes – see Fig. 17-1 – the turnpike to Dell Quay, the canal and Basin Road; the cattle market and Market Avenue; the railway and the gas works and finally the Avenue de Chartres by-pass.

4. East Gate.

This suburb developed very early and appropriately had its own church, St Pancras, which was demolished in the Civil War (1642) and rebuilt in 1750/1. Needlemaking and other industry was included in the built-up area near the walls. Further out were the large fields: Portfield and Guildenfield, an ancient open-field strip system of 188 acres which survived to 1849 outside the East Gate.[6] (See Fig. 1-5.)

The 93 strips, many of them as little as an acre, were divided among 12 landowners and frequently sub-let. The earliest reference to the names Portfield and Guildenfield are in the 12th century. There is some doubt about

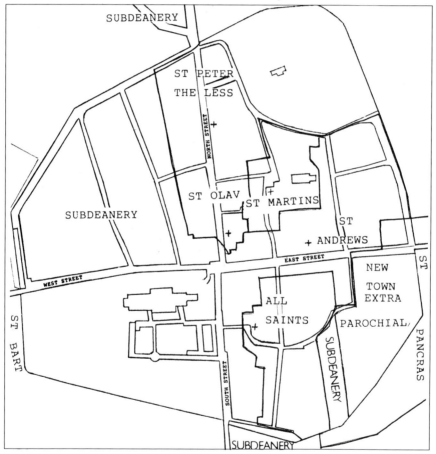

Fig. l-7 The old parish boundaries

the origin of the names; the word 'Guild' suggests ownership of the Guild merchants, but whilst it is certain that the lands of the Guild of St George were purchased by the City in 1548/9, only a small part of Guildenfield (5 acres out of 27) was subsequently in City hands. 'Port' in Old English means 'a market'; in Latin 'portus' means 'a harbour', and 'porta' 'a gate'. The most

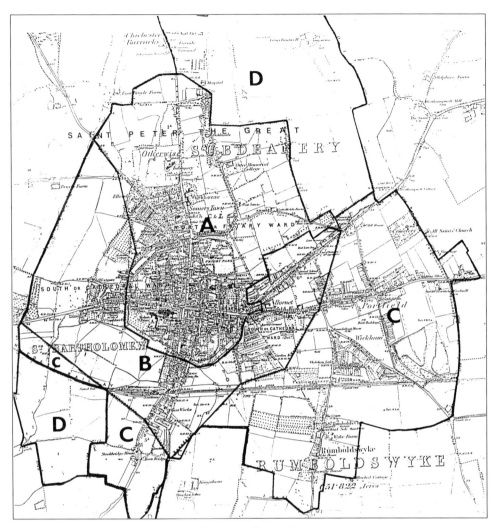

Fig. 1-8 Boundary changes

likely explanation is the simplest – a field near the gate. What is certain is that the fields were open and that few landowners or tenants had two adjoining strips. By the time of the Enclosure virtually the whole of the land was arable; small plots for pasture, with problems of fencing and economics, were unthinkable.

Other trends were emerging in this area which dictated the need to move to larger units: gravel working and the demands for housing. After enclosure the City owned over 26 acres in 6 plots, but by 1862 all except 3 acres had been sold, and this last amount was used as the cemetery.

The Enclosure Award was made in 1847 and implemented 2 years later. In total the ownership remained the same, and the area of holdings also, but the total number of plots was reduced to around 30 and most of the new allotments became economically viable units.

Boundaries

Parish boundaries everywhere appear to have little reason and so it is in Chichester. Parish areas vary from the minute, huddled around parish churches such as St Olav, and the vast residual areas of Subdeanery (St Peter the Great).

Fig. 1-8 shows the widening of the City's jurisdiction. The inner line A is the boundary which had been unchanged since the 13th century.[7] Next come the changes – area B – proposed in 1831.[8] In the application to Parliament the condition of the City was lauded as 'well built, lighted, watered and drained' (not exactly true – see Chapter 3). The principal streets were described as spacious with many large houses. The area then to be included was St Bartholomew, St Pancras (outer) and the Hornet. They were added in 1837.

A further extension in 1893 – area C – added Portfield, Wickham, Rumboldswick and St James[9] to enable the City and the Parliamentary constituency to coincide. Finally in 1895 area D was added.

CHAPTER 2

POPULATION AND WEALTH

Population Estimates

Estimating population before 1801 is notoriously hazardous and is likely to remain so until there is general agreement on definitive multipliers for use with other criteria (e.g. number of houses, number of males over 15). The graph which follows is the best that can be achieved at present. In the sources at the end of the book the bases of the multipliers used are given, and the authorities for such are quoted.

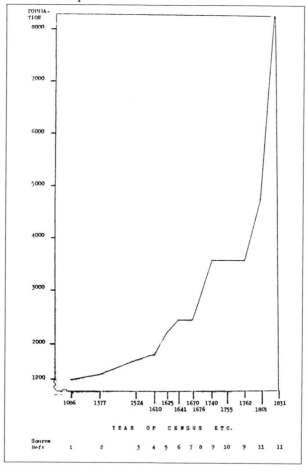

Fig. 2-1 Estimates of Population

There were no significant boundary changes until 1837. Where possible the suburbs have been included in Fig. 2-1 although they did not all come within the city until the 19th century.

The Rich and the Poor

To find out how the available cake was shared out we can examine tax lists before 1850: in 1851 the census tells us how every breadwinner earned his bread and something about lodgers and servants.

The earliest taxes were in the Lay Subsidy Rolls of 1295, 1524 and 1586-1638 and the Poll Tax of 1380.[12] The later rolls identify streets, and so give an idea of which streets were more or less paved with gold.

The Lay Subsidy figures for 1524 are useful in providing a detailed return of those liable to tax. Like all taxes based on income (as opposed to real property) the possibilities for fraud were well exploited by those being plundered, and the taxpayer eventually achieved ascendancy over the tax collector, thereby depriving economic history students of a useful series of data. Those with wages of under £1 a year or goods of less than £2 were, not surprisingly, exempt. This indigenous sector has been estimated at one-third of those assessed. In Chichester[12] the tax distribution was:

Assessed on	% of those taxable	No. of taxpayers	Description
Wages £1 per annum	32	95	Labourers
Goods/wages £2	33	101	Small craftsmen, husbandmen
£3 – 9	21	64	Lower middle class
£10 – 19	7	21	Substantial middle class
£20 – 39	4	12 }	
		}	Affluent
£40 +	3	8 }	
	100	301	

Chichester ranks as the wealthiest town in Sussex,[13] but nationally was not in the top 30[14] in 1524.

Ranking	Town	Yield £	Population
1	Norwich	1,704	12,000 +
5	Exeter	855	8,000
6	Salisbury	852	8,000
17	Gloucester	307	4,000
23	Southampton	224	
26	Shrewsbury	220	4,000
36	Chichester	138	1,600
37	Winchester	132	

Taken street by street the figures show:

	1524[12]			1586/7[15]		
	No. of Assessments	Average Tax paid p. a.		No. of Assessments	Average Tax paid p. a.	
		s.	d.		s.	d.
East Street (with St Martin's Lane & Little London)	74	4.	6.	20	13.	0.[B]
North Street	85	4.	5.	15	12.	10.
West Street (& Lanes)	64	6.	0.[A]	14	14.	3.[C]
Pallant	41	2.	5.	7	10.	2.
South Street	37	1.	7.	14	11.	9.
	301	4.	4.	70	12.	8.

A or 2s. 10d. (14p) if one very large taxpayer is excluded
B or 10s.   (50p)   "   "   "   "   "   "
C or "   "   "   "   "   "   "   "

With these large payers excluded North Street emerges as the consistently most affluent street.

This question of affluence must be put in perspective. The 1524 tax
excludes perhaps 150 persons earning less than £1 a *year*. A man earning £1
paid 4d. (2p) of it in tax. Inflation was very bad in Tudor times. If the year
1501 is taken as a 100, the price index reached 437 by about 1600, but wages
did not rise proportionately. In 1586 a mason might earn 6s. 5d. (32p) a
week.[16]

Hearth Tax as an indicator of wealth

Hearth Tax was imposed in 1662 at a rate of 2s. (10p) for every hearth
and stove. Exemptions were given 'by reason of poverty or the smallness of
his estate', or to those who were already exempt from Church and Poor Rate,
or whose house had an annual value of less than 20s.

As a guide to the relative wealth between one house and another, one
street and the next, one town and another, it is of considerable use, as long
as due allowance is made for evasion caused by its unpopularity. The tax
involved inspection of homes by constables who might well observe a plethora
of illegal or undesirable activities[17] which made deceit even more attractive.
Nevertheless avoidance was probably on a constant scale within an area.

Pepys records in his diary 'They clamour against the Chimney money
and say they will not pay it without force.'[18] It was abandoned in 1689.

As a guide, one or two hearths indicate a humble dwelling; conversely
seven or more suggest affluence, with hearths in each room, sources of fuel
and servants to tend the fires.

The Hearth Tax list for 1670 has been preserved at the Public Record
Office[19] and is partially reproduced in *SAC 24* where the editor, W.D. Cooper,
comments that the record is so specific that the houses should be identifiable.

The author of the present book has worked out how the street order has been made and most properties have now been identified.

The list gives occupiers, not landlords. For Chichester the poor are listed even though exempt.

An analysis of the Hearth Tax shows:

Street	No. of houses	No. of poor ass-essments	Average hearths per house	Spread poor 1-2	modest 3-6	affluent 7-12	13+
Close	22	-	5.77	6	10	5	1[A]
West Street	77	-	4.37	29	34	10	4[B]
Pallant	46	-	4.00	22	16	8	-
North Street	96	5	3.92	37	45	13	1[C]
East Street	69	6	3.85	22	38	9	_[D]
St Martin's/Lion St.	25	5	3.44	10	14	1	-
Little London	12	-	3.33	6	5	1	-
South Street	85	30	3.30	55	22	6	2[E]
Chapel Street	19	-	2.47	12	7	-	-
Tower Street	10	-	2.20	8	2	-	-
Within walls	461	46	3.82	207	193	53	8
St Pancras[20]	38	20	2.58	23	14	1	_[F]
Westgate[21]	31	6	3.71	10	17	4	-
Total	530	72	3.72	240	224	58	8
			%:	45	42	11	2

Comparison with[22]

		poor	modest	affluent
	Lewes	49	39	12
	Rye	64	32	4
	Midhurst	58	33	9

Notes: A The Bishop-25
       B Bragg (Dolphin)-23; Henry Peckham-13; Dr. Dobell-13; Major Hurst-13.
       C William Baldwyn-12
       D Swan Inn-12
       E John Bing-12; Edward Hobjohn-14
       F Inn (William Hudson)-11

Conclusion: Chichester had a lower proportion of poor and a higher proportion of modest dwellings than the three other Sussex towns. If the Close and the Dolphin in West Street are excluded then the Pallant and North Street emerge as the areas with the highest average number of hearths.

Poor Rates

Rates provide another indicator of relative wealth. Being a tax on property, rates are very difficult to avoid, which doubtless was a prime cause of the clamour for their removal. First established in 1601, it became the practice for parishes to raise money for the relief of their poor through overseers' and churchwardens' rates.

In 1755 these rates were consolidated in Chichester[23] and for the first time the whole city was assessed on a uniform basis. This provides a firm measure of the wealth of individuals using their properties as a mirror, and of the relative wealth of various parts of the city. For over 1,100 properties a rate income of £200 was produced for the upkeep of the Northgate almshouses. It is significant that newcomers had to produce security to show that they were not likely to be a charge on the parish and would be able to pay their rates.

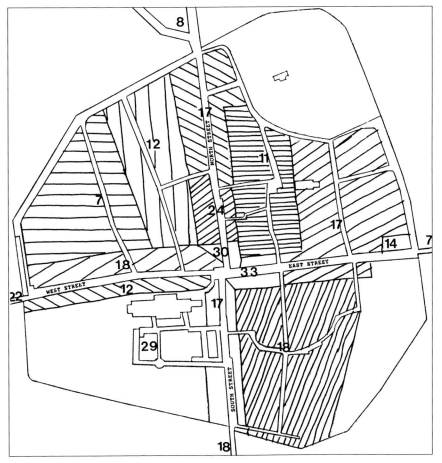

Fig. 2-2 1755 Rate

The charges per property are plotted here with the amounts converted into decimal pence.

If the number of assessments is divided into the rate levied, and if poor are excluded, the highest valued properties are:

	s.	d.
East Street near the Cross	6	7
North Street near the Cross	6	0
The Close	5	10
North Street, next segment to Crane Street	4	9

And the lowest are:

	s.	d.
Outside Northgate	1	7
St Pancras (outside city)	1	6
Tower Street	1	5
North Walls	1	5

– And the poor. How were they cared for?

Cawley's Almshouses were founded in 1625 as the Hospital of St Bartholomew for the maintenance of 12 decayed tradesmen.[24] In 1753 the building became the united workhouse for all the parishes. 30 guardians were appointed and the buildings repaired. Finance came from the new poor rate.

Before 1753 every parish had its own poor house. For example St Martin's had St George's House, which was a poor house until about 1744 when it was found to be ruinous. The first record is in 1492 (see Chapter 13). St Peter the Great had a house in Tower Street (opposite the Library).

In the 16th century, particularly, many wealthy wills contained legacies to the poor of various parishes, and invariably to the one in which the deceased died.

Other establishments concerned with the needy were:

St Mary's Hospital, which had vast endowments. The Charity Commissioners' investigation of 1815/39 lists over four pages of property held, including about 100 houses and much land in Chichester and suburbs, and other land at Eartham, New Shoreham and Birdham, mainly derived from legacies in the 13th century.[25]

St Mary in Foro of the 13th century, at the junction of East and South Streets.

St James' Hospital – founded before the reign of Henry II, mainly for lepers. In 1596 it had 13 inmates (5 male, 8 female) all cripples, idiots or impotents. It was supported by property in East Row, St Pancras and Colworth and in earlier centuries by bequests. By 1618 the building had almost completely fallen down.[25]

The poor of Rumboldswhyke were provided for by Elizabeth Gubbett, who bequeathed £20 in 1617 with which her overseers and executors bought a house in Tower Street to provide an annuity.[26]

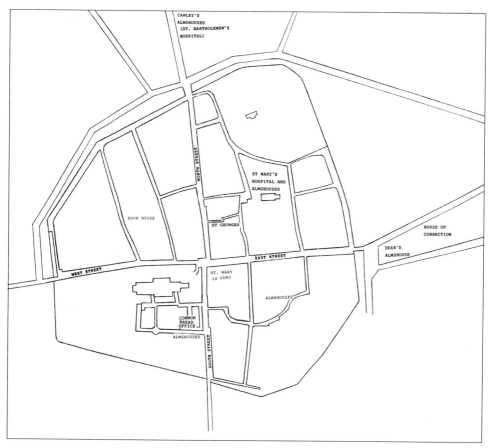

Fig. 2-3 Almshouses and poor houses

There were almshouses in Canongate[27] in the 16th century and six almshouses in the Hornet, which were unoccupied in 1786, being dilapidated and used as sheds. The almshouses were rebuilt and Dear's Charity provided £1,000 for the work. There were almshouses on the south side of the Hornet in Oving Parish in 1848.

There was a House of Correction in St Pancras in 1647. The County Quarter Sessions sent Mary Nightingale, who had a bastard child, there in 1649. Between 1612 and 1695 there are a number of references to burials from the House of Correction, the Bridewell and the almshouses in St Pancras.[28]

Then there was the Common Bread, or 'Dole Bread'. There is mention of the dole in the 12th century. Bishop Hillary is credited with its inception from estates at West Dean for the distribution to clergy and the poor. By 1718 it was clearly laid down that the person appointed to the Office of Baking should receive all wheat, corn and grain due to the Dean and Chapter and from this should deliver to the Bin Room in Canon Lane bread for the use of the officers of the Cathedral, and in addition, for the distribution to the poor, 42 casts of bread each of 22 ozs. It is a matter of record that there was a queue waiting to go on the Bread Dole List. [29] In 1872, by which time money had replaced loaves, the system started to be wound down.

The 1851 Census in Chichester[30]

The first official national census was taken in 1801, but the first one in some detail was in 1851. The totals for England and Wales at ten-yearly intervals from 1801-1901, with those for Chichester, are shown later in the chapter. The comparisons show clearly that the growth of Chichester kept pace with national growth from 1801 to 1851, but that there was no further significant growth within the boundary for the next 50 years.

Closer examination shows that there was an actual drop in population in St Olav, St Peter the Less, St Andrews and All Saints, suggesting that the denuding of the city central areas had begun at the same time as the suburbs were starting to grow (see Fig. 1-6).

The 1851 census provides a great deal of detailed information about the population – full name, sex, age, occupations, relationships to head of household and place of origin; also the number of houses and whether occupied, empty or building, and the number of households. It is thus possible to make all sorts of statistical analyses for Chichester in 1851, breaking the results down to streets, or quadrants, in or outside the walls, or by occupations, or by origins.

Accordingly an analysis has been attempted using, as its basis, the occupation of the head of household. This has been allocated to one of six socio-economic classes. The results have then been examined geographically, to try to establish how the city divided in 1851 by occupations. Corollary statistics have been injected relating to lodgers, servants and numbers of children. The results have been examined in relation to shops, trade, schools, churches and the condition of the city.

The whole study depends heavily on the validity of the analysis by socio-economic classes. It is only too obvious that 'class' means something different to each person, with the modern inclination for the vast majority to allocate themselves somewhere within a 'middle' class.

For our purposes Chichester in 1851 was refreshingly free of 'aristocracy' which would create an 'upper class'. The labouring poor of the 18th century were not the same people as the 'working class' of the 19th. To avoid pointless dialectic it has been decided to apply backwards in time the classes devised by Dr. Mark Abrams of Research Services Ltd. which identifies the six socio-economic classes. This was a natural successor to that used by the British Market Research Bureau in 1955 and the five classes identified in the 1951 Census. In so doing, precautions have had to be taken to avoid imprinting 20th-century conceptions on the 19th century.

The classification used is:

A   Upper middle: higher managerial, professional, administrative (doctors, clergy, barristers, solicitors, army officers, fundholders, annuitants, large scale farmers, bankers, administrative civil servants)

B   Middle: intermediate management, professional or administrative (executive civil servants, apothecaries, fellmongers, brewers, vets, school principals)

C1   Lower middle: supervisors, clerical, junior managerial, professional or administrative (clerks, teachers, small farmers, shopkeepers)

C2   Skilled working: (tradesmen, bricklayers, carpenters, coopers, nurses, NCOs, dressmakers)

D   Semi-skilled and unskilled: (shop assistants, gardeners, ostlers, labourers, servants, postmen)

E   Lowest grade: casuals, state pensioners (washerwomen, laundresses, chars, on relief)

No two sociologists would agree with the above – nor all the individuals concerned. The analysis by occupation of the *head of household* shows:

(1) that the four main streets all had the highest proportion of lower middle class, i.e. clerks, teachers and shopkeepers, and similarly had a high level of classes A and B, and of servants. It is not difficult to deduce that the wealth and influence was heavily concentrated on these main streets. By contrast the quadrants behind these streets (always ignoring the Cathedral quadrant) had their highest concentrations of occupations in the C2 and D classes.

(2) The total percentage for the city of semi-skilled and unskilled was 31%.

(3) The suburbs outside the walls are very uniform in their results: a high concentration of C2, D and E, totalling about 70% compared with 21% in North Street, 18% in East Street and only matched by the north west quadrant (81%). These suburbs and the north west quadrant were the poorer areas, occupied by low cost housing, but providing the great number of the essential service workers – bricklayers, coopers, gardeners, servants, washerwomen and laundresses.

The north west quadrant had long consisted of gardens and small holdings, and outside the walls had been largely agricultural immediately before the 19th century. When the building boom and the effects of the industrial revolution were felt, the new town workers could not be housed easily within the walls and the low cost Victorian suburbs of terraces sprang up because there was nowhere else to put them, and with inadequate transport they had to be near to the town.

Census Totals

	England and Wales 000	% growth over 1801	Chichester	% growth over 1801
1801	8,893	100	4,752	100
1811	10,164	114	6,425	135
1821	12,000	135	7,362	155
1831	13,897	156	8,271	174
				__Boundary change
1841	15,914	179	8,512	179
1851	17,298	194	8,647 +	182
1861	20,066	225	8,884	187
1871	22,712	255	8,205	173
				__Boundary change
1881	25,974	292	8,569	180
1891	29,002	326	7,877	166
1901	32,528	366	8,934	188

Sources: Census returns and *VCH.*

+ Chichester had no soldiers at the Barracks in 1851.

1851 Census – Analysis of Chichester population
Number of houses: 1745, of which 1654 were occupied, 83 were empty and
8 being built.
The 1654 occupied houses contained 1812 households.
The total population of 8,647 was divided between 3,915 (46%) males and
4,732 (54%) females.
There were 450 lodgers (6%), about 700 servants (8%), and 3,300 children under
21 (40%).

	Occupation of head of household by percentages						Household average	
	A	B	C1	C2	D	E	Lodgers	Servants
Four main streets:								
North	20	5	54	18	2	1	-	1.0
West	20	4	47	18	5	6	0.2	0.9
South	11	9	46	26	8	-	0.2	0.7
East	10	11	61	10	5	3	-	1.0
Quadrants								
N.W. quadrant	4	3	12	35	38	8	0.3	0.1
N.E. "	12	3	21	22	21	21	0.4	0.4
S.E. "	24	4	10	25	30	7	0.1	0.7
S.W. "	38	-	35	12	15	-	-	1.2

Suburbs:

West suburbs	13	4	25	26	21	11	0.2	0.2
North "	9	3	23	26	26	13	0.3	0.1
South "	6	3	23	30	33	5	0.1	0.2
East "	5	4	23	39	19	10	0.5	0.2
WHOLE CITY	11	4	27	27	21	10	0.2	0.4

General Conclusions

Chichester was the wealthiest town in Sussex in the 16th century but did not rank high nationally. In the Hearth Tax accounts it had a bigger middle class than other towns in the county. As will be seen in Chapters 5 and 6, the energetic were favourably placed in the 17th century to take advantage of the wool trade; when this collapsed the bounty of the hinterland and the availability of the port enabled a thriving corn market to flourish. A number of modest families had become affluent and landed by the end of the century.

CHAPTER 3

HEALTH

The Plagues, the Black Death and other visitations of the Middle Ages have been thoroughly argued over by professional historians – and few of them agree, particularly over what the diseases were, so I do not propose to tread long in these quagmires.

The Parish Registers for 1608/9 contain many burials attributed to 'the Plague'. Compared with a normal year of 20 burials there were 88 in St Peter the Great, and 72 instead of about 12 in St Pancras.[1] The City's Quarter Sessions gave notice of adjournment in September 1608 until January 1609 'because of the plague'.[2]

It would have been remarkable if there had not been any epidemics. The City Court books for 1574 to 1641 reveal many cases of careless hygiene – which shows a dichotomy. It was realised by some city leaders that leaving dung in the streets was not a good thing, but many of those arraigned for doing it were leading lights in the city. A few examples:

1574[3]   Mr. Hargrave to carry away his dounge in Savery Lane.
John Lowe layeth his shaveings of his shop in Savery Lane in the Queene's hye waye. We find the fysh shambles are greatly decayed. Mr. Mayre leaving his timber logges in East Lane of West Street. Hence's wife for throwing owte of her fylthy watter and for other of her fylthey doungs in West Street. Robert Benet to remove dounge lying before his Slaughterhouse doore [in the Vintry]. John Benet the bucher is anoyed by a gutter that cometh from Mr. Mayor's backsyde.

1604[4]   Mr. Booker and Mr. Pikkem for a dunghill before their stables [in West Street] Francis Chatfield for dung lying in the Street nearby the water canal [in West Street].
Filth in the lane going by the South gate in the Pallant. Henry Bragge to remove a hill of Earth and Dong before his door [in South Street]. William Wale and William Ollifer have laid 2 dead horses at the stile entering into Scuttery Field. Thomas Swanne doth annoy the passengers by the High Cross by pouring out water and washing clothes without his door. The whole Upper Ward of North Street was warned to cause doors to be swept clean and the dust carried away.

1627[5]   Thos Diggons for dung against East Walls. George Bennett for laying soile against the towne hall gate. Doctor Frye for a dunghill lying against his stable in the Pallant.

1628[6]   William Smyth for a dung hill lying under the West Walls, being noysom to the passengers and inhabitants. Mr. Clifford for throwing dung in lane in Little London. Gyles Browne for keeping of a slaughterhouse within the City being very noysome to the inhabitants and passengers. George Addisone [Pallant] for making a dunghill and skalding of porkers in the street. Chandler Clark for feeding of his swine [in the Pallant] before his door.

1641[7]   Seven residents of South Street for laying dung in the street. Mr. Binstead [Pallant] for gutters running into the street. Inhabitants of the Pallant for casting of soil against the Pallant Cross.

Thomas Leberd casting soyle in the Street exceeding noysom.

The great plague of 1665 was brought to the city probably by a traveller from London. It spread so rapidly that the Mayor decided to close the city. Near starvation resulted from this cordon sanitaire until relief was provided by the people of Bosham who brought food and left it outside the West Gate and collected their money from within buckets of water.[8]

The Plague, as such, has featured less in epidemics of the last 300 years: opinions differ on the reasons – weakening of strains, immunity, better housing (which excluded rats from dwellings) or even more specific diagnosis.

Smallpox peaked in Chichester in 1722 (168 deaths); 1740/1 (66); 1759 (180); 1775 (24). Inoculation played an increasing part in controlling the disease from 1722 onwards.[9]

Surprisingly, in the 19th century, the health of Chichester often lagged behind the rest of the country. Various diseases of a water and sewage origin – enteric fever (typhoid) and cholera – attacked regularly.

A water supply by conduit from the area north of Bishop Otter College was of ancient origin, and when it arrived in the city it was prone to pollution. The only drainage was the open gutter in the middle of the street.

The sanitary condition of Chichester in the late 18th and the 19th centuries.

Only when a standard for comparison is available are people likely to comment critically. James Spershott[10] was able to do this by remembering in his late years (in 1783) how poor was the condition of Chichester in the early 18th century. In his childhood he remembered the city having a 'very mean appearance', particularly in the back lanes. Little London was not pitched and was very dirty, with deep cart ruts. The street had no paved footwalks.

Despite Spershott's feeling of satisfaction about the situation in 1783, in the year before he wrote his memorial there was a petition to the M.P. by citizens requesting 'the paving, repairing, cleansing, lightening, watching and widening of the streets and lanes of the city and the removal of nuisances, obstructions and annoyances therefrom.' However, as the implementation would have required higher taxation there were objections, and the petition was withdrawn.

Among the duties of the Paving Commissioners, established in 1791, were the cleansing of streets, lanes and public ways and passages within the walls.

As early as 1794 the streets were swept twice a week.[11] However the inbuilt resistance of the town leaders to spending public money, which was to bedevil progress for a century, was expressed in 1803: 'The expediency of covering the streets and lanes with gravel and keeping them repaired therewith for the future was taken into consideration and it was unanimously resolved and ordered that it would be extremely inexpedient to adopt such a measure.'[12]

The sweeping of streets involved the removal of 'soil'. This is a euphemism for what follows any Lord Mayor's Show and doubtless, in no small measure, was the end product of the frequent beast markets in the streets. The richness of the product is evidenced by the tenders for removal: people were not paid for removal – in 1819 there was a tender of one pound per week for the removal concession.[13]

So there was a considerable will to keep the streets in a reasonable condition but it was ever thwarted by the cattle markets, and the standard of cleansing varied. In 1859 attention was drawn by the Town Clerk to the inefficient cleaning of the streets especially after cattle markets.[14] It may be no coincidence that this was the year in which the Bishop had protested at the introduction of the Beast Market into West Street. Sheep had encroached as near as three yards from the Cathedral west gate.[15]

Fig. 3-1 Market, East Street, mid 19th century

Six years later (1865) a memorial prayed for the removal of the street cattle markets as being 'injurious to the health of the inhabitants'. This was partly due to the difficulty of treading safely but also to the 'profane and disgusting language of the cattle drovers and their wanton cruelty to the cattle.'

The Daily Telegraph expressed astonishment that Chichester should retain a custom 'so singularly behind the century as to suffer a cattle market within its walls' and went on to describe how 'cattle rush into shops and one animal got wedged behind a shop counter and could not be released until the counter was taken to pieces.'[16]

By 1867 the town's leaders were disposed to meet the cost of the removal of the cattle market and the new market was opened to the public on the 9th May 1871.

Thus one of the more obvious causes of concern over health in Chichester was finally removed. The more hidden problems concerning water supply, sewage disposal and housing cleanliness were not to be so easily resolved; these were more fundamental and yet less visible, thus accounting for Spershott's satisfaction with the overt state of the city.

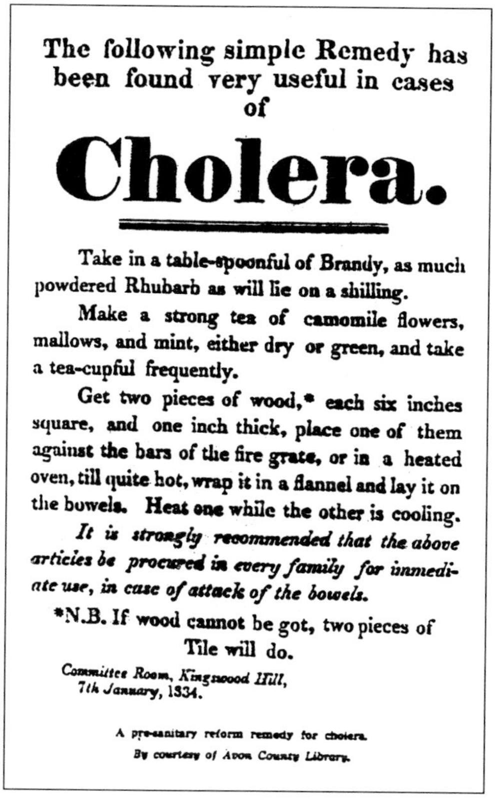

> **The following simple Remedy has been found very useful in cases of**
>
> # Cholera.
>
> Take in a table-spoonful of Brandy, as much powdered Rhubarb as will lie on a shilling.
>
> Make a strong tea of camomile flowers, mallows, and mint, either dry or green, and take a tea-cupful frequently.
>
> Get two pieces of wood,* each six inches square, and one inch thick, place one of them against the bars of the fire grate, or in a heated oven, till quite hot, wrap it in a flannel and lay it on the bowels. Heat one while the other is cooling.
>
> *It is strongly recommended that the above articles be procured in every family for immediate use, in case of attack of the bowels.*
>
> *N.B. If wood cannot be got, two pieces of Tile will do.
>
> *Committee Room, Kingswood Hill,
> 7th January, 1834.*
>
> A pre-sanitary reform remedy for cholera.
> By courtesy of Avon County Library.

Fig. 3-2

The state of public health had been a cause of great concern to medical men before the end of the 18th century. The immigrants from country to town brought with them the primitive sanitary standards of the countryside, where much could be neglected with impunity; such neglect became fatal in the crowded, infectious, festering alleys and courts of the towns. The towns already had endured bad standards for centuries; disease was a constant part of daily life. The first outbreak of cholera in Chichester – a disease intimately connected with dirt, bad sanitation and contaminated water – was in 1831-2, and there were to be renewed outbreaks in the next decades.

Doctors could not agree on the way the disease spread: contact, air, miasma from refuse, water, were all blamed by lobbies.[17] The water theory advanced, in a pamphlet of 1832, was described as 'a fanciful theory' by a Scottish doctor. Prophylactic devices included wearing a belt of thick warm material around the stomach and keeping the windows closed. The Bristol remedy of 1834 (see Fig. 3-2) must have also led to some urgent and moving experiences.[18]

A report by Edwin Chadwick[19] in 1842 showed that the expectation of life in Leeds for a member of the gentry was only 44 years, a tradesman 27 years and a workman 18 years. The report led to the Public Health Act of 1848 and the requirement for all towns with a death rate of over 23 per 1,000 to set up Boards of Health. But the Boards were allowed to lapse when the worst of the cholera epidemics were over. Chadwick set out to enlighten both public and politicians on the urgent need to provide pure water, adequate sewage disposal and properly ventilated homes with a view to checking the ravages of cholera, typhoid, typhus and dysentery. Bristol was one city which adopted the advice. In 20 years from 1850 to 1870 there was a dramatic improvement in the health record, with a reduction in mortality from 28 to 22 per thousand, being transformed in that time from the third most unhealthy to nearly the most healthy city in Great Britain.[20]

In Norwich a detailed report by a Government Inspector in 1850, after a cholera epidemic, showed that the city was a very unhealthy place to live in. There was some piped water but this was only available for 2 or 3 hours a day on 2 or 3 days a week and the water came unfiltered from a filthy river. Poor people depended on pumps and wells. There were no sewers: just overflowing cesspools. A new water works was begun immediately and the first sewer was laid in 1869 and slum clearance commenced in 1877. At this time Norwich was not prosperous and money was difficult to find, and the sewage scheme was bitterly attacked. Nevertheless sufficient progress was made for the death rate to have been reduced to 21 per 1,000 in 1873: below the national level.[21]

It is strange that it is necessary to make much of the successes of Norwich and Bristol – after all the Palace of Minos at Knossos had an elaborate drainage system in 2,000 BC; and most Roman villas and cities in Britain had carefully engineered water and disposal systems. Chichester was not alone in this: major Roman public baths and water supplies have been excavated in the city centre, which precede present occupation by some 18 centuries.

In the middle of the 19th century the citizens of Chichester fell ill and died in their squalid houses in Tower Street and Chapel Street, with their polluted wells sunk down into those magnificent Roman baths and drainage channels.

The city minutes from 1850 onwards are a sorry chronicle of the decadence which was to be a matter of talk, but not of action, until the turn of the century.

In 1852 it was decided that 'drains, closets and sinks shall be trapped so as to prevent the effluvia coming up from the sewers and cesspools.'[22]

In 1855 following the passing of the Sanitary Nuisances Act a notice was prepared by the Town Clerk[23] which the City Council decided should be distributed to all citizens. After commenting that there were now ample powers to render the city more salubrious and that improvement of public health would 'render less probable the recurrence of fevers and virulent diseases' it went on to say that the Act was stringent, and that the Council felt it imperative to exercise their powers but did not wish 'to be compelled … to come into collision with their fellow citizens' and suggested to owners and occupiers 'the propriety of immediately and closely inspecting their relative premises and the removal of … noxious accumulations, the judiciously providing and keeping in good and clean condition sufficient drains, the providing of receptacles for filth of every kind.' The Council also strongly recommend 'pains be taken to provide ample supplies of wholesome water' and that houses be ventilated and cleansed.

Significantly the Council stated its awareness that in making this appeal they were calling on owners and occupiers to take trouble but also to incur expense – this was to rule thinking for years and it was made clear that the statement was somewhat under duress of the overhanging threat of Parliament to take default action.

A Sanitary Inspector was then appointed at an annual salary of £30.

The Lavant was thought, with good reason, to be the cause of much trouble – it was the receptacle of privy soil from all adjacent houses; after notices were issued in 1856 all but two were connected instead to cesspools. However, the Lavant was to continue to give intermittent trouble for years to come, and in 1865 it was reported as being the main sewer. The same report[24] proposed that sewers should be laid at such depth as would enable all cellars to be drained; that gullies be provided for surface water; that 90 acres of land be used for sewage irrigation from outfalls (the water would drain into the Lavant after passing over the land).

If the Lavant had not been there it would have had to be invented.

The report also proposed a water supply from a 100 foot well at the Barracks. The cost of sewage works and water supply would be £27,500 giving an annual cost at $4\frac{1}{2}\%$ interest of £1,500.

A letter from Secretary Walpole[25] in the following year to the Town Clerk called attention to the level of sickness in the district and issued a warning that he might direct work to be done and charge the authority in default. Complainants had pointed out that there was no public water supply, other than two public pumps, for 8,000 inhabitants; that the wells within the city drew supplies from the gravel bed; that there were no sewers in the district and therefore the whole of the sewage was discharged via cesspools into the same gravel bed. The complainants (30 leading citizens) were driven to their action by the Council's decision on 13th April 1866[26] to defer any action

SHAKESPEARE

REVISED FOR THE

NON-DRAINERS.

Hamlet III. 1.

TO DRAIN, or not to Drain, that is the question:—
Whether 'tis better in this town to suffer
The Smells and Odours of the City Cess-pools;
Or to take arms against the grim non-drainers,
And by opposing end them. To purge,—to drain,
No more, And by these drains to say we end
The fever and the thousand foul diseases
That cess-pools breed. 'Tis a consummation
Devoutly to be wish'd. To purge—to drain;
To drain! perchance we shall, ay, there's the rub;
For when the City's drained, such good will come,
When we have rooted out this present system,
Must give us thanks. Health's the reward
That crowns the efforts of the Drainage Party.
Why should we bear these foul existing cess-pools,
The fever's scourge, disparaging statistics,
The want of proper drains, the long delay,.
The ignorance of some folks, the contempt
That drainèd cities, healthier, hold us in,
When we ourselves might renovate the City
With proper Drainage?

Fig. 3-3

(by 9 votes to 8) for 6 months on the report on water supply and sewerage.

A house-to-house survey revealed that of 1739 houses

> 42 were dirty
>
> 34 had prevailing sickness
>
> 39 had full cesspools
>
> 97 had full privies
>
> 75 had bad water

At this time there were horrendous reports[27] of bad sanitary cases, e.g. 8th December 1866: 2 houses in Somerstown with long back gardens sloping upwards from houses. 'In heavy rain the water runs down to the houses, fills and overflows the cesspools, which then flood the houses.' It was stated that the smell was 'rather strong'.

The pungent comment was made[28] that for a small city of 8,000 people, with no noxious trades or factories, with a favourable natural situation and wide, well ventilated streets and houses not closely overcrowded, Chichester had a yearly mortality rate all but equal to the Metropolis.

The death rate in 1864 was 24.12 per 1,000. The death rate per 1,000 in England and Wales (1861-65) was 22.6.[29]

Although the water supply was basically pure and wholesome it had become polluted because the whole underbelt of the town was honeycombed with cesspools and the gravel bed had been charged with cesspool material for centuries.

Nevertheless the Mayor noted that there was a considerable majority on the Council opposed to any form of water supply or sewerage and that there was ample room available for fresh cesspools without danger to health and a memorial from 460 ratepayers confirmed this view.

And so it went on.

Government niggling continued with a further questionnaire in 1869 asking what had been done about sewerage and water supply and the Lavant.

The Finance Committee retaliated by calling the attention of the Council to the tendency of the legislature at the present day 'to speedily and recklessly increase local taxation.' Chichester was clean; Chichester had a low death rate.

Again in 1873 the Local Government Board commented on deaths from fever (4) and diarrhoea (5). The Sanitary Inspector thought this was due to rain and wind.

In 1874, at last, a water supply was brought to the centre of the town and supplies started in 1875.

But still no system of drainage.

By 1888 the Council were still talking about it. Some were still very much opposed to drainage and by now were polarised into 'drainers' and 'non-drainers'.

In 1889 a report was published[30] showing the effect on the death rate per 1,000 in other towns before and after the construction of drainage works. These statistics, taken as a comparison over a short period in the same town, have more validity than crude death statistics per 1,000 population shown between various towns of different age structures.

Saving of Life

Rugby	$2\frac{1}{2}$%	Warwick	$7\frac{3}{4}$%
Salisbury	20%	Dover	7%
Cardiff }	32%	Ely	14%
Newport }		Leicester	$4\frac{1}{2}$%
Banbury	$12\frac{1}{2}$%	Merthyr	18%
Croydon	22%		

The Anti-Drainage Party met at the *Unicorn Inn* in October 1889 to decide steps to oppose the proposed scheme of main drainage. One of their more fascinating quotes was that 'a bucket of urine thrown on the ground would spread itself over the ground, be dried up by the sun, and in short time there would be nothing to see or smell'.[31] The argument went on to prolonged discussions in the Council Meetings in April and October 1890. A large majority of Non-Drainers admitted that drainage 'must come one day but that they could not afford it now'!

Statistics were produced by the Drainers[32] showing the incidence of typhoid fever in Chichester compared with other districts in Sussex for the 8 years ending 1888. Four districts were 5 times better than Chichester, three 4 times, five 3 times, five twice, and the remaining two were still better. For consumption also, no district was as bad as Chichester and in the previous 10 years, 1871-1880, Chichester was amongst the very worst in England (including London) for typhoid and consumption cases.

Finally the Drainers reached the ascendancy; tenders were obtained in 1895 and by 1896 half the houses were connected.

Chichester was being dragged reluctantly towards the 20th century.

Even so, the saga was not quite finished. The incidence of typhoid fever remained high.

In 1896-8 there were cases of fever at 257 houses:[33]

	No. of houses in 1898	No. affected by fever			Comparison of deaths in	
		1896	1897	1898	1870/4	1885/91
Within the walls	682	4	6	13	22	2
Somerstown	303	18	36	8	8	11
Portfield	335	13	26	21	11	7
St Pancras/ Hornet	253	21	12	9	11	6
Orchard St./ Franklyn Place	180	11	10	10	5	3
Other	817	12	11	16	24	10
	2570	79	101	77	81	39

Plotted on a map a dot represents the actual or approximate location of every case in 1896/8 (see opposite).

Within the walls there was now a piped water supply and drainage. Private wells were still in use outside the walls, and were sunk into the gravel. The public wells were sunk much deeper, although for a while it was suspected that the chalk in which they were bored had been polluted by a stream. One proved cause was the consumption of cockles gathered from the harbour and contaminated by raw sewage from the harbourside settlements. Some private wells were still polluted and in St Pancras some cottages obtained water from a well polluted from nearby privies.[34]

Professional health care

Besides the hospital of St James and Mary Magdalen (see Chapter 2), the Pest House[35] was in College Lane and was used for all epidemics until it was superseded by the Infectious Diseases Hospital in Spitalfields Lane. The Infirmary[36] opened in 1826 following the Dispensary which was established in 1784 for out-patients. Graylingwell[37] opened as a mental hospital in 1897 on a 245-acre site.

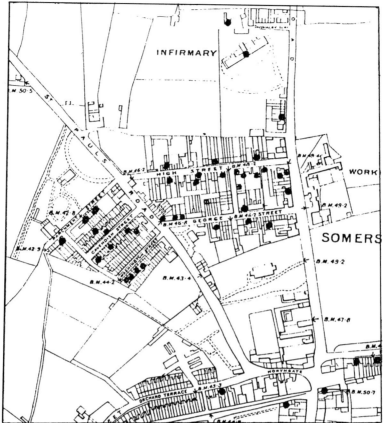

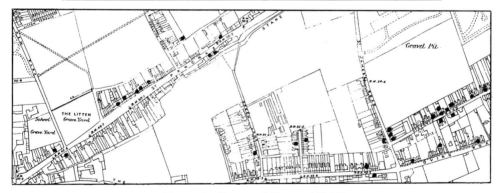

Fig. 3-4 Cases of Fever 1896/8

Where are they now? – The bodies under Chichester

In a city like Chichester, of small compass, and with nearly continuous occupation for 1,900 years, disposal of bodies cannot ultimately be unplanned. The Romans, typically, buried outside the gates, primarily in St Pancras and near the Litten. Later generations buried often within the walls and in the course of archaeological exploration and redevelopment skeletons relating

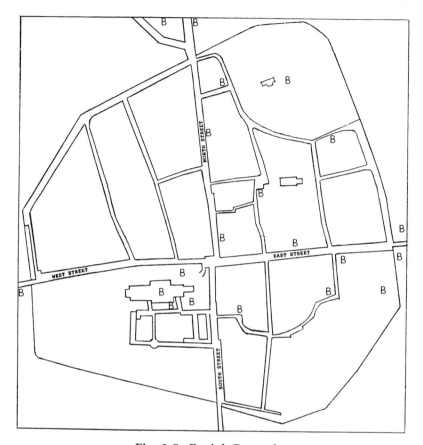

Fig. 3-5 Burial Grounds

to most of Chichester's history have been uncovered at one place or another. Our ancestors are all around us, and after the Romans left there were no cremations.

It can only be guesswork to calculate how many bodies there have been since Chichester began, but it could be in the order of 60,000[38] from AD 1000 to 1800.

It is not surprising that an Order in Council was made concerning burial of the dead, with public health in mind, in 1854.[39]

This discontinued burials:

under the Cathedral

under the Church of St Peter the Less

in the burial grounds of St Andrew's, All Saints and St Bartholomew

in the Cloisters and Paradise and the Cathedral churchyard

in the Friends Burial Grounds in Rumboldswick and St Andrew's

in the Baptist Burial Ground in Rumboldswick (opened in 1852) in the Unitarian Burial Ground in Baffins Lane.

Limited exceptions were made with regard to existing family vaults.

Other burial places were St Paul's (19th century) and Whyke Lane; and Roman sites outside the gates; within Eastgate Chapel and the major site at the Litten. Portfield was consecrated in 1859.

Small numbers were buried within other churches – St Olav and St Martin's; also at Cawley Almshouses.[40]

The Blackfriars had a large burial ground in East Street (excavated recently – 127 bodies recovered)[41] and the Greyfriars would have had a similar site.

A large number of plague and other burials were at St James's.

CHAPTER 4

COMMUNICATIONS

The Romans, having military minds and engineering skills, provided Chichester with good communications.

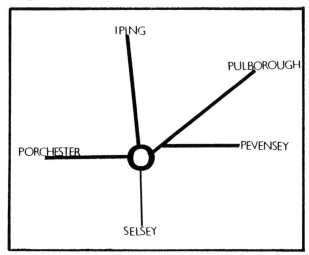

Fig. 4-1 Roman Roads

By 1603[1] it was cheaper to move goods by water rather than by road. Parish residents had to provide labour and carts for repairing their stretch of highways from 1555 (4 days each in 1555 and 6 in 1563)[2] but roads deteriorated through neglect and increasing and unsuitable traffic – heavier carts with narrow wheels – and by the incompetence and ignorance of those required to do the work. There were also attempts to restrict the right of passage which led to a narrowing of what was available.

Turnpikes

Contemporary descriptions[3] of journeys in the area in the 18th century are horrendous to our sophisticated sensibilities:

'overturned twice'

'journeys better measured by days rather than miles'

'roads were abominable, sussexian'

'our horses could not keep on their legs'

'last nine miles took six hours'

Continuing dissatisfaction nationally had led to the introduction of the turnpike system. The first turnpike had been established in 1663[4] and in 1702 the need to send goods overland increased because of enemy ships in the English Channel. Early Trusts dealt with repairs and improvement, not construction, and introduced the idea that travellers should contribute towards the costs. Toll gates were erected and collectors appointed.

A local Act in 1749 described the road to Midhurst as ' in many parts … so very ruinous and deep in the winter season that carriages cannot pass without great danger and difficulty, and are in many parts very narrow and incommodious.'

So Turnpike No. 15 was born. It was known as the Fernhurst, Midhurst, Chichester and Dell Quay Turnpike. The Dell Quay stretch was not completed at this stage.

The road left the Northgate by the New Broyle Road and cut out the old road which went through West Dean village, taking the route still used today. It was 21 miles long and had 8 toll gates. £8,325 was borrowed for its construction. The toll for a coach pulled by 6 horses was one shilling (5p)[5]

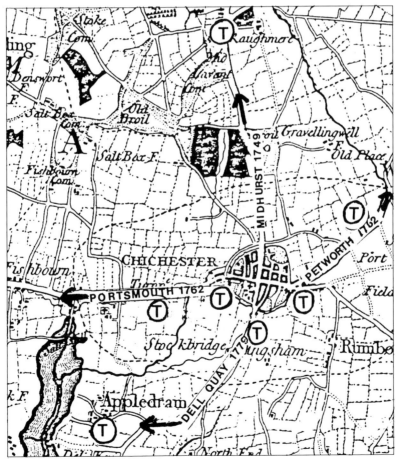

Fig. 4-2 The turnpikes and tollgates (T)

The Turnpike to Portsmouth (No. 10) was started in 1762. It was to be 12 miles long with 3 tollgates. £12,901 was borrowed. By 1778[6] it was shown as fenced with, already, signs of ribbon development. There was a toll gate at Westgate and one at Fishbourne. Turnpike No. 36 went out of Eastgate to Petworth with a branch to Pulborough. There was a toll bar at St James.

Toll tickets were issued and were valid for return journeys and for other gates. Corruption was rife and many trusts resorted to farming (leasing) their tolls, thus ensuring a steady income.

The final stretch to Dell Quay (No. 15) was built in 1779.[7] The toll cottage was in Stockbridge Road and was demolished in 1956.

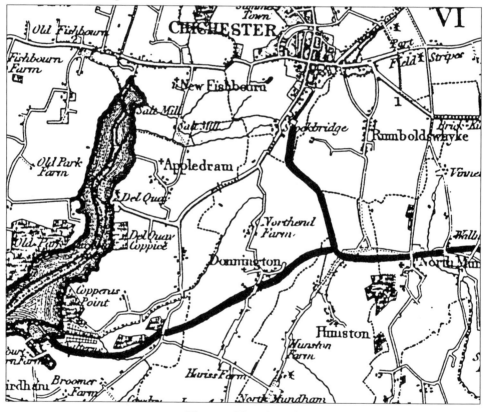

Fig. 4-3 The Canal

Canal

Dell Quay's importance was supreme during the centuries of poor road communications and may have been the City's salvation. It was the main landing place in the Port of Chichester and the only legal entry for foreign trade.[8] Its earliest recorded use in Post-Roman times was 1226.

A considerable element of the city's prosperity depended successively on wool, cloth, grain and malt being funnelled in through the market and out through the port.[9] Imports – slates, coal, pipe-clay, portland stone and wine – were not so voluminous, but an important fillip to the market.

The need for a good link from Chichester was foreseen in 1585 [10] when an Act was obtained to make a canal from Dell Quay. It was not proceeded with. The bad state of the intervening roads was quoted. An Act of 1770[11] authorised the building of the short turnpike.

When the canal was built in 1818-1822 it was already too late. Capital was eagerly subscribed, but such was the rapid change in road standards, and the competition from the railways in 1846, that no dividend was ever paid. The section from Arundel to Portsmouth was abandoned in 1868. The section from Birdham to the Canal Basin carried on until 1898. The Canal Company owned the Basin and roadway, 2 houses nearby, some yards and pounds, land and a timber store in Stockbridge Road and an iron bridge.[12]

The Streets

The medieval layout of Chichester's streets was largely as it is now – four main streets, leading to gates and crossing at the centre. These contained the shops and better houses.

The ruling condition in the 16th century was neglect. In 1534 the Mayor and Citizens of Chichester sent a petition to the King 'touching the ruin and decay of their town'.[13] In 1540 there was an Act for the 're-edifying of decayed towns'. Chichester, Canterbury, Winchester and Southampton were among those cited. In 1596 an anonymous petition [14] to the Lord Treasurer of England emphasised 'the multitude of poor who would certainly drive out the better sort of inhabitants.' Repair of the ruins of the city was requested. The walls were broken and thieves went at will.

In the Middle Ages every householder had been required to pave and clean his frontage up to the centre of the street.[15] This duty was taken over by the Guardians who had the power to levy a rate. In the 16th century Chichester's streets were described as 'very mierie, full of water and dirty places both loathsome and noysome'. Large areas were then paved. In 1575 another Act re-introduced the frontagers' obligation to pave and the four main streets are recorded as being paved at this date.

In 1711[16] the townspeople were required to sweep in front of their houses and to clean the gutters each Saturday evening. In 1735/6 an Order[16] prohibited the blocking up of streets with wagons, carts, wheelbarrows, bricks, timber, dung, rubbish or other noxious things. However, despite the rebuilding of houses in the 18th century the streets and pavements remained in poor condition throughout until the Paving Commissioners were set up in 1791 with power to levy a 9d. rate. They were charged with better paving, repairing and cleansing streets and preventing encroachments. During their existence and until the duty was again taken over by the City in 1872 they:[17]

Paved the main streets, providing cambers and removing central drains and made gutters at the sides;

Forbade bow window obstructions where the footway was less than 4½ feet (1.4 m.);

Gave notice for various projecting inn signs to be removed (*Bell*, *White Hart*, *Kings Arms*, *Little Anchor*, *Wheatsheaf*, *George*, *Sun*, *Royal Oak*, *Great Anchor*) (1792);

Negotiated for land outside the Southgate to be used for depositing road sweepings and soil (1793);

Moved and repaired pumps in North and West Streets;

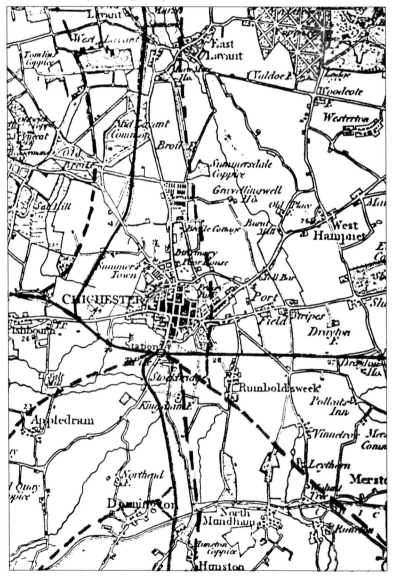

Fig. 4-4 Railways

Lines completed _____   Lines proposed[18] but not completed _ _ _

Replaced the footpath opposite St Olav's church because rats had undermined it;

Filled up holes in streets with 'good gravel' (1804-5);

Agreed various cellars under footpaths;

Provided crossing places in streets with flatteners;

Extracted penalties for emptying of slaughterhouses and having dung-hills in the streets (1810);

Had a report that it would cost £606 8s. 9d. to put various streets, lanes and passages in good order. As rates were insufficient £450 had to be raised by public subscription (1813);

Considered lighting streets with gas (1823).

Railways

The railway came to Chichester in the form of a link from Brighton to Chichester and on to Portsmouth in 1846. A further line, now discontinued, ran via Lavant to Midhurst in 1881. A series of other lines were proposed, and some are shown in Fig. 4-4.

Selsey Tramway[19]

The railway, known as the West Sussex Railway, ran 7 miles from the main line station to Selsey beach, leaving south-westerly, crossing Terminus Road and stopping at Hunston, Hoe Farm, Chalder Farm, Mill Pond, Sidlesham, Ferry, Golf Club, Selsey Town and Selsey Beach. The railway ran from 1897-1935. (See Fig. 4-5.)

Fig. 4-5 Selsey Tram, a cartoon by Cynicus

Postal Services and Coaching Inns

Until the roads improved the link to London was by pack horse. In 1804 the London post came in every day at 8 a.m. except Monday, and went out daily at 4 p.m. except Saturday.

London coaches left Monday, Wednesday and Friday and returned Tuesday, Thursday and Saturday. There were daily coaches to Portsmouth and three a week to Brighton. Wagons went thrice weekly to London with large quantities of wool which then went on to Yorkshire.

Even back in 1616 Chichester had been a principal post town and in 1669 a postal stage town; in 1683 post was received daily.[20]

CHAPTER 5

TRADE AND INDUSTRY UP TO 1700

The Setting

There was a mint at Chichester as early as about AD 930,[1] and moneyers were recorded with the mint, with some gaps, up to 1207.

There was a market place in the Roman period, near to the intersection of the four main streets. A subsequent market place was established by 1160 – it was burned down in that year. It was originally a collection of stalls in the area of the present Cross and was a large open space which was gradually encroached. A market was held, from the 12th century, on Wednesdays and Saturdays;[2] the first fair (Sloe Fair) was held about 1107-8.

The Hinterland

Chichester was in the fortunate position of being the only town for many miles, in being surrounded by good flat land, and by being close to an access to the open sea.

Large and small farms were established on the Broyle to the north, land which was owned by the Bishop.[3] The Broyle was described in 1388 as having 135 acres of wood and 17 acres of water-meadow, and 182 livestock, mainly sheep. The Dean had a farm to the south and west, the Prebendaries to the south east; the common fields of Portfield and Guildenfield were to the east and other early common fields to the west. Produce and livestock were brought to Chichester market, and surpluses were bought there for transport to other areas.

A mill was recorded in Domesday (and 11 at Bosham and 2 at Fishbourne). The Dean owned a mill outside the Westgate up to 1649.[4] The water mill at St James dated from 1231.

This favoured situation between Downs and sea led to Chichester's three great trading successes: wool, grain and cattle.

Wool : Cloth

The Downs were suitable for sheep farming. Chichester had exported wool in 1273[5] and a Staple was established in 1353. The quality was modest and the quantity large. The cloth industry was well established by 1536.[6] Yeomen and farmers sold wool to clothiers, who employed casual labour to spin, weave, full and dye.[7] The clothiers were, thus, early industrial entrepreneurs, and Chichester was heavily involved in England's second largest industry (after agriculture).[8] The clothiers needed few fixed assets – buildings or plant – and cut down involvement and expenses in a slump.

In 1550 Chichester and 3 areas in Kent were among the main areas of cloth manufacture; it is at this time that the Miller family moved from

Kent to Chichester, where they operated as clothiers, and became founder members of the new Guild in 1616: then when it was expeditious they changed to malting and became merchants. They married well, accumulated land and property, became baronets and M.P.s and country landowners, friends of the Duke of Richmond – all within 150 years. The Spencers of Althorp paralleled this upward movement and went on to even higher things.

Cloth remained a major industry until the mid 17th century. Tariffs, wars, and protectionism abroad by Holland, France and Spain led to a crisis: exports declined by one-third in the 1620s.

The Guilds

Those established in Chichester,[9] with the number of members at formation were:

1477	Weavers	13
1497	Tanners	not known
1504	Tanners and cordwainers	6
1528	Barbers	3
1562	Woollen drapers	7
1562	Cappers	4
1567	Joiners and shopkeepers	7
1608	Barbers (7), surgeons (1), and glaziers (4)	12
1609	Blacksmiths and cutlers	11
1616	Clothworkers and dyers	37
1622	Mercers	6
1633	Sadlers and collarmakers	10
1663	Blacksmiths (23), cutlers (4) and goldsmiths (1)	28
1685	Merchant tailors	19
1685	Barbers, surgeons and periwig makers	15
1686	Sadlers (3), ropemakers (3), stationers and bookbinders (2)	8
1686	Goldsmiths (1), cutlers (1) and blacksmiths (7)	9
1687	White tawyers and glovers	7
1698	Mercers	4

The blacksmiths and cutlers complained, in 1609, that 'there were blacksmiths and cutlers not inhabitants within the city who do not bear any scott, lot or other charge within the city, who do daily repair into the same city and set up shop ... and do put to sale there all kind of iron wares and knives of all sorts … many of them being not apprentices nor having served seven years'. The trade threatened that they would not be able to maintain their families if this persisted, or pay taxes or maintain apprentices.

The clothiers, in 1616, had similarly complained that they were 'greatly hindered and impoverished in their several trades and occupations by reason that divers farmers and out dwellers do daily repair into the city and exercise their trades … some of them keeping shops openly, others working secretly in private houses … they nor any of them bearing or paying any scott, lott, or other charge.'

Fig. 5-1 Malthouse

Merchants

The development of the city as a commercial centre can be measured by the number of merchants and mercers. During the 17th century 288 were recorded, concentrated in the 4 main streets. They were wholesalers, operating in several areas, controlling the fortunes of many who produced raw materials. They were often involved in trade through the port at Dell Quay. They were upwardly mobile and often to be found in city affairs and in land ownership. Grain was gaining in importance and many merchants had malthouses. In these malthouses barley was soaked in a large vat and spread on a large floor to germinate and convert the starch into sugar. It was then put in a kiln to dry and bake.[10] It was now malt. The fuel for the kiln was originally wood and straw, but for fear of fire no person was allowed to use burning straw after 1709.[11]

The 17th-century Port Books [12] show that many cargoes of malt were exported by the merchants. Much of the barley from which it was made came from land adjoining the city. The trade so developed that Thomas Miller was sending out a cargo to the west country once a fortnight in 1662. He monopolised one ship, *The Francis of Chichester* which did a round trip in 5 weeks and it is likely that he had a share in the vessel.

Cargoes of malt in 1662:[12]

Ref. on map		Dwelling & Malthouse	No. of Cargoes
1	Thomas Miller	Pallant	23
2	Thomas Clarke	St Martin's & Pallant	12
3	Robert Miller	North Street	6
4	Francis Page	East Street	9
5	Anthony Williams	" "	8
6	Richard Rables	North Street	6
7	John Bartholomew	South Street	4
8	Henry Jennings	North Street	3
9	William Stamper	East/West Street	4
10	George Stamper	East Street	4

William Stamper had a quarter share in the barque *William and Mary*.[13]

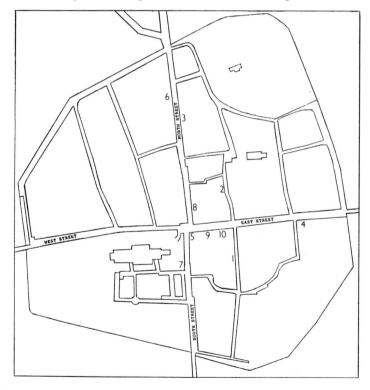

Fig. 5-2 Location of major merchants exporting malt in 1662

The malt exported in the year, at the current price of 13s. a quarter, was worth £6,500,[14] i.e. over £400,000 now.

THROUGHPUT AT DELL QUAY

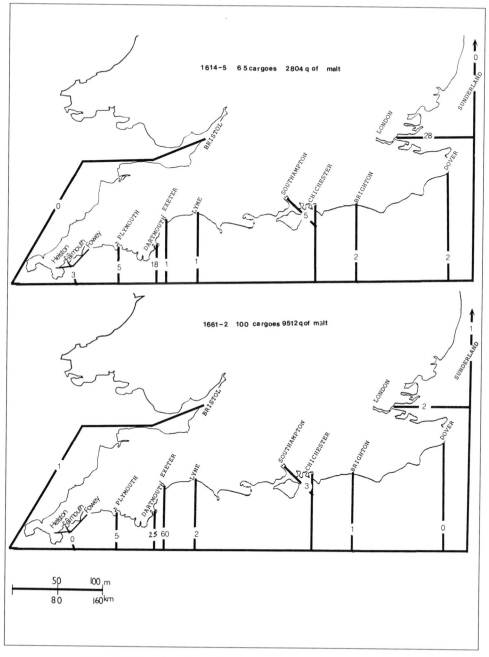

Fig. 5-3 Destination of cargoes from Chichester and
number of journeys involved.

Imports through Dell Quay[12]

	1614/5	1633/4	1654/5	1661/2	1674/5
sugar	+	+		+	
salt	+			+	
starch	+				
groceries	+	+		+	+
raisins	+				
vinegar				+	
cheese		+		+	+
cod/herrings	+	+	+	+	
aniseed					+
soap		+			+
household goods		+		+	
glasses		+		+	+
earthenware pottery	+	+		+	+
French & Malaga wine		+		+	+
strong water					+
cyder					+
brandy					+
hops	+	+			
sea coal	+	+	+	+	
pipe clay				+	+
tobacco pipes		+		+	
Virginia tobacco				+	+
calf skins				+	
paper				+	
feathers for beds				+	
stones (rub, grind and quorn)					+
slates			+		
nails				+	
ironmongery		+			+
wrought iron					+
gault		+			
allum	+	+		+	+
madder		+			
bird shot		+			+
canvas		+		+	
pitch and tar	+	+			+

Trades and Occupations in the 17th century

The importance of the markets and the growth of the cloth industry and of malting led naturally to the need for the supportive trades of a market town. Every available documentary source has been searched and has led to a card index of over 2,000 persons carrying on trades. These are the active – not the submerged – members of the community; it is reasonable to accept that most of those with a trade or occupation have left their fingerprints on one record or another. The records which have been searched are: wills, inventories, leases, conveyances, rentals, tax lists, marriage licences, parish registers, port books, protestation returns, guild indentures and court records. The emergence of 2,000 names over a hundred years from an average population of 2,400 is as much as can be expected.[15]

Of the 2,000 names the place of work and home of about 65% has been located. The cards have been analysed to identify the trades in groupings and to where they were concentrated; also an indication when trades emerged, if ascertainable.

In these analyses the drink trade includes innkeepers, alehouse keepers, huxters, tipplers, victuallers, brewers and vintners. Food trades are only revealed as butchers (124), bakers (34), grocers (8), fishmongers (2), cheesemongers (2).

Of the other retailers the leading ones are: coopers (19), collar and harnessmakers (18), chandlers (18), tallow chandlers (12), sadlers (12), cutlers (11), upholsterers (8), booksellers and stationers (8). There were also tobacconists (second half of the century), clockmakers, ropemakers, basket makers, soap boilers and hoop makers.

The metal workers include blacksmiths (81), wheelwrights (16), needlemakers (14), braziers (11), goldsmiths (12); also pewterers, gunsmiths, locksmiths and farriers.

Processors are: maltsters (55), clothworkers and weavers (77), tanners (11), millers (11) and turners (10). There are also curriers, pipemakers, felt makers, silk weavers, fellmongers and a parchment maker.

Building workers increase after 1650. Not surprisingly carpenters (90) are the most numerous, followed by bricklayers (51). Glaziers (21) are increasing in importance.

The crude totals for the period 1600-1700 are thus analysed:

| | Number | Percentages | | |
		of total	within walls	in suburbs
Food and drink	560	27	87	13
Clothing	303	15	79	21
Other retail	145	7	75	25
Metal working	151	7	55	45
Building	182	9	59	41
Service trades	26	1	94	6

Medical	79	4	90	10
Merchants/mercers	288	14	91	9
Processors	184	9	66	34
Agriculture	116	6	54	46
Miscellaneous	42	1	93	7
	2076	100		

Of those located within the walls the breakdown is:

	%
North Street	27
East Street	23
South Street	14
West Street	18
Pallant	9
St Martin's	6
Remainder	3

– making North Street the busiest street (see Chapter 9), leading significantly in food, drink, clothing and merchants, mercers and processors.

The busiest suburb was St Pancras (206 recorded). The next, West Gate, was only half as busy. The figures for these suburbs would doubtless have been higher were it not for the disruptive hiatus of the Civil War (see Chapters 16 and 18).

In common with other towns some people could only survive by having several occupations: often the wife would run an alehouse whilst the husband carried on his original trade; there were alehousekeepers and innkeepers who were also cordwainers, tailors, bakers, maltsters. Several combined the trades of butcher and baker. Others moved up the scale from tippler to innkeeper, or maltster to merchant, retail to wholesale.

Similarly analysis cannot be done in 20th-century terms. Division of labour was not yet fully worked out; many retailers were manufacturers. Tailors did not buy in ready made goods; shoemakers produced where they sold; most inns and alehouses made their own beer, although some was bought in from surpluses. Conversely the manufacture of malt, a constituent of beer, was already a major industry with much of it for export.

In addition to the major industries of clothing and malting, needle-making was important in Chichester.

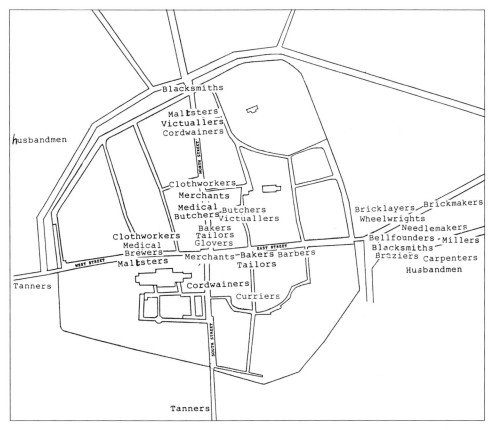

Fig. 5-4 17th-century trades plotted geographically

Needlemaking
The Chichester needlemaking industry has loomed large in published literature yet, in terms of the total economy of the town, it was nowhere near as vital as wool, or grain, or cattle.

It was mainly carried out in St Pancras, and was probably at its peak by the Civil War. The destruction of part of the suburb, combined with competition from cheaper midland manufacturing methods, led to decline.

It had been a cottage industry, obtaining its supplies of iron from the Weald. Availability of water may have decided the siting, close to the ubiquitous Lavant.

The needlemakers did not aspire to Guild status, possibly because they were too poor; more likely they were the one industry which could not easily be threatened by local competition.

Although the industry is supposed to have declined after 1650, needlemakers are recorded through to 1788 and one, Isaac Hammond, who lived on the Lavant Bank in St Pancras, left a detailed inventory in 1733 which is summarised later in this book.[16]

The following list gives the names of needlemakers who have left records, with the dates of references. Those marked + have been discovered since *Chichester Paper No. 31* was published.

1621	John Mounsloe (1)	All Saints
1640	William Lucas	St Bartholomew
1647/78	Robert Hitchcock	St Pancras
1666/72	John Mounsloe (2)	St Pancras (corner New Park Road)
+1667/77	William Winston	Pallant
+1670/75	John Hitchcock	East Street
+1671	John Hammond	St Pancras
+1671	Thomas Saunders	
+1677/8	Daniel Hitchcock	
+1677/8	Samuel Hitchcock	
1682	Joel Farnden	St Pancras
1685/1701	Thomas Belchamber	North Street
1686/1706	Edward Dollman	
1687/98	Abraham Collicke (1)	St Pancras

For completeness, the later needlemakers are also listed; those marked * have been located to one area of St Pancras on the south side near the *Ship and Lighter*, and backing on to the Lavant.

+1701	William Dollman	
1704/23	Joseph Smith	St Pancras
* 1707/33	Stephen Vicars	St Pancras
1709/33	Isaac Hammond	St Pancras
1715/6	John Blackwell	East Street
1716	William Vicars	
1716	Thomas Raymond	
1717/18	John Newman	St Pancras
* 1718/28	John Farrenden	St Pancras
* 1724	Robert Clinch	St Pancras
* 1725	Magdalen Roill	St Pancras
1727	Abraham Collicke (2)	St Pancras
* 1728	William Valentine	St Pancras
1732	Thomas Dollman	
+ 1737	John Newsham	St Pancras
1774	William Powell	St Peter the Great
1788	James Dollman	St Pancras
+*18th century	Scale family	St Pancras

Tanning

In market towns like Chichester, tanning had been significant from medieval times. There was a Guild of Tanners in 1497, but tanners are recorded living in West and South Streets in 1402 (see Chapters 8 & 11) and outside the Eastgate in 1232-4 and 1327.[17] Tanning needed a water supply – available again from the Lavant, and numerous streams in the south-west suburbs – and bark as a tanning agent. It also needed space, as the process, which involved the use of a smokehouse and a series of pits and hanging areas, could take up to 18 months. It also required a supply of cattle.

The next tanners who can be located were in St Bartholomew's.[18] From 1549 to 1649 they were the Undershill family – John, Thomas, Simon and Edmund. Also there were John Payne (1612), Henry Woolgar (1624), Thomas Bridger (1639), Thomas Sandham (1640) and Nicholas Trevett (1641). Chapter 18 gives further details.

Tanners were also recorded in the Pallant in 1600/4 – Richard and William Brooker.[19]

In 1649 there was a tanner at Stockbridge House outside the Southgate. He had come from Havant where he had also been a tanner.[20]

Curriers worked the hides after tanning, reducing their thickness, and increasing softness and flexibility. Five are recorded in the 17th century, mainly in the East Street area and in the Pallant,[21] where they had their own Market Cross. The output would go in the direction of cordwainers, shoe-makers and glovers, of whom there were 172 in the century. Such a number of craftsmen must have been supplying an area larger than Chichester.

Other end products of the industry were soap boiling and candlemaking – two of each were at work, as well as 12 tallow chandlers.

Bell-founding[22]

A surprising activity, discovered during the excavation of Tower Street. There had been bell-founding in St Pancras around 1594-1622 (Thomas Wakefield, a bell-founder, received £9 for casting the bells of Amberley church in 1622). Medieval bell-founding was carried out mainly by itinerant founders who travelled from site to site, making their foundry as near to the relevant church as possible and there they cast new bells and repaired the old ones. Thus it was that they settled briefly at the Cathedral's own store and workshop, and left behind traces of their moulds (see Chapter 12).

Hoopmaking[23]

Two hoopmakers, James and Jasper Robinson, were active in the lower end of West Street between 1625 and 1680. Large numbers of hoops were exported to Rye, Plymouth and Dartmouth by various merchants for use in the cider industry.

Blacksmiths and metal working

This industry was common to most market and other towns. Horse-drawn transport needed the equivalent of the modern garaging for servicing. Dominating the trade in Chichester were the Butterly family.[24]

Thomas Butterly, a blacksmith, married twice (1573 and 1593) and produced 9 children. All the boys – William, John, Simon, Thomas, Roger, Stephen and Edward – became blacksmiths. The stage was thus set for domination of the trade. Fourteen Butterlys were blacksmiths between 1573 and 1693.

The Butterlys were members of the blacksmiths' guilds of 1663 and 1686. Their own production of sons forced some of them to move out of Chichester into other villages nearby:

William to Boxgrove. Produced 2 sons, both blacksmiths who went to Patching;

John to Northgate;

Simon to Northgate. Produced 8 children;

Thomas to St Pancras. His son Richard, a blacksmith, was in the Hornet;

Roger to Bosham. His son, William, was a blacksmith;

Stephen to St Pancras. His son Edward was a blacksmith;

Edward to the Hornet. His son Thomas, a blacksmith, was also in St Pancras.

Although Thomas's 9 children produced 23 children between them, 13 were girls and several boys did not produce issue. After major dominance there is no record of a Butterly as a blacksmith in Chichester after 1732.

Inns and Alehouses

It is necessary to set out the accepted distinction between various echelons in the drink business, although the edges are sometimes blurred.

Inns: usually large establishments selling wine, ale, beer and good food, with lodgings for travellers, horses and carriages; often with a court or backside approached through a carriage entrance. Inns had large rooms which could be used for functions, and employed a variety of staff. An intermediate class was the Tavern.

Alehouses: small premises, which sold ale and beer and provided basic food and accommodation, usually only for travellers on foot. The proprietors often had to rely on other employment to survive. At the bottom end of the scale was the sale of beer in one room of a house. Ale was also sold by full and part-timers, without necessarily formal premises; they were described as huxters, regrators or tiplers. Often the ale was sold in the open, on market days, by women.

For information on this industry the licensing records of the 16th and 17th centuries can be consulted.[25]

In 1574 there were 5 inns in Chichester. Four were in North, East and South Streets near the Cross; the fifth was in North Pallant. At the same time there were 32 tiplers, huxters, vintners and victuallers.

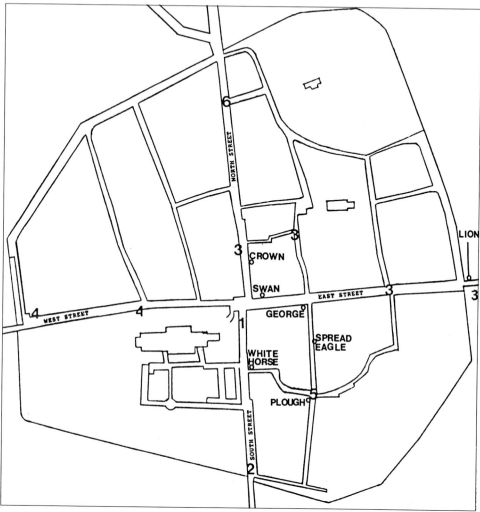

Fig. 5-5 Location of Inns in 1604
(the figures relate to alehouses in various parts of the city)

By 1604 there were 7 inns – *Swan* and *George* in East Street, *Crown* in North Street, *White Horse* in South Street, *Spread Eagle* in North Pallant and *Lion* immediately outside the East Gate. Another inn was also in the Pallant: it was probably the *Plough* in South Pallant. The Court Leet recorded 34 alehousekeepers and tiplers in 1604, of whom 9 were in North Street.

The pattern of the number and location of the inns remained virtually unchanged until the Civil War, with only one – *The Star* in lower North Street – being added in 1628.

In 1651 the tally was still 7 inns, with the *Dolphin* in West Street now added and the *Crown* in North Street now gone, plus 41 alehouses and 9 huxters.

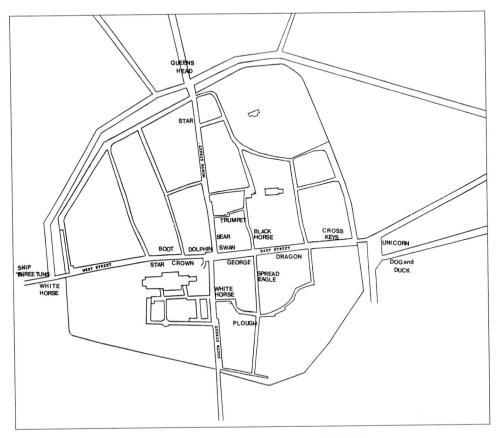

Fig. 5-6 Location of Inns in 1670/1700

Three inns were destroyed in the Civil War – the *White Horse* outside the West Gate, the *Lion* at East Gate and the *Dolphin* in Eastgate Square. All were in highly vulnerable positions. The *White Horse* was re-established.

Taking the whole century there were 88 persons recorded as innkeepers, 124 alehousekeepers, 30 huxters, 18 tiplers, 78 victuallers, 28 brewers and 11 vintners.

CHAPTER 6

TRADE AND INDUSTRY FROM 1700 ONWARDS

The products of farming continued to dominate the city into the 18th century. Grain, cattle and sheep still provided work and wealth: the wealth eventually needed an outlet and this led to the evolution of local banks and the establishment of a new minor aristocracy.

Grain and milling

Defoe reported in 1722[1] that granaries had been set up near the harbour and that mills reduced the grain to flour which was then exported by ship. The mills[2] (with dates recorded in documents) were at:

King's Water Mill – demised in 1231 by Richard, Earl of Cornwall, to St James. City water mill up to 1745, when it fell into decay.

Adjoining Eastgate – horse mill (1697).

Portfield (see Fig. 16-7) – post windmill (1719, rebuilt 1721, 1813-1861, 1875).

St James – post-mill (1724-1778). Smock-mill (1813-1823, 1862).

Broyle (East Breach) – windmill (1741, 1854). Field called Mill Post 1633.

Westhampnett – water mill burned 1773 (1826); windmill blown down 1748, rebuilt.

Dell Quay – a large square-built post-windmill which could grind 7 loads a week. (1785-1867). Recorded in a painting by R.H. Nibbs (1815-1893).

Old Broyle (Great Oak) – windmill (1802, 1852).

Appledram: two salt mills (1813, 1825).

Some flour milling took place from about 1693.[3] The trade continued in importance leading to the building of the Corn Exchange in East Street in 1831 (see Fig. 10-10).

Conversion of barley to malt continued. Exports, as in the 17th century, were initially to the west country; however, by 1731 the trade, still considerable, was all to London. The Poor Rate of 1755 is useful in listing 31 malthouses in the city. Spershott had thought there were 32 in 1725 and about half that number in 1770.[4] The export trade in malt declined over the turn of the century.

Cattle and sheep

Chapter 5 demonstrated the importance of the livestock trade up to 1700: this continued. Beast markets continued to be held in East and North Streets (see Fig. 3-1) and in 1759[6] an observer commented that they supplied the great demand in Portsmouth. In 1755 there were 3 slaughterhouses in Chapel Street, 2 in the Pallant and 1 each in St Martin's and St Pancras.

Fig. 6-1 Location of malthouses in 1755

By the early 19th century increasing fastidiousness led to the move to establish a cattle market out of the town. The preamble to the Act of 1807 remarked that ill-disposed persons, out of wantonness and malice, frequently destroyed the street market pens; that cattle were frequently, negligently and improvidentially driven in the public streets and the inhabitants exposed to great danger. It was also felt that there was a great advantage in building a new market in East Street for the sale of meat, fish, poultry, eggs, butter, herbs, roots and vegetables, fruit, china and glass.[7]

Tanning
There were tanneries still, outside the South and West gates,[8] the former ceasing about 1790 and the latter carrying on until the middle of the present century on the site still known as 'The Tannery'.

Woolstapling
Woolstapling was carried out in Tower Street. Ebenezer Prior was a woolstapler and fellmonger, dealing with the fleeces of sheep after shearing, and with sheep skins from the slaughterhouses. Another woolstapler, Charles Parsons in the Pallant, was bought out by Prior. Prior took over the site of the Lancastrian School in Tower Street (see Chapter 12) and erected a 3-storey building on that site and that of the adjoining *Fighting Cocks* public house (Fig. 12-5). The skins were put into washing pits and left to soak. These pits were still in existence, buried, when the recent archaeological excavations were carried out. Prior lived at Northleigh House.[9]

Brickmaking

The new growth industry was brickmaking and building. Using the London clay beds, brickfields and kilns were established all around the city. Some of those recorded were:[10]

Spitalfields: this covered 6 acres and was closed by 1730 when John Royle was required to recompense the owners – the Dean and Chapter – £7 in damages to make good. In 1755 an area was described as new brick kilns.

Westhampnett: Brick Kiln Farm on both sides of the road in 1790 and on the Tithe Map of 1838. 'Clay Pit Lane' enshrines the memory.

Old Broyle Farm: Kilns in 1772.

Vinetrow: Brick Kiln Farm and works on the O. S. map 1912.

New Fishbourne.

St Bartholomew.

Rumboldswick (1852).

The Goodwood brick accounts show a production of 99,000 bricks in May 1817 supplying 150 different customers in Chichester, Halnaker, Oving and Tangmere.[11]

Many small brickmaking operations were carried out for short periods where the new houses were built. An example is in East Pallant, where a relatively small operation provided bricks from a clay deposit.

The peak of building and re-building was from 1700 to 1730.[12]

Tobacco Pipemaking

A parallel industry to brickmaking was pipemaking which had started in Chichester in the 1660s, and thrived through to the 19th century. Pipe clay was imported in large quantities from Dorset and turned into pipes in a series of small kilns.

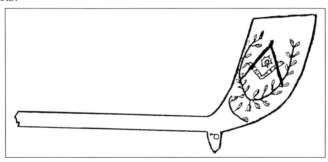

Fig. 6-2

The pipe illustrated is marked IP – James Pitt (died 1810) being the maker. On one side of the bowl is a masonic emblem and on the other 3 tuns within a cartouche and trailing leaves. The pipe was excavated in Crane Street. The *Three Tuns* inn was a few yards away in Chapel Street in 1800 (see Chapter 12).

The following list is of pipemakers who were active in Chichester. The nucleus of this list can be found in *Sussex Clay Tobacco Pipes and the Pipemakers* by D.R. Atkinson, FSA. Some additions, marked +, have been made.

Pipemaker	Date active	Location where known[13]
William Artwell	before 1700	1693 'of Chichester', later at Arundel
Mark Briant	1841	Described as journeyman pipe maker but only 14 at time. Tower Street
+Daniel Gardner	1693	West Street
+Robert Gardner	1693	" "
James Harrington & Son	1855-66	Canal Basin
+John Jones	1689	'of Chichester'
Henry Launder	1823	St Pancras
Thomas Launder	1823/7	"
Andrew Leggatt	1851/61	Basin Cottage. Journeyman
+George Leggatt	1851	Canal Road
Henry Leigh	1836	Canal Basin
Stephen Leigh	1845-62	Southgate
Samuel Lucas	pre 1686	'of Chichester'
+William Peck	1871	Basin Road
Pitt family James I & II } William I & II }	1770-1841	St Pancras
+John Russell	1686	
+Henry Ryle	1697	St Pancras. Described as brickmaker and as a pipeburner.
Taplin family, William, Henry I & II, John	1716-1800	Chapel Street. One son set up in Emsworth, Hants.
+ - Tapner	1738	St Martin's Street
Henry Weston (father and son)	pre 1715	

In 1661/2 16 tons of pipe clay were imported into Dell Quay by John Dyall, in 1674/5 12 tons by Henry Smith, and in 1683 12 tons by Dennis Smith. It is reasonable to assume that some of this clay was for use by Chichester pipemakers. The earliest traced pipemaker is Samuel Lucas, a Quaker.

Inns and alehouses

In 1810 there were 25 inns licensed in the city and immediate suburbs, and 6 inns and 34 taverns and public houses in 1839.[14] The Beerhouses Act of 1830 led to 40,000 new pubs being opened nationally in 5 years and this was reflected in every town.

The changing trade structure

With the trend of industrialisation came division of labour, specialisation and the growth of capital. A poll book of 1782[15] gives not only who voted for whom but also the prime occupation of those entitled to vote. The analysis, compared with that for the 17th century in the last chapter, was:

	% 1782	% 17th c.
Food and drink	19	27
Clothing	18	15
Other retail	17	7
Metal working	7	7
Building	14	9
Service trades	5	1
Medical	2	4
Merchants & mercers	3	14
Processors	3	9
Agriculture	5	6
Miscellaneous	7	1
	100	100

Too much should not be read into the 1782 analysis, for, like that obtained from trade directories, there is a tendency to exclude the lower end of the social scale.

New Industries
Shippams

In 1782 Charles Shippam had a storehouse outside the Westgate (see Chapter 18) and by 1846 had a large house there. In 1786 there was a shop near Eastgate. In the 1840s a grandson had a pork butcher's shop at 48 East Street, and by the end of the 19th century there were already buildings at East Walls, forerunners of the present factory, with an output of 500 lbs of sausages a day. There was also a retail shop at 3-4 South Street up to 1961.[16]

Coachbuilding

This was established by John Turner in St Pancras in 1738 and sold to Cuttens in 1821; it carried on in the Cutten family to 1930 when it was sold to Rowes, who demolished the old buildings and eventually moved to the present site in the Hornet.[16] William Shayer the painter was employed here by George Parsons in 1810.

Postal[17]

The postal history of Chichester has been admirably covered by Brigadier G.A. Viner in his *Chichester Paper No. 47*, so it is only necessary to summarise, in context here, and add supplementary information. Chichester was a principal post town in 1616 and in 1669 it served Petworth, Midhurst and Arundel. An early (deputy) post master was Robert Tayer (to 1690) and his successor, John Barnes, was appropriately a carrier, with premises in Little London. His joint manager, Francis Greenfield, was an apothecary in North Street. The Barnes family continued to be involved until 1761.

William Carlton, the postmaster from 1783-98 and 1799-1800, had a business in East Street (North Pallant corner) as a chinaman. Joseph Redman, a wine merchant of the Vicars' Hall in South Street, was postmaster in 1812, and Joseph Angell, also of South Street, 1816-1833; and John Attree Fuller had the post office in East Pallant (north side) 1834-1856. Adhesive stamps were introduced in 1840. In 1856 the post office was next to Vicars' Hall and the first purpose-built post office was in South Street and this survived until the present building was erected in West Street in 1937.

Finance

The increasing wealth, from trade, of the middle classes in the 17th and 18th centuries was paralleled by an increasing sophistication in retailing, with the emergence of merchants and entrepreneurs, as seen in the last chapter. The profits produced capital for the new opportunities provided by the re-building. The *nouveaux-riches* moved both into land and investment.

The early banks[18] were all in East Street and are still predominantly there:

Nos.

9-11   The first so-called country bank: Chichester Old Bank was established by 1779 by Griffiths, Chaldecott, Drew and Trew. Now Lloyds.

88   Sussex and Chichester Bank – Francis and John Diggens described as 'bankers' in 1791; joined by Thomas Dodd by 1795.

73-4   Chichester Bank, 1809, established by Hack, Dendy and Farenden, each of whom subscribed £2,500 capital. Now Barclays.

30   Capital and Counties, 1834.

94   London and County, 1842. London and Midland, 1928. Now Midland.

5   Founded 1898. London and Westminster 1928. Now Nat-West.

21   National and Provincial, 1928.

Conclusion

With the advent of the turnpikes, the canal and the railways, Chichester was no longer dependent on its old jewel – the port of Dell Quay, which in any case was about to fail the city through silting. Chichester was ready to move forward. The traditional industries based on agriculture and a market centre have lost their importance and a new one has taken over, based on the old sea and Downs connection – and the very facts of a long history – leisure and tourism.

CHAPTER 7

THE BUILDINGS OF CHICHESTER

There is very little information on the domestic buildings of the city before the 16th century. From evidence elsewhere we can assume that Chichester, like other walled towns such as Salisbury and Leicester, had its merchant class living within the walls at their places of business, with ample warehousing and orchards at the rear. Some of the poorer elements were in the extra-mural suburbs, packed tightly around the gates. There would have been extremes of wealth with a broad based pyramid and a small pinnacle. Greatest crowding and intensity would have been closest to the market place.

The small town houses were timber framed with frontages from 6 to 12 m and a depth of 8 m (and a long plot behind) with a shop or parlour in the front and a detached kitchen behind, and perhaps one chamber above. The base frame would have been probably on bare earth with no foundations other than stone, leaving little of the building for the Chichester archaeologists to find as evidence of plans. Much more survives of the Roman buildings beneath them.

These flimsy timber houses rarely lasted more than 50 years, even with constant repairs. They were continually being demolished and rebuilt and each time the decayed relics survived. The city rose on the residue of its own history, as archaeological excavation shows. Individually they have few footprints because of their flimsy nature. Man's impermanence is emphasised by the number of people who have lived successively on many sites.

In 1533 the Dean and Chapter owned and repaired a considerable number of small houses in the city. We are fortunate that detailed accounts survive for the years 1533-38.[1] Some of the houses on the south side of West Street and the west side of South Street, particularly, were on leases which did not require the tenants to repair, and they were occupied in many cases by the craftsmen who spent much of their time repairing the Cathedral and other ecclesiastical buildings.

This map shows the location of houses for which there are repair records in 1533-38. Where the tenant was required to keep the premises in good repair he also had to pave the street outside his dwelling.

The record gives a valuable picture of the small house at that date, and its needs. The accounts list the names of the tradesmen, occupiers, materials used, and the rooms in houses.

The trades involved were:

masons	smiths	plumbers
carpenters	thatchers	joiners
sawyers	helyers (who worked on roof coverings)	

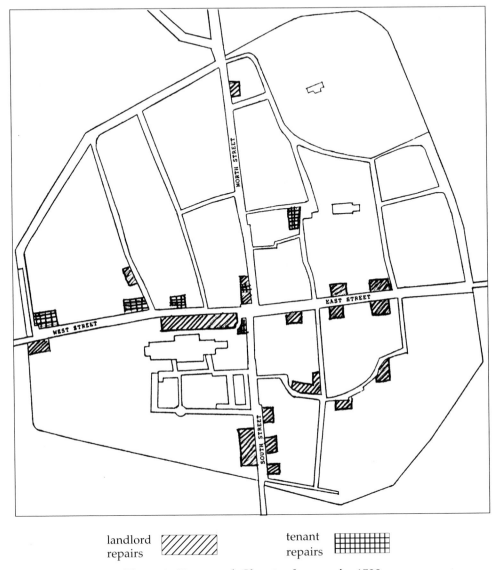

landlord repairs   tenant repairs

Fig. 7-1 Dean and Chapter houses in 1533

They were often assisted by labourers and boys. No bricklayers, as such, were mentioned.

The materials included:

tiles – roof, hip, crest, gutter; tile pins; blue slates; timber – laths, eaves-boards, sills, braces, twiggs, planks, sleepers; lead; daub – whitewash; bricks, stones, sand, mortar, lime; locks, keys, hooks, garnets (T-shaped hinges), twistes, staples. Earth for underpinning and for covering wattle.

Rooms, etc. named:
hall, chamber, great chamber, kitchen, shop, bakehouse, buttery, lime house, privy house, cellar, barn, stable. Other structures mentioned – entries, gables, chimneys, wells.
Repairs described include:

Walls and frame: stud, brede and daub (i.e. the upright posts, the wattling and whitewashing the timber frame).
Pointing – filling up the gaps.
Underpinning foundations, with stones, sand and earth. (Foundations on rough stone or wood were prone to settlement.)
Laying on rafters and sills.
Making windows with timber and board (particularly shop windows).
Providing hatches, door furniture.
Making and repairing brick chimneys. Timber for chimney mantle.
Bastard chimneys.

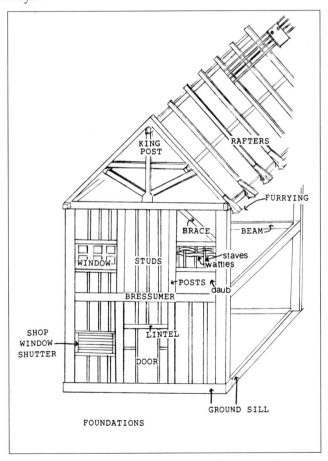

Fig. 7-2 Timber framed house – the named parts

Inside timber work: new joists, setting hammer beams, furrying rafters (nailing in extra pieces of timber; the shaped ends of rafters); making partitions, repairing stair steps, replacing floors and joists; providing innumerable locks and keys. Repairing doors, wicket hinges, bracing.

Roofs: thatching kitchens, barns, bakehouses and storehouses; tiles and slate (many thousands used); laying on and making castings for lead gutters; repairing eaves boards for 'defence of watter'; weather board for gables.

Outside and backside: repairing foundered walls; iron 'wench' for well; making up sinks, replacing bricks under ovens; five foot pale fences, with post and rail; make pentice (lean-to building or passage); new privy houses.

From these records a picture builds up of the appearance of these small rented houses in Chichester in 1533. The houses were timberframed, often 2 storeys, not necessarily jettied, with whitewashed walls, brick chimneys and ovens, but no other brick, built on wooden sills. The roofs were mainly tile or slate, but outbuildings were often thatched and include kitchens, barns, bakehouses and stores. Gutters were of lead; windows were not glazed, the openings being covered with hinged board or sliding shutters. It was to be another hundred years before glass was used regularly in vernacular houses.[2]

In the short period covered by the accounts – no more than 4 or 5 years – 15 houses required underpinning, and filling in gaps in walls was repetitive. Timber and tiles were being replaced all the time, particularly after storms.

The impression of life in the houses is clear – they were cold, damp, draughty and insecure.

Other leasehold houses of the Dean and Chapter were mainly on sites away from the Cathedral: they had come into their ownership usually as gifts in the 13th century rather than as development of convenient Cathedral street frontage, and rarely appear in the repair accounts. These houses were often larger than those previously considered and were frequently occupied by merchants. It may be assumed that some were jettied and had decorated fronts with a range of separate buildings behind, all in timber framing, and with a gable to the street.[3]

The remainder of these important repair records concerns the Cathedral and the Close buildings. Works mentioned include:

Repairs to bells and wheels; mending great organ; painting and glazing. There is a record of a glazier at work in the Cathedral in 1171;[4] for 1240 Salzman[5] quotes an agreement made with John the Glazier by which, in return for a daily allowance of bread and a yearly fee of 13s. 4d., he and his heirs were to keep the windows of the Cathedral in repair.

Such a large repair organisation needed a store and a workshop. This was in Lower West Lane (Tower Street) on the east side and north of the Army & Navy store.[6] This building was timber framed and thatched.

Blue slates came to Dell Quay from the west country[7] and were carted to the store, split by helyers for use, and carried to sites. 22,000 are listed in store at one point in the accounts; also 2 tons of timber, and sand, lime, laths

(400 of 4 foot and 300 of 5 foot) and nails. There is a record of a delivery of 28,600 'blew' slates bought for store at 4s. 4d. per 1000 (i.e. £6 4s. 0d.) and carted in 14 separate loads at 8d. a load.

In reading the accounts[8] for work it is possible to hear the voices of Chichester craftsmen. In most cases they would be unable to write; the clerks who wrote out the accounts would be unfamiliar with building terms: the coming together of both to prepare accounts meant that words were written as they were spoken. Thus we get:

ovyse board	for	eaves board
bussyll lyme		bushell of lime
gotter		gutter
kechyng		kitchen
flowar		floor
bottery		buttery
bordyng		boarding
rowbryshe		rubbish
fott of tymber		foot of timber
roffe		roof
lowght		light
comyn barns		common barns
warkes		works
hokes		hooks
betwyne		between
grett		great
watter		water
hapse		hasp

We are probably seeing Middle English as it was spoken. Regarding the last item, *The Dictionary of Sussex Dialect* comments that this reversal was common.

The end of timber

When James I arrived in London he was horrified by the crazy timber structures of his new capital after the ordered stone of Edinburgh. He decreed that, in future, city house fronts were to be in brick; this spelled the end of the jetty.[9]

Chichester was slow in following fashion. It is conventional to think of the city as without brick before 1690. There were brickmakers and brick-layers active in the 16th and 17th centuries, but their products were mainly used for chimneys and ovens, and for ecclesiastical buildings. The new availability of coal as a fuel led to the building of stacks to take away a smoke which was more objectionable than that from wood. Coal had rarely been burned away from the producing areas before the 16th century, but by 1605 seven times as much coal was imported by sea to London from Newcastle as in 1580.

Speed's map of Chichester (1610) indicates a general use of chimneys and by 1614 coal was certainly being delivered to Dell Quay.[10] Records of early brickworkers include[11]

Denys Hicks (a Frenchman)	bricklayer	North Pallant	1517
William Lane	tilemaker		1533
William Kewell	bricklayer	West Lane	1604
Charles Crossingham	"	West Street	1607
Thomas Wheeler	"	St Pancras	1619
Thomas Marner	"	Pallant	1625
William Austeds	"	Southgate	1626
John Fuggator	"	St Pancras	1627
Thomas Colden	"		1630
Raphe Allen	"		1638
Edward Piper	"		1641-7
Richard Cooper	bricklayer	St Pancras	1641
Anthony Browne	"	Tower Street	1641/1666
Richard Tracey	"	St Pancras	1647
Richard Linfield	brickmaker	St Pancras	1649
John Chase (1)	bricklayer	West Street	1665
John Crossingham	"	"	1663
Henry Bullock	"	"	1666/70
Thomas Aylwin	brickmaker		1673
John Royle	brickburner	St Pancras	1674
John Bailey	brickmaker		1677-94
John Sowter	bricklayer	Pallant	1679
Thomas Wittman	"		1679/80
John Chase (2)	"		1681
John Grigg	brickmaker	St Pancras	1684
James Joy	bricklayer	Pallant	1694
James Allen	brickmaker		1696
Henry Roile	"	St Pancras	to 1716
John Blunden	"	"	1729
John Randoll	"	"	1736

The above list is not exhaustive. It does seem to confirm that up to 1649 bricks were imported and after that date there was an increasing tendency towards local manufacture.

The Parliamentary Survey of 1649[12]

Whilst little more is recorded on the repair of small houses, the Parliamentary Survey of 1649 for Chichester is particularly detailed in its survey of all buildings owned by the Dean and Chapter and Vicars' Choral at the Interregnum. It records the rooms and appurtenances of houses which are on the same sites as those in the repair records of 1533. The houses are still timber framed and tiled, but doubtless in the intervening period would have been rebuilt – or have fallen down more than once.

Two examples are:

On the south side of West Street. A house consisting of a hall, wainscotted parlour, kitchen, washhouse, buttery and cellar with 3 chambers over.

On the east side of North Street (No. 66). A dwellinghouse which consists of a hall and two parlours, one whereof is well waynscotted and a large study and a kitchen and a large washhouse with a well of water in it and a pantry and buttery, a coal house and cellar and a little low room used for malting, over which said rooms forward to the west side of the house are 3 fair chambers and on the east thereof are 3 other chambers and on the north side of the house is a large gate and gateroom leading into a large courtyard: in which is a stable and hay room adjoining to which yard and stable is a large fair garden fenced on the north and east side with a new brick wall which garden contains 1 rood. The property was leased for £10 10s. 0d. per annum to William Baldwyn a gentleman and is now the site of North House. It was rebuilt in 1696.

The Rebuilding

The so-called Georgian city that we see today (i.e. where it has not been destroyed) is a product of the 18th century. Brickwork came late compared with the rest of the country. One cause was the indecision in the Civil War, when the townspeople were largely for Parliament, but the prominent citizens supported the King: the resulting siege by the Parliamentary forces led to demolition of much of the east and west suburbs and some of the industry. There was a moribund situation for some years after the Restoration with the St Pancras suburbs particularly depressed.

Eventual recovery came, following Chichester's emergence as the main Sussex port to export grain from the fertile plain behind the city.

In 1687 city minutes ordained[13] that no houses, barns or outhouses in the city be roofed with thatch and that all existing thatch be removed.

Contemporary descriptions[14] include:

1696: In new building of some of their houses they have encroach'd onto the street (Celia Fiennes)

Early 1700s: Of mean appearance with old low-timber built houses with shops open to the street. There were few new houses with solid brick fronts, only 4 in East Street had sash windows; the Pallant was very old with few good houses (Spershott)

1739: The buildings are mostly brick and covered with tiles (Philpott)

Chichester is probably unique in that there is virtually no vernacular English bond brickwork because of this late start: brickwork is universally Flemish bond.

The encroachments observed by Celia Fiennes had become such a problem by 1705 that the Council instructed the Mayor to view them and report.[15]

What was happening was that the timber framed houses with some remaining life were being encased with brick, not unlike some 1945 pre-fabs. The alternatives were:

(1) the jettying of the upper floors could be cut back and allow brick to be built up flush: however this defeated the whole idea of jettying if its purpose was to give stability to the floor itself, or

(2) to build flush with the upper floor at street level and so come out into the street by a good few inches.

A long stream of minutes follows where the Council accepts the inevitability of the loss of some street frontage and makes the most of it by levying an encroachment rent on the freeholder. A second wave of more acceptable applications then comes from those who lagged behind and whose properties were left out of line. The Council at that time were conscious of the appearance of the streets and encouraged a lining up of buildings.

Some of the present appearance of Chichester as a 'Georgian City' is accounted for by this encasement. In towns where brick arrived earlier it was used there to replace the wattle and daub interstices. Chichester's greater sophistication comes from its tardiness.

By 1700 everyone was beginning to have glazing. A Dean and Chapter reference of 1725 refers to the glazing of poor peoples' windows.[16]

By 1784 James Spershott[17] was able to record that the City had a very mean appearance in 1720 but by now it was much improved.

The rebuilding and refronting doubtless conceals many timber framed buildings. A few show themselves with residual jetties:

1. The Punch House, East Street
2. Bookshop, 24 South Street
3. 62 North Street
4. White Horse, South Street (side)

Good examples of refronting (timber frame behind):

5. St Martin's Square (Fig. 13-3)
6. 41/2 North Street
7. 58/60 East Street
8. 3/4 Tower Street

The first specifically major new brick buildings were:

9. John Edes House, West Street, 1696 (Fig. 8-3)
10. Pallant House, 1712 (Fig. 14-7)
11. The Deanery, Canon Lane, 1725
12. Farrington House, 1696 (55 South Street)

Fig. 7-3 Building Types

The Poor Rate of 1755[18], discussed in Chapter 2, gives a picture of non-domestic buildings. There were:

- 7   slaughterhouses
- 32   malthouses and 5 brewhouses
- 81   stables
- 11   chaise and coach houses
- 14   workhouses
- 19   storehouses

The location of the malthouses is plotted in Chapter 6 (Fig. 6-1).

The City Walls

As now seen these are largely of medieval or later material, but are on the original Roman line. Repairs have ever been a problem, whether in the 14th century for defence or later for preservation of the heritage. A breach in the 12th century by the Dean (see Chapter 15) was the precursor of a weak point, in the Civil War. In the 17th and 18th centuries the City Council clearly made the Mayor responsible for repairs (in 1687/8 'Mayor to take care to have the walls of the City mended'); 1786 ordered that the East Wall of the City be put into sufficient repair under the superintendence of the Mayor. Reports come every few years, e.g. 1795, reported that the City Walls are decayed in many places and in a very ruinous state.

CHAPTER 8

WEST STREET
Genteel Elegance

Domesday listed 11 haws on the north side of West Street.[1] The earliest map (1595) shows ribbon development from the Cross to the Westgate on both sides – as it must have been for a considerable time previously. The only break in the line came with the demolition of the buildings in front of the Cathedral in the last century.

Parts of the street consistently attracted wealthy occupants with big houses. On the north side between Chapel and Tower Streets seven houses accounted for 54 hearths in 1670: an unusually high average.

In 1851 West Street matched North Street in its high percentage of professional residents; and so it is today. After all, the south and west areas of a town receive the prevailing wind first.

North Side

1-4 What is now visible is a group of small 19th-century buildings on a cramped site. Even in 1808 traffic problems were acute and it was represented to the Council[2] that it was most desirable to obtain sufficient room to form a passage for carriages on the north side by pulling down properties which at that time ran square across what is now a modest sized opening. Cellars of the old buildings remain under the pavement. Even then the Market Cross was a mixed blessing.

Dolphin and Anchor: Evidence in 1486 and 1534 points to an earlier inn called *The George,* roughly on this site. A stone once in a chimney in the *Dolphin* was dated 1519. Earliest records for the *Dolphin* suggest it started in 1649; the owner in 1666, Henry Binsted, was referred to in Henry Chitty's will of 1641 as being a vintner and living in Chitty's house near the Cross at that time; it describes brewing vessels in the house. Chitty's widow is mentioned in the 1641 Court Leet for brewing and selling ale without a licence: the drink trade is not new to the site.

The Dolphin and *The Anchor* were originally two separate inns. The *Dolphin's* first mention by name – in 1649 – is in a conveyance from Thomas Phillips to Richard Collins. By 1670 it was a big establishment with 23 hearths, owned by Richard Bragge, a notary public, and Chapter Clerk, who also had *The Swan* in East Street. In 1662 an old ruined house on the east was purchased and a coach entry made. The inn was rebuilt in 1768. *The Anchor* was on the corner of Chapel Street; the property was also owned by Bragge in 1671. It was the *Blew Anchor* in 1737, described as 'new built' in 1768. The two inns were amalgamated in 1910.[3]

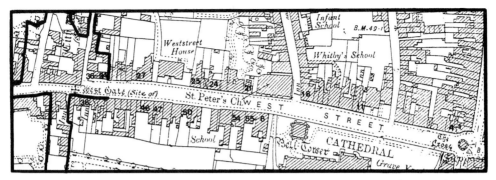

Fig. 8-1 1875 O.S. map overlaid with some modern street numbers and also showing the area since demolished to form the Westgate roundabout

Post Office site:[4] In the 18th/19th centuries this was the site of two houses (one called 'The Willows') with a coach house and stable and a long second frontage to Chapel Street.

11-18 (A & N)[5] No. 12 was the house of Lady Undall (1612), Lady Jarrett (1615) and Sir Henry Peckham in 1670, when it was a sizeable mansion with 13 hearths. In 1824 it was 2 newly built houses. Subsequently became the *Royal Oak* public house which was not demolished until 1962. Nos. 13-14 were Dean and Chapter property. Occupants included John French, goldsmith (1402), Michael Durrant, chirurgion (1612). The latter's house was described as 'old' in 1618. Seven hearths in 1670, *The Boot* alehouse in 1682 and a new house in 1731. No. 15 was owned by John Farrington up to 1608 and descended to Dr. Dobell by marriage (1670) when it had 13 hearths. Oliver Whitby's Free School 1712 (rebuilt 1904). In 1851 it had 38 resident pupils. Closed 1949. No. 18 was the *Marquis of Granby Inn* in 1798, the *Eagle Inn* 1830-1903[6] subsequently 'Tudor' then 'Tower' Cafe and A & N in 1959 (then Morants).

Fig. 8-2 Townscape showing *Eagle Inn* and Oliver Whitby's School

Subdeanery Church (now St Peter's Arcade),[7] was built in 1852. The eastern half of the site was the city custom house in 1790. The western half and also including No. 21[8] was a Dean and Chapter site with 4 cottages on it in the 16th century. The side wall of No. 21 is in English bond brickwork and the street front in stretcher bond. Between No. 21 and 24/24A was the Chichester Library prior to 1967.[9] This was a freehold site.

24-24A Site owned by St Mary's Hospital probably from the 13th century. Was three houses in 1685; encroached on street, 1724, probably when refronted; four houses 1763. In 1806 east end house taken down and rebuilt as one 'good substantial and complete house' (No. 24). In 1848 described as 'all messuage lately erected by Stephen Wise'.[10] Nos. 24 and 24A are butted on to each other.

25-25A Up to 1871 was two houses owned by City, when sold to William Norman who built Oriel Lodge. In 1842 had extensive yards, stables and workshops to the north. City lease of 1758 refers to 'The Old Storehouse'.[11] There were two old cottages straddling the present roadway on the west which were pulled down in the 19th century.

John Edes House:[12] This building once contained most of the records on which this book is based. It was built in 1696 and has been known, erroneously, as Wren House (Wren was not its designer). First occupied by John and Jane Williams and passed through successive generations of the family. In 1848 it was bequeathed to Dr. Joseph McCarogher. With the house were coach houses, stables and outhouses and 3 acres of meadow land behind. In 1916 it became County Hall, and when the new County offices were built it became the County Library.

Fig. 8-3 John Edes House as it was in the 19th century

There are no deeds before 1696 so it is necessary to try to reconstruct previous use from the Hearth Tax and other records. These suggest a group of several small houses on the site, occupied in 1670 by John Allen (2 hearths), William Gardner (3), Robert Green (2), Richard Peirce (8). The Dean and Chapter accounts for 1534 indicate that this site, between the modern 25A and 27, was owned by the City and the Chantry of Bishop Arundel: the latter certainly had land all the way up the rear of the Tower Street frontage before the Dissolution. Finally, the eastern abuttal to No. 27, in 1534, points to a city tenement on that site.

27   Eighteenth-century house with additions. John Aylwin was there in 1534, Richard Dally, a butcher, in 1661 (5 hearths in 1670), and Robert Raper in 1851.[13]

29-31: 29 – an early 19th-century house; 30-31 – 18th century. The site of these 3 houses was owned by the Vicars' Choral. In 1670 Thomas Booker, a baker, was occupier, taxed for 6 hearths and an oven. It was a large house described as a mansion with outhouses and stables in 1708. In 1785 three tenements were in the place of the original house. At the rear in 1649 was a malthouse and a wood yard.[14]

32-33 18th century. Vicars' Choral site. Site records from 1334 (John Stubbe and Master William le Ray); Thomas Patching and others 1402. Was liable for a quit rent to Canongate Manor.[15]

Sadly everything west of No. 33 is now under the roundabout and surrounding cleared area. (see Fig. 8-1)

What was 34-36[16] next to North Walls Street was recorded back to 1402. It was a Dean and Chapter property known as 'Brinkhurst' with a 20m frontage and 38m depth. Doctor Lewkenor, a recusant, lived here in 1611 and there is a graphic description in his inventory of 1618: it had a great and little parlour, a study, 9 chambers, a larder, kitchen, malthouse, buttery, garret, a little house, a footman's room, stable and well house. A previous occupant, Thomas Westmyll, had been a goldsmith. By 1763 the building contained 4 houses and in 1818 two are shown on a plan, but with a store and many outbuildings, and two cottages behind. In 1856 it was again divided into four.

West gate. The gate was demolished in 1773.

South Side

38 (*Castle* P.H.); the site was owned by the Dean and Chapter with a house in 1227; in 1534: 'two little tenements and garden plot adjoining'. A 1624 inventory records a great chamber, cellar, parlour, hall, wash house and kitchen, but significantly in 1649, after the Civil War, it was described as 'ruined and decayed' – for it had been a 'court of guard' when the city was a garrison and by 1670 was reduced to 1 hearth. House again in 1692 and was occupied by a bricklayer in 1704. By 1754 it was an inn, *The Three Kings*, subsequently *The Duke of Richmond*. The sign was removed by the Paving Commissioners in 1793 (by which time it had become *The Castle*).[17] The ground between this site and the wall was the Porter's Lodge in 1534[18] and a building was newly erected there in 1785. Now called, late 1992, *The Chichester*.

39-41 Two houses recorded in 1640/41, with stables and garden.[19]

44-45 Domestic buildings from the 16th century. No. 44 was *The Coopers Arms Inn* in 1766. In 1816 Gatehouse Bros. (new owners) pulled down all buildings and erected new public house called *Red Lion*.[20]

46 Property of Guild of St George until 1549. Bought by the City in 1550; subsequently freehold house (with shops in 1779). Present building early 19th century.[21]

47-51[22] Site owned by Dean and Chapter from earliest days of the Cathedral. Shop at No. 47 in 1534. 48 (formerly 'South Lawn') 18th century. 17th-century earlier house occupied successively by a singingman, merchant, baker: it had a hall, wainscotted parlour, kitchen, wash house, buttery and cellar, 5 chambers over; 6 hearths. 49 was a merchant's house in 1610. Combined with No. 50 in late 17th century and became separate again soon after 1700. Present house late 18th century. 50 late 18th century. Records from 1558. Merchant's house 1610, shop in 1644 with a hall, kitchen, buttery and also a stable and hayroom. 51, records from 1402 (Henry Greneliffe, tanner). Two houses in 1649. Frequently occupied by building trades – plumber, glazier, painter, joiner, bricklayer, carpenter.

52-53 Prebendal School and School House.[23] Original school dates from 13th century; reconstructed 1497, largely renovated in 1830 and much altered over the years. No. 53 was the house of the Master of the School.

Fig. 8-4 Townscape south side of West Street

54 Subdeans Place. Was the house of the Subdean of the Cathedral. Present house 18th century. In 1643 the Vicar and Subdean was ejected and it was thenceforward occupied by poor people of the city. In 1672 the vicar leased it to Dr. Stradling, a Prebend (as Subdean he already had a house in good repair), the house having fallen into decay, and Stradling undertook to rebuild it. However, when John Parke became Subdean in 1720 he found the house in the possession of John Shore, a Doctor of Physic. Parke claimed that the lease was illegal and void and that as it was the ancient Vicarage House it could not be leased. Parke made an entry in 1721 and ejected Elizabeth Shore, now widow of the Doctor.[24]

55-56 Another Dean and Chapter property with records from 1402. There is a long series of leases up to the 19th century. In 1649 it had four low rooms – 2 wainscotted, a cellar under one of them, 6 chambers over (1 wainscotted) and at the west end a little stable with a hay loft over and it had 10 hearths in 1670. Present building 18th century with alterations. Described as '2 tenements' in 1832. In 1562 it was occupied by Edward Ayres, a chapter clerk, who was suspended for misconduct.[25]

Bell Tower There is no other English cathedral with a detached medieval bell tower. The present tower was built between 1375-1435. It is 33 m high and 13 m square at the base. The walls are 2.5 m thick.[26]

Fig. 8-5 Cathedral Bell Tower

The Cathedral Frontage

On the 31st October 1205 King John gave leave for the building of houses 12 feet wide onto the highway in front of the burial ground on the north side of the Cathedral. Thus the townscape of this part of West Street was then very different. This otherwise continuous stretch of buildings was broken in three places: to the east was the Paradise Gate; in the middle the Middle Gate; at the west end the Tower (or Sun, or Churchyard) Gate. The whole of the property was leased by the Dean and Chapter and by the Bishop at different times, to a conglomeration of householders, butchers, bakers, blacksmiths, and for stables, slaughterhouses and a lime house. There were 3 inns: *The Sun* (also called the *Coach and Horses* in the late 18th century); the *Star* in the middle (later known as the *Royal Oak*); and the *Crown* (or *Crown and Sceptre*) at the east.

The city resolved on 7th June 1825 to vote £400 'for the removal of houses on the south side of West Street from the Cross to the Sun Gate' as a desirable objective – the area was finally cleared in 1848/52. A row of trees which replaced the buildings has also gone now, in its turn.

The front row of properties lay on what is now the pavement in front of the Cathedral, i.e. well in front of the present building line from Rapers onwards. Behind were more properties (see Fig. 8-6). In the 18th century even more encroachment took place as the jetties (overhangs) were filled in down to ground level.[27]

William Shayer, the painter, lived in the row in about 1800.

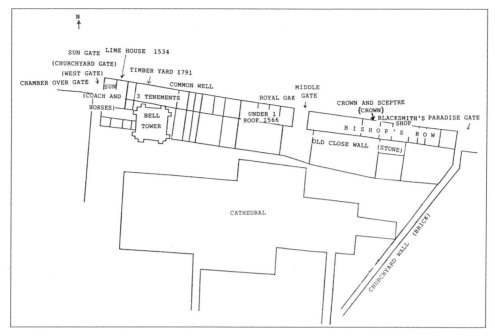

Fig. 8-6 Map showing various developments on the Cathedral frontage

In the middle of this stretch was a group of three houses under one frame in 1650, for which we are fortunate in having the will and inventory of the occupier, Edmund Southcott, a surgeon, and his wife. Whilst not large, there was a great chamber, bedchamber, kitchen, bakehouse and cellar. The contents in 1653/4 are exceptional (value £528) and include the usual tables and bedsteads, but also 20 pictures, 4 skutcheons, books, glasses, a harpsichord, silver tankards, gold pieces, a picture of his father 'with a curtain to draw over it', silver tobacco box, silver porringer, wrought silver teapot, silver bowls and candlesticks and crystal bottles.[28]

CHAPTER 9

NORTH STREET
Bustling and Busy

Documentary evidence is convincing that North Street was the predominant of the four main streets. For much of the time right up to 1974 it contained the administrative offices; it had two of the small churches, St Peter the Less and St Olav, and many inns; also important houses. The main market was there. Above all, its communications were supreme – far better than the other main streets. Fig. 9-1 shows that in addition to linking to East, South and West Streets and to a turnpike, it had east-west routes which ensured that passage right across the city went more easily through North Street.

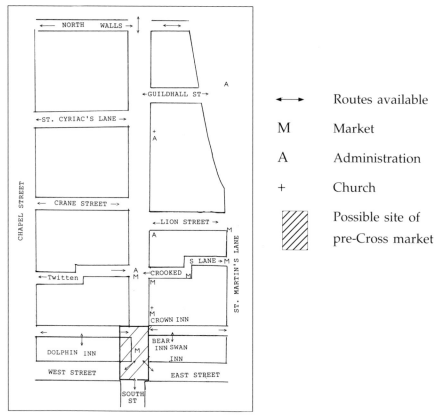

Fig. 9-1 Showing the churches, administration centres, markets and communications

Fig. 9-2 North Street early 20th-century view

Early documentary sources for the market at the south end of the street show:

12th century: reference to land of the Deanery in the Market Place[1] (and in 1160 'market burnt by fire').

13th century: 'all the land in the market place'[2]
'plot in Chichester market'
'all his stalls in Chichester market place with the space adjoining'
'Plot in market place 36 feet x 14 feet.'

14th century: tenements in Market Place[3]
'Certain shops situated in the Market'

15th century: 8 shops under 1 roof in the middle of the market place (9m x 4m).[4]

Stall-holders would try to leave their stalls on site between market days and gradually these became permanent buildings with let-down shutters and living premises behind. Shop fronts were edged forward in front of houses.

There is a case for the original open area taking in the sites of the present numbers 1-8 North Street, the first 49m on the west side to a depth of perhaps 15m. This would explain the misalignment of North and South Streets (see shaded area in Fig. 9-1).

Bishop Storey's Market Cross dates from 1501[5] and was provided so that the poor people should have somewhere to sell their wares, which tends to confirm the ever narrowing of the market area by merchants' shops.

Fig. 9-3 The old central Corn Market House before 1731

The Market House (A M in Fig. 9-1) is described by Spershott in *Records of Chichester* as follows:[6]

'The Old Corn Market House stood in the North Street, on the West side; it was pretty long from South to North, one side of it was close to the Gutter in the middle of the street, and the other was within about six or seven feet of the Houses, it stood upon posts or fram'd timbers. Pannel'd up about Breast high, it had an Entrance on each side, but its Chief Entrance was at the south end about half its width next the Houses, the other Half being the Cage which was Boarded up Breast High, and wood Barrs Perpendicular above. Behind the Cage was the stairs up to the Council Chamber, which was low, and had low old windows, it was a very old Building; the North End was nearly opposite the South End of the new Market House.' The old Market House is shown on the Norden Map of 1595: it was demolished in 1731. Further evidence of its appearance comes from the city records of repairs carried out.[7] An account of 1668 records the use of sand, lime, a hundred bricks, tiles, laths, tile pins and the employment of a joiner. In 1672 glazing is recorded and the payment of 'chimney money' i.e. Hearth Tax, for 1 hearth. There were tiles on the roof in 1574 (Court Leet). There was glass in the few windows upstairs, and a fire up there to ensure that members of the Council did not get cold.

Services

As in all market areas, services grew up all around. To provide for the
thirsty on market day there were the inns and beer-houses – *The Wheatsheaf,
Queen's Arms, Heart in Hand, Crown, Queen Anne, Benham's Beer House, Bear,
Little Anchor, Swan Tap* – could all be found between the Cross and Crane
Street (see Fig. 9-2).

The Council Offices were next to St Peter's Church from the 14th century
to 1541; subsequently in Priory Park; then over the timber Market Hall; and
finally in the Assembly Rooms building. The whipping post and stocks were
originally by the Cross and removed to the old Market Hall in 1714.

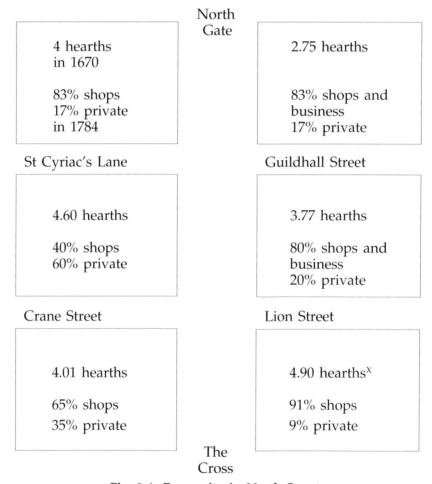

North
Gate

4 hearths in 1670 83% shops 17% private in 1784	2.75 hearths 83% shops and business 17% private

St Cyriac's Lane   Guildhall Street

4.60 hearths 40% shops 60% private	3.77 hearths 80% shops and business 20% private

Crane Street   Lion Street

4.01 hearths 65% shops 35% private	4.90 hearths[x] 91% shops 9% private

The
Cross

Fig. 9-4 Prosperity in North Street

'hearths' = the average number per property in 1670
[x] includes 1 large inn with 11 hearths
1784 percentages are derived from Trade Directory

Property

With its market, churches, administrative offices and inns North Street was bustling and busy. It is a long street and its character was not constant throughout. Examination of trade directories, censuses, leases and hearth and land tax records shows that the area from the Cross to Crane Street had a preponderance of shops with day-to-day trades. By 1784 there were more food and clothing shops in this stretch, suggesting less dependence on markets and more on permanent shops. An analysis of the hearth tax assessments gives an indication of the way the wealth of the street was segmented, if the number of admitted and assessed hearths can be taken as a guide to size of house.

The stretch from Crane Street to St Cyriac's, on the west side, emerges as the area with a high number of hearths, least businesses and trades, and most private houses. Many of these houses had large gardens which extended through to Chapel Street: this allowed for coach entrances from the rear. It is likely that this area was equally favoured right back to the 13th century when John de St Cross had a large area north from Crane Street with his own house, barns and tenements let out by him.

West Side

1-8[8]   This block of property, originally the site of market stalls, is recorded in the ownership of the Dean and Chapter from the 12th century; all the stalls in Chichester Market Place let by the Dean to Geoffrey Butcher 1227-41; shops (1338); specific shop leases from 16th century. The properties next to the Cross were pulled down in 1808/10.[9] Nos. 1-8 now much altered but mainly early 19th century.

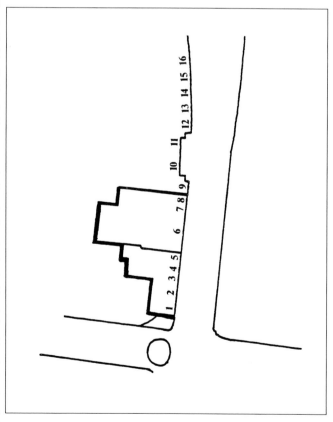

Fig. 9-5 Outline of Dean and Chapter and demolished properties

9   Recently Bastow's the chemists, had been in the occupation of doctors and apothecaries for well over 250 years: Farhill (1716), Phillipson (1804), Pile (1874).[10] Building early 19th century.

10-11[11] (Woolworths) Northern part was *Queen's Arms* public house in 1706 and *King's Arms* on accession of George I in 1714.

15   Land of Bishop Arundel's Chantry up to Dissolution.[12]

16-17 (W.H. Smith) Land of Guild of St George[13] which passed to the City in 1549.

20   *Heart in Hand* public house from about 1826 into the 20th century.[14]

21 $_{W}^{P}_{M}$ 1736 on rainwater pipe refers to William Pannell and his wife Mary who owned the property in 1732.

23 and **24** Early 18th-century pair. Large house in 1670 (13 hearths, Robert Anderson).[15]

25[16]   Young Ladies boarding school in 1804.

Fig. 9-6 Old houses at corner of Crane Street and North Street

27-28 Built as one house about 1700 and divided into 2 houses by 1710.[17] (See Fig. 9-6.)

29-30 All one building, built 1760. Joseph Briday, gunsmith, to 1672.[18]

31   (Purchase) 18th century. Maltsters in 1650-1700 (John Watts then David Wells.) House, malthouse, stables and gardens back to Chapel Street.[19]

32 and **32A** (Laura Ashley) 18th century. Tenement granted to John de St
   Cross in 1283/4 (see Chapel Street and Crane Street); in same family
1305-1335; had dovecote in 1402-14; occupied by a tailor, 1435; Richard Rables,
maltster, 1690; William Page, maltster, to 1738.[20] New built in 1772.

33-34 *City Arms* public house early 19th century. In 1829 anticipated
   pedestrianisation – Paving Commissioners recognised 'frequent nui-
sance occasioned and public put to great inconvenience by Mr. George
Seymour supplying his customers with beer and placing seats for them on
the foot pavement in front of his house particularly on Beast Market Day'.
Became Prince Albert in 1845 (reverted to *City Arms*, 1846).[21]

37   18th century. Purchased by Thomas Ball, archdeacon, about 1780 and
   rebuilt.[22]

38-39[23] Built as one house mid-18th century.

40   Fernleigh. Plot of ground in 1534 adjoining the 'Fire Rack'. House of
   William Cawley in 17th century. In 1788 described as a malthouse (later
brewhouse) with banqueting house which were pulled down and rebuilt by
1807[24] using mainly flints and yellow brick dressings and with a Tuscan doric
porch.

St Cyriac's Lane. Whilst the name has only recently been bestowed, a lane
   existed here in the 13th century – 'a messuage in the Street of St Cyriac'
awarded by Boxgrove Priory to Alexander Bole.[25] It led to the Chapel of
St Cyriac which was established in the 12th century but declined rapidly to
become the residence of a recluse. The lane is still referred to in 1649, and
ran on to Chapel Street up to 1769.

41-42[26] House in 1225/6; in 1521 a tenement granted to William Fleshmonger;
   garden in 1627; a pair of small houses on the site from about 1700
(probably 1 house from 1684-1691). Described, in 1742, as 'two dwelling houses
under 1 and same roof or frame, many years ago built on the site of 1 messuage.'
Thus whilst the date on the rear (1665) has no relevance, it is fairly near to
the truth. The two houses then were among the early brick phase using
probably part of the earlier frame.

43[27]   Dates from about 1700 and often had land at the rear included with
   it ('land called Cherry Garden') through to Chapel Street and North
Walls. Known erroneously as 'St Cyprians' in 1890.

   The final block from Nos. 44-49 consists of 18th- and 19th-century
properties:

44   18th century. The Butterly family were here in the 17th century with
   a blacksmith's business; the *Star Inn*, probably 1628, certainly 1641, had
6 hearths in 1670. It was a large building, and in 1679 had a hall, kitchen,
parlour and buttery, 4 chambers upstairs, a gallery, a milkhouse, brewhouse
and cellars. **46** *Bell* public house in 1780. **47** *Forresters Arms* beer house for
nearly 100 years up to 1934.[28] **49** new built in 1831.

   The North Gate was demolished in 1773.

East Side

In 1592 the site of Nos. 51-3 was 'a great house next to North Gate' and known as the *King's Head Inn*. A contemporary description mentions 'a chimney room, stairs, closet and rooms on the said stairs and closet'. Thomas Brigham had it in 1581 and owned most of the land inside the street framework north of Guildhall Street (excluding Nos. 54-56).[29]

51   *Dog and Partridge* 1721; George, 1745,[30] now *George and Dragon* public house.

52   Early 19th century. Robert Quennell (carrier) occupier in 1780 was obviously affluent – he had 6 servants. The family was virtually decimated about this time – 16 members died in 20 years.[31]

53   Early 19th century.

54-56 Dean and Chapter owned the site from 15th century or earlier. 55 and 56 have, at various times, been one or a divided pair. There have been cottages on the site back to 1402 or earlier.[32]

Ship built 1780. Was two cottages in 1581. Richard Godman's house 1689-1755. Home of Admiral Sir George Murray 1804-19. He was chief of staff to Nelson 1803-5 and was famed for his navigational expertise.[33]

58   Described as 'new built' in 1747 (previously a malthouse).[34]

59-60 18th century. Previously a merchant's house in 1629; malthouse added 1649; occupied by a carpenter in 1671 and a bricklayer in 1760.[35]

61   Greyfriars 18th century. House of Exton family (butchers, merchants and mayors) 15th-17th centuries. Alderman Smith, 17th century. Site included a large garden at the rear and, in the 17th century, the lease of small cottages at the rear in Priory Road.[36]

Fig. 9-7 St Peter the Less Church in 1852

62-63 16th-century timber framed cottages. Blacksmith in 1592. House of
       Margery Wilkinson 1669, used as a meeting place by Quakers. In 1699
'tenement, malthouse, stable, garden, sometime 3 messuages.' Robert Miller,
who was unmarried, lived here as tenant and died here, 1669. He was a
maltster/merchant who often sailed with cargoes to Devon.[37]

Church of St Peter the Less now demolished. Had various names (the Great,
       by the Guildhall in North Street). Church built pre 1347. Where the road
is now there was the Parsonage Garden. This stretched behind the Church
also and contained a barn.[38]

64 Guildhall in 1300, survived to 1541 when Corporation acquired Grey
       friars. In 1548 described as 'void plot where old Town Hall stood'.
Slaughterhouse and town pound here at that date. 1611 newbuilt house.
Owned by City Council until 1880.[39]

65 (*Old Cross Inn*) Was land given to Bishop Arundel's Chantry in
       1501/2; two tenements on plot 1585, one occupied by Hugh Jones a
tailor; came to the City Council. Known as *Dragon*, or *Green Dragon*, 1688.
In 1738-48 described as leasehold stable, formerly dwelling house called *Green
Dragon*. In 1753 *Dragon* alehouse. *Old Cross* built 1928.[40]

66 Vicars' Choral property. For very full description in 1649 see Chapter 7.
       Rebuilt 1696.[41] Now North House, built 1936.

70-70A Early 19th century, was Dean and Chapter property, known as
       'Collins'. Records from 1585. In 1649 shop, hall, kitchen, buttery,
4 chambers over, stable and yard and garden (occupier the Mayor). 1679-99
occupied by Richard Faithful, distiller, by now a malthouse.[42]

Assembly Rooms. Basic building, north and west parts, erected 1731, with
       extension to rear in 1783 and to south in 1880. Home of Thomas Miller
to 1635. He had been a clothier and the house was wainscotted and had glass
windows; also a dye-house. Occupied by his third son Mark in 1670 (5 hearths).
Sir John Miller (who by now lived at Lavant) agreed to sell to the Corporation
in 1730 so that a new market house and council chamber could be built on
the site to replace the old wooden market house.[43] The accounts show that
the cost, including land, was £1,271 15s. 11d. In 1733 the pavement where
the old Market Hall stood was pitched and put into repair.

74-75 Probably 16th century and timber framed. Thomas Hammond's in-
       ventory, 1727, lists a kitchen, cellar, workhouse, 3 chambers and a
glazier's shop. 74 was the house of Thomas Ghost, citizen and alderman. 1670:
8 hearths. 75 was Benham's Beershop in 1851.[44]

78-80 Adjoins Crooked S Lane (Shamble Alley). City properties. 79-80 were
       occupied by Abraham Howard, a victualler, in 1670 (5 hearths). It was
a jettied house: permission had to be obtained from the City to build under
the overhang.[45] 80 was the *City Arms*, and by 1755 the *Wheatsheaf Hotel*.
In 1787 still timber built, with tiles. In 1792 a decaying site; by 1804
substantially rebuilt, and now had a large market room, dining room, several
bedrooms, good yard and a corn store. The original canted bays are still
visible on the upper floors.[46]

Fig. 9-8 The Wheatsheaf

St Olav's,[48] 11th-13th century (now bookshop). The church consists only
of a chancel and a nave, both small. Construction is flint rubble with
stone dressings. The church was enlarged in the 13th century, altered in
the 14th and restored in 1851.

Fig. 9-9 St Olav's Church (19th century)

81   Was Parsonage House of St Olav's. Jettied up to 1700 when it encroached
      upon the street.[47]

Market House.[49] *Crown Inn* in 1574, John Buckingham, innholder, and in 1628
      Richard Bragge. Merchant's house by 1648 with a malthouse in 1663.
In 1720 it was divided into 2 parts (north part a house, shop and malthouse;
south part a brewhouse and shop. Both had garrets, chambers, cellars and
outhouses). The Butter Market was built in 1807 on land already owned by
the City Council.

83-85[50] Timber framed building behind a modern facade. Swan Tap here,
      also *Little Anchor Inn* (pre 1780 to 1963). John Greenfield, a mercer, had
a shop until 1663. His inventory (£1,204) reveals the large affluent house of
a successful mercer (5 major rooms downstairs and 8 hearths). Listed are many
tables, chairs, pictures, carpets, featherbeds, etc.[52]

Fig. 9-10 Butter Market as it was in 1830

86-87 Site belonged to the Brotherhood of St George pre 1550. Probably
      the site of the *Bear Inn* 1670 (11 hearths: Richard Young, innholder).
There is a fine plaster ceiling (16th-17th century).[51]
Corner site owned by St Mary's Hospital from 13th century (5 shops).
      Shops in 16th and 17th centuries and rebuilt in 1767 (still a shop).[52]

CHAPTER 10

EAST STREET
The Street of the Moneylenders

East Street, like North Street, has always been an important, busy commercial street. It has not enjoyed the administrative involvement of its neighbour, except for one limited exception, and there has not been a church directly on the street. Nor, too, has it had the same influence as a communications link – there was no cross-town routing. St Martin's Lane and Little London were extensions of East Street, rather than routes which led anywhere – the same is still largely true; and to the south were the Blackfriars and the Pallants which certainly led nowhere and were largely self-contained.

With its street markets came the inns, especially two major houses. Significantly it has had banks on seven different sites and still has four.

Documentary and archaeological sources reveal:

The street existed in Roman times and formed the route out to London (Stane Street).

Houses are recorded in the 12th and 13th centuries.[1]

There was continuous development from the Cross almost to Eastgate (see Norden Map).

Cattle markets were held in the street (see Fig. 3-1) from medieval times,[2] and in 1804 Seagrave records that it took up the whole street on alternate Wednesdays. The sheep market, which was not large, was moved from the area between East Walls and Little London and set up against the Priory wall on the south side of the street.[3]

The Gaol was located in the street.

The average number of hearths per house in 1670 was 3.85.[4]

In the early 1700s there were only 3 houses with sash windows;[5] (*Swan Inn*, *Coach Inn* – subsequently *Fleece*, and Mr. Sandham's house).

North Side

4   City property built about 1719. Site belonged to Guild of St George up to the Dissolution.[6]

5-6 National Westminster Bank. Present building 1899 for London and County Banking Co. Ltd. In 1402-14 a shop and principal messuage of Stubbe's Chantry in Litten Chapel. *Swan Inn* on site before 1527 (John Mathew, tenant). Thomas Bird, innholder and vintner 1599, Thomas Salloway, 1621. His son Edward's inventory in 1638 lists: kitchen, larders, hall, dining parlour, little dining room, ostler's chamber, chambers called Spread Eagle, Lyon, Rose, Bell, Angel, Green, Fox; gallery, yard, lodging chamber. The valuation was £347 9s. 6d. Among the contents were carpets for tables, 7 pictures, 2 maps

**Fig. 10-1 East Street showing the *Swan Inn*
and the conduit house in the 18th century**

and 42 beds. Richard Bragg (see *Dolphin* also) was keeper in 1655. The inn had 12 hearths in 1670. Thos Bury innkeeper, 1684. Thomas Peerman a merchant, had it up to 1703/4, Amos Peerman 1713, John Peerman 1733, Kemp 1784, William Ridge 1790, Richard Trigg 1798. Was described as 'quite new with sash windows' in 1718. Ceased to be an inn in the 19th century. Whilst occupied by Edney's in 1897 there was a disastrous fire. Sold to the Bank in 1898 (see Fig. 10-1 and Fig. 10-3).[7]

Fig. 10-2 Moulded plaque 5-6 East Street

7-8   House with a brewhouse 1736; mercer's 1804; new built 1795. Behind it was *Swan* stables 18th-19th centuries.[8]

Fig. 10-3 East Street, Edney's fire in 1897

11 Occupied by a cutler 1696, then a glover. Edney had his Poor Peoples' Furnishing shop here before moving to 5. Known as Old Bank House (Griffiths, Chaldecott and Drew)[9] and now Lloyds Bank.

14-15 City property known as 'White Oven' 1651. New built as 2 houses. Shops 1837.[10]

16-20 Marks and Spencer site (see Chapter 13).

21 Dean and Chapter property (records from 1402); 1556 Robert Norris shoemaker; 1609 Robert Cawley, alderman, father of William Cawley, MP; 1649 Stephen Humphrey – the house had a hall and wainscotted parlour, a kitchen, lower lodging chambers, little buttery, cellar, wash house, a fair dining room, chambers over and a garret; also a large malting floor at the rear 17m x 7m, with a malting loft over it. Had 9 hearths in 1670. William Collins 'the Chichester poet' was here. Through hands of a series of printers (Andrews, Seagrave, Mason, Wilmshurst, Charles Knight) in 18th and 19th centuries. Lottery office 1804. National and Provincial Bank 1928 (new building 1927).[11] A passage to the east of 21, leading to St Andrew's Church, is recorded in 1402.

St Andrew's Church[12] is at the rear of the street. Was known as St Andrew-in-the-Oxmarket. Surrounded by a small churchyard. Burials recorded 1563-1854. There was a little street to the east of the church variously called

Fig. 10-4 Church of St Andrew-in-the-Oxmarket about 1850

Cow Lane and Ox Street (1249).[13] Church built in the early part of the 13th century.

22-23 *Red, White and Blue Inn* at 23 in the mid-19th century.[14]

25   Built 1756. 'DW' inscription relates to Davis Wall (see note under 26).

26   Built about 1763. Mr. Beeding, a whitesmith, seems to have been disputatious. He made a cellar which encroached onto the street without the permission of the City Council, and his neighbour, Davis Wall, a butcher, complained that he had 'placed a gutter so that water ran off Beeding's property and into Wall's, making it damp', and he had dumped bricks causing Mr. Wall's wainscotting and lath and plaster to bulge inwards.[15]

29-31 John Lewis, a currier, merchant and victualler, was here 1621-1632.

In 1670 John Peachey had a large house (9 hearths) with a stable, yard and garden, and the lease of all the Great Garden of St Mary's, at the rear. In 1794 there was a cabinet maker and upholsterer here. In the 19th century the Capital and Counties Bank was at 30.[16] *The Bell Inn* was at 31 in 1736, but had gone by 1788 when the site was rebuilt.[17]

32-37 Site No. 220 of the Dean and Chapter. Site history starts in the 13th century (grant to Dean and Chapter of houses of Peter Cooke and William English – the latter's a stone house) and follows with Juliana Say and Robert Denecombe as tenants in 1402/14. In 1534-7 the building repair accounts mention repairs to a chimney, studding and daubing the walls and making a pentice to cart away the fall of water from the chimney; in 1649 when William Stamper, a merchant, was in occupation, the property consisted of 'all those little tenements'. Starting from the west there were 2 shops with 4 other low rooms and 4 chambers over, and next another property with 4 rooms, and an old former stable behind.[18] In 1790 John Dearling rebuilt and altered the 8 tenements and brewhouse on the site. 33 rebuilt mid-19th century, and 34-5 refronted.

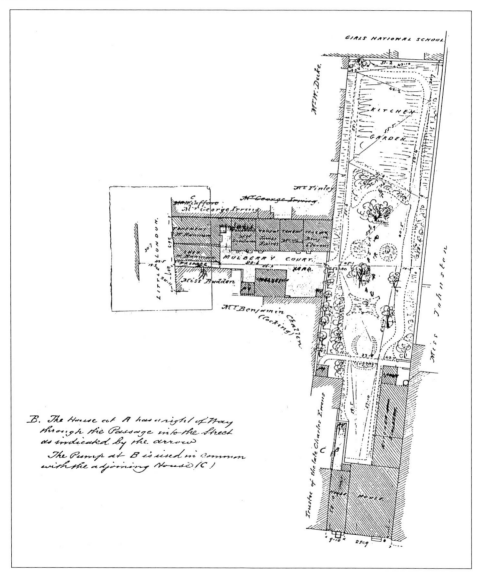

Fig. 10-5 A 19th-century plan of 42 East Street and property under same ownership in Little London

38 This largely rebuilt property dates from the 18th century. In 1750 James Dearling informed the City Council that his dwelling house and the one opposite were greatly exposed to wind and weather and in danger of being blown down in case of extraordinary tempest and therefore desired to put and fix one or more pieces of timber across [Little London] from one house to the other in order to strengthen and steady both houses at such proper and convenient height so as not to be an annoyance or inconvenience to coaches, carts or any loaded carriages.[19]

41 18th-century house. In 1769 Henry Curtis, a tobacconist, left a detailed inventory which shows that he also sold tea, coffee and drugs. The contents of his house included china coffee cans, blue and white cups and saucers, spoon boats, enamel painted tea-pot and saucer and coffee pot and pictures.[20]

42 A pair of 18th-century houses.[21]

43-44 Site owned by Guild of St George and occupied by Mr. Dunstall in 1549. Bought by City. Sir William Morley 1698, Sir John Miller 1718. Parish boundary (St Andrew's : St Pancras within) ran through the middle of the property. With the house went a garden containing much of the back land 73m x 15m plus 52m x 43m).[22]

45 *Cross Keys* 1721 and through to the late 18th century.

48-50 Site owned by St Mary's. Charles Shippam, pork butcher, had a shop at 48 in 1866; 49, Lucy Foster, beer retailer; 50, Budden, plumber.

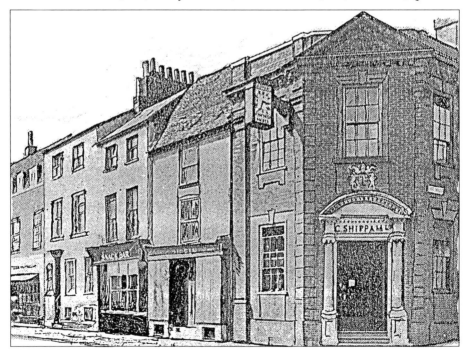

Fig. 10-6 Shippams corner site before its expansion along East Street

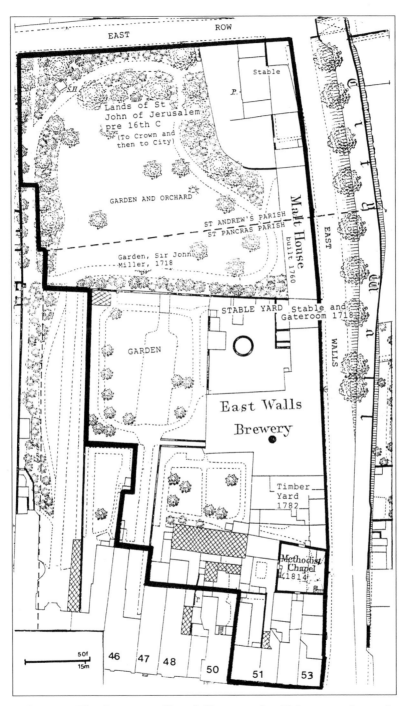

Fig. 10-7 The heavy outline delineates the Shippams site and shows what was there previously

In 1663 the whole was occupied by Robert Hitchcock, described then as a pinmaker, and as a woolmaster in 1673. In 1718 Edward Sanden occupied the house, which by 1739 was divided into two and by 1769 into three (one occupied by James Spershott in 1755). 49 was a beer shop in 1866, *Swan Inn* 1900, also known as *White Swan* and *White Horse*.[23]

51-55 This corner site was owned largely by the City Council. On the East Street frontage and for 30m up East Walls it was a jumble of houses, stores, a chapel (1814) and a stable, and a timber yard (18th century). In 1865 a shop there was called 'The Little Teapot', selling china, glass and earthenware.[24] Between 1650 and 1678 it was a house occupied by Edward Lacklott, a merchant.

Rather like the Marks & Spencer site, Shippams have 'spread' over a large slice of the town which had previously been in various sorts of occupation.

Gate Gaol and Gatehouse. On the east side of the East Walls the gate linked the city wall, until it was demolished in 1783. The City Gaol had stood over the gate and on the north side was the gatehouse (see Grimm's drawing, Fig. 10-8) where the porter originally lived, but which was handed over to the gaoler in 1744 'the better to enable the Gaoler to look after the Gaol and premises'. A new gaol was erected in 1783 on the south side of the place where the East Gate stood. The gaol was recorded in 1363 and was described as often wrecked (*prostrata*) by the prisoners.[25] Nothing changes.

Fig. 10-8 1782 Grimm's drawing of Eastgate and into East Street, showing the fencing in front of Page's house

South side

The land from the East Gate to Baffins Lane formed part of the site of the Blackfriars (see Chapter 14). Before they took over the site in the 13th century there was a lane (Pouke Lane) which ran from the East Street southwards along the inside of the city wall.

Wall to St John's Street. Houses recorded 1239/47[26] and in the 14th century.

There was a forge just inside the walls in 1473 and 1502.[27] The Old Police Station was here to 1937, with a gaol.

Fig. 10-9 The Old Police Station

St John's Street to Baffins Lane. Under what is now Stockland House was the burial ground of the Blackfriars, mentioned in 1363 as open and unfenced.[28] This was excavated in 1965 (see Chapter 3).

Before the Corn Exchange there was a mansion house[29] built after the dissolution of the Blackfriars. A capital messuage called 'Blackfriars' is recorded in 1600. It was in the occupation of the Page family from 1649 to 1809: in 1670 Francis had it – 11 hearths were taxed. It was rebuilt just before 1777 when it was described as a capital messuage. Before its final sale it was described:

> Basement: excellent cellarage, butler's pantry, dairy, larder.
>
> Entrance by flight of stone steps and doric portico, handsome hall and staircase 39ft. x 49ft., eating room 23ft. x 18ft.6in. by 11ft.6in. high, marble chimney piece, stucco cornice, dadoed and plain stained paper.
>
> Dining Room 25ft.6in. x 16ft.6in. with rich cornice, marble chimney piece.
>
> Library 15ft.6in. square.
>
> Housekeeper's room with presses.
>
> On the first floor a cheerful morning room, 3 bedrooms, 4 excellent attics, dressing room, closets.
>
> Detached kitchen, brewhouse, wash house, laundry, man servant's room.
>
> Flower garden, shrubberies, meadow, double carriage house, 5-stalled stable, harness room, orchards, pigeon houses.

Fig. 10-10 Corn Exchange, East Street, in mid 19th century

This house was pulled down and replaced by the Corn Exchange (see Fig. 10-10) in 1833. The facade of that building has survived, but altered inside to become a cinema and later, a café. The land behind was sold for building plots which became St John's Street, New Town and Friary Lane (see also Chapter 14).

57   Site owned by Dean and Chapter. Front is 19th century. Core is mid-17th century, when it was converted from a little house and stable into a dwelling house. The stable is recorded in 1581.[30]

58-60 *The Fleece Inn* (now closed) is now only one part of this building, but
     originally occupied the whole site. Previously under the name of
The Golden Fleece, The Bell, The Coach and Horses. Was refronted in 1715 when
the underhang of the jettying was filled in. Earliest record as an inn is 1710
but was an alehouse in 1641.[31]

61-61A 18th century. Wheelwright in 1637/8, then a shoemaker.[32]

63-64 New built 1776.[33]

66   18th century. *Catherine Wheel* (alehouse) in 1690.[34]

67   18th-early 19th century. William Smith, baker, in 1670 (8 hearths).Pre-
     viously John Butler, gent, was arraigned in 1627 for having dung before
his door. Had malthouse in 1637. Jetty overhang filled in 1723.[35]

68   18th century. In-fill of jetty, also, in 1724.[36]

71-72 Pair of 18th-century houses, encroached on street, 1724.
     At rear was a court of 7 houses in 1800.[37]

73-75 73 was the *White Hart Inn* in 1784. Richard Holmes, a baker, here in
     1573. In 1678 Roger Eyles, a maltster, left a detailed inventory (value
£902 13s. 11d.). He had a windmill at Westhampnett. Debts owing to him
made up half his valuation. Chichester Bank 1809-1900. Previous house built
1791/3.[38]

76-77 Dean and Chapter site. Records from 1402/14. Known as Millwards.
     John Holmes, glover 1573; Richard Manning, fishmonger and chandler
1624; in 1649 described as a house with little parlour, kitchen, buttery and
3 chambers and garrets over.[39]

78-79 In 1573 stable of Ralph Westdean and in 1604 of Richard Triggs, the
     innholder of the *George* at 80. Was two dwelling houses 1784, subse-
quently Tudor Cafe and Tylers.[40]

80-82 The Hall of the Fraternity of St George was here from 1368 to 1547
     when it was appropriated[41] and became known as The Old Council
Room. William Royce had his house here in 1534 and an inn was known from
1573. It was *The Anchor* in 1573 and then *The George*, one of the seven major
Chichester inns, and was still in existence in 1664. Innkeepers included Richard
Triggs and Emme Clarke. Her inventory in 1652 lists a hall, kitchen, Red
Parlour, a little buttery, malthouse and well, and Anchor, George, Rose and
Lyon Chambers, also 2 garrets, a large cellar and stables. It was well furnished
– wainscotting, tables, cupboards, 14 beds, arras carpet, brewing and malting
equipment and a turkey carpet. John Miller had the Old Council Room in
1754 and John Chaldecott, a gold and silver smith and cutler had the premises
in the late 18th century. Halsted's iron-monger's shop, which was there in
1871, was destroyed by fire.[42]

83   The site was given to the Dean and Chapter by Henry Eyre and William
     atte Dene in 1492/3. They previously had it from Thomas Frank of
Tortington. By 1533 it was a substantial building – the repair accounts list
300 lead castings for a gutter; 2,500 lath nails and 700 tile pins were used.
From this house a passage led southwards and then turned east through a
court into North Pallant in the 16th century. In 1649/50 it was a shop with

Fig. 10-11 East Street, Old Punch House

5 other rooms and 3 cellars, and above were 4 chambers and 2 garrets. Behind was a yard and pump and a malting floor 15m x 6m. with a malting loft over it and behind this was the passage mentioned above. Merchants occupied it in the 17th century: Thomas Billet (1607-1626), Bernard Harmwood, George Stamper, and by 1793 William Carlton a postmaster and chinaman. The present building dates from 1713.[43]

84-86 House of the Diggons family[44] for about one hundred years from 1557.

 84 is 18th century.[45] Occupants have included a tinplate worker and brazier (84) and a mercer, bookseller and corkcutter (85).[46]

87-89 Dean and Chapter site, new built 1536/7. *Star Inn*, John Holland inn-holder 1573, then Thomas Bird, who subsequently crossed the road to the *Swan*. Inn ceased by 1597. Partly rebuilt 1655, divided into 3 in 1675. Rebuilt again 1709. Occupants have included merchants, butchers, an apothecary, barber, brazier, watchmaker, sadler, grocer, surgeon and latterly The Sussex and Chichester Bank.[47]

90-93 Block owned by St Mary's Hospital. Between 91 and 92 is an entry (The Horse Entry) at the end of which was the old Church of St Mary in Foro. 91, east side of the entry, was its parsonage house, measuring 6m x 4m. It is first recorded in 1534 but is doubtless earlier.[48]

92-93 House, formerly two, built into one by William Holland before 1595.

 His widow married Viscount Lumley and it became his town house. It had a backside, garden and a great vaulted cellar under the late Church of St Mary and a great chamber built on the south side of the cellar. The house contains a fine 16th-century plaster ceiling. Now the *Royal Arms* public house (*Ye Old Punch House*)[49] (see Fig. 10-11).

94 18th century. Midland Bank, previously London and Counties Bank and later the London and Midland.

 The common water conduit stood at the Cross end of the street. The conduit house was a large round heavy building leaded over and in pyramidal form. Its position between what is now the *Royal Arms* and the Cross meant that only pedestrians could edge past it and the houses. A new conduit was built in South Street in 1777[50] at a cost of £92 17s. 10d. after allowing for the sale of the old lead. Subsequently a cornice (£9 9s. 5d.) and a statue (£15 15s. 0d.) were added.

CHAPTER 11

SOUTH STREET
Escape to the Sea

This has been a busy commercial street from the 13th century, when there was a row of little shops running south from the Market Cross on both sides of the street as far as West Pallant. By the 16th century the shops on the west side had spread further south, whilst on the east side a number of large mansions began to appear down to the south wall.

The fish shambles were here in 1604 and the conduit head was moved from its awkward position by the Cross in East Street in 1777, forcing the fish shambles to move southwards. The conduit, with its stone statue (now in Priory Park) had a large reservoir underneath.

Excepting for the *White Horse* (16th century) and, much later, the *King's Head* (mid 18th century) there was a dearth of inns and the early banks never settled here. The Theatre was founded at Southgate and two early post offices were in the street.

The street never had the importance of North Street (market, administration, churches) or East Street (market, banks, largest inns) and not until 1779 was it a significant route out to the south when it was turnpiked, but the developments of the 19th century (canal and railway) increased its importance.

West Side

Almost the whole of this side from the Cross down to the old Congregational Chapel was for centuries in the ownership of 3 bodies: the Dean and Chapter, Vicars' Choral and St Mary's Hospital. It is unique, even in Chichester, that a stretch of over 200 metres had only one freehold property.

Even the remaining properties southwards to the wall were originally owned by the City Council. The ownership pattern is logical. From the Cross to the churchyard entrance backing on to the churchyard was mainly property of the Dean and Chapter; the next stretch to Canon Lane was of the Vicars' Choral (for these properties were originally the backs of houses in Vicars' Close); the final section – all Dean and Chapter – backed on to Close properties south of Canon Lane.

Behind what is now 1-13 was a great brick wall known from 1534 and probably much earlier: in 1589 the Chapter Acts record that the tenants in this row should enter into covenants to repair the wall within one month of a warning, on pain of a forfeit of 3s. 4d. per month. A graveyard wall is recorded in 1247 but the material used is not given.[1]

1-3   This much altered site was owned by the Dean and Chapter and had been used as shops ever since they were formed out of market stalls.

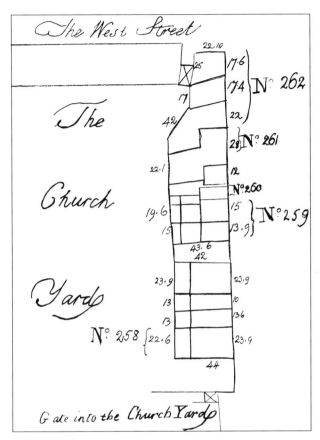

Fig. 11-1 A plan of the Dean and Chapter of 1763 showing the ownership of their properties (258-262)

The corner plot was granted to the Dean and Chapter in 1246 for the anniversary of John Neville junior and in 1402 there was another shop backing it (facing westwards at the old churchyard gate, which is now part of the footpath). In 1644 it was a shop with a lodging garret above. **2** was two shops in 1402. Rebuilt in 1776. In the 18th and 19th centuries occupiers included Charles Jacques, a watchmaker, William Smithers, a stationer, and William Potter, a fruiterer. **3** another shop in 1402; repairs in 1533 were to the kitchen and buttery and privy house, 2,500 bricks being used and it refers to a new chimney; in 1670 5 hearths. Occupants included: baker (1574), fishmonger (1604), glover (1628), tallow chandler (1699), cordwainer (1722), printer (1783), china dealer (1804), dealer in stays (1840). In 1604 Mr. Roman was reported to Court for a dunghill which 'annoys the fish shambles'.[2]

4   Another Dean and Chapter property. Shops recorded from 1220. In 1623 occupied by James Pilbeam, a merchant. It was in this shop that Pilbeam's mother, Elizabeth Wright, allegedly called Mary Chitty a scurvy queen. Chitty retaliated by calling Wright a filthy bause. This led to a defamation case.

In 1649 it was described as a large shop, with kitchen, wash house and cellar and a fair dining room (wainscotted) over the shop and three other chambers and garrets on the top floor. Later occupants included a butcher (1790) and Shippams (1881 until recently).[3]

5-6   This plot, partly owned by the Dean and Chapter and partly by St Mary's Hospital, was a shop in 1220 when it was granted by William of Keynsham to the Hospital and was still a shop in 1402. **5** was occupied by a tailor in 1577 and a chandler in 1628. Occupants have included a barber (1697), peruke-maker (1760), grocer (1796). The two plots were combined in the same building by the 18th century.[4]

7-8   In 1247 Nicholas Pupet granted this plot with buildings on it to the Dean and Chapter for the anniversary of Sir Walter de Giles. Pupet had acquired it from William de Audesbury. It was a shop in 1402; in 1565 Richard Mann had a mercer's shop. Before 1649 it had been two tenements but now became three shops with kitchens, halls, cellars and chambers and garrets over. Subsequent occupiers: glazier (1661), tailor (1666), patten maker (1742) – when it was newly built as 3 messuages – sadler (1787), basket maker (1812), hat maker (1851), grocer (1854).[5]

9-10   Early 19th century. Belonged to St Mary's. Three shops in 1402. Shoe maker (1691), grocer and tea-dealer (1780), draper (1831) to modern times.[6]

11   Early 19th century. Dean and Chapter property occupied by John Est, a mercer, in 1534. He had to do all repairs except those requiring lime and tiles. Occupiers included mercer (1569), fishmonger (1574), cordwainer (1610), bricklayer (1697), butcher (1776), chemist (1851). In 1649 there was a shop, hall, kitchen, buttery and 4 chambers and a garret over.[7]

12-13 18th century. The only freehold property. To the south was stone stile to the churchyard. First recorded occupier was John Est (of 11) in 1534, then in 1592 it appears in the will of Richard Bennett, a cordwainer, who had purchased it from Rowland Starkie. John Bartholomew, a merchant, had it prior to 1666 when it had 4 hearths. In 1869 the northern half was the *Crown* beerhouse.[8]

Vicars' Hall and Undercroft. The Hall which fronts the street is late 14th century. It has an open timber roof. The brickwork is 18th century. The original range of the Hall was 11m east-west by 7m, the eastern end being the Vicars' parlour. In the 14th century a building called La Guldenhalle was on the site. In 1394 the premises were conveyed to the King and thence granted to the Bishop for the Vicars' Hall and Residence. In 1402 it is recorded that the buildings were pulled down for 'the vicars' new building'. It was used as a post office in 1812 and a school in 1853. The undercroft was probably part of the original Guildhall (late 12th century), and survives. It may have long been used for storage. By 1649 the Vicars' leased it to the occupier of the *White Horse Inn* opposite for use as a cellar. In 1686 the tenant Mr. Booker kept swine there. In the early 19th century it was a wine vault. It has also been a horticultural store, an antique shop and a restaurant.[9]

Fig. 11-2 Vicars' Hall building

14-23 Part of this row (17-23) suffered unprecedented vandalism in the 19th century. Originally these were houses facing westwards into Vicars' Close, with their back walls to South Street. In 1825 they were made to face eastwards and turned into shops, and were sealed off from the Vicars' Close by a 3-metre flint wall. The whole stretch from the churchyard to Canon Gate remained in the ownership of the Vicars' Choral.[10] The history of the buildings up to 1825 is discussed in Chapter 15.

Fig. 11-3 Vicars' Hall Undercroft

Canon Gate. This was originally of 16th-century date and was restored in
        1894. In 1649 it was described as a large house and gateroom and
contained the porter's lodge.[11]

Fig. 11-4 Canon Gate

        From Canon Gate southwards to the wall the property again was mainly
in the ownership of the Dean and Chapter. The frontage land was leased for
shops and houses, probably soon after it was acquired in the 11th century.
24-29 In 1402 this group consisted of five newly-built tenements all under
        one roof.[12]
24-25 Tenant was Stephen Stonham in 1402. In 1534 repairs consistent with
        a timber-framed building – laying syl and plate, 2 postes and it is
described as a shop. In 1569, as was customary, it had a detached kitchen
and the tenant shared a well with his neighbour. For a period around 1600
it was used for ale-brewing and tippling. In 1649 it had a hall, a wainscotted
parlour, kitchen and wash house, cellars under, 4 chambers over the parlour
(1 wainscotted) and 2 garrets above. In 1665 a gable end was newly erected
and used as a stable. Richard Collins (grandfather of the poet) was occupier.
It had 6 hearths. Later occupiers were a baker (1760), butcher and baker (1851).
It was divided into 2 by 1812. A bakehouse in 1822 was described as 'recently
erected'.[13] Present building is 17th century or earlier under modern work.
26   The earliest record is 1402 when it was newly built and occupied by
        William Lovent. In 1533/6 George Ives was having frequent repairs –
studding, bredding and daubing, new tiles, new guttering, work on covering
his kitchen. In 1558 William Frend had a shop and subsequent occupants were
Philip Wisdome, cordwainer (1609), Thomas Pollard, tailor (1625). In 1783

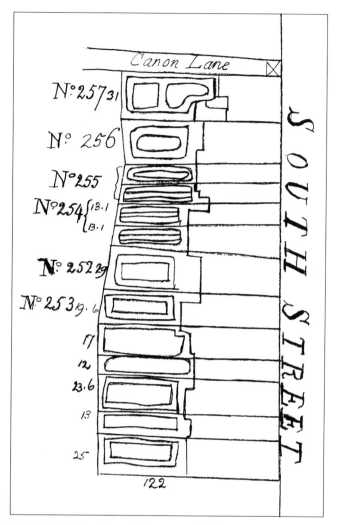

Fig. 11-5 24-29 in plan of Dean and Chapter properties, 1763

Mary Pay left the property divided into 2 tenements to Thomas Capel and it went via his widow to her daughter Catherine Luffe who was a cordwainer.[14]

27 New built 1402 (Richard Pryde, occupier). 2 tenements in 1608 and described in 1649 as 2 separate shops with respectively 2 and 4 chambers over and detached kitchens and in 1670 each had 2 hearths. Later occupiers included: William Kelway (1755), James Shippam, grocer (1796) who was described in 1809 as ' late a tailor now a shopkeeper ', Thomas Howe Clarke, leather cutter and magistrate (1845). Present building about 1770.[15]

28-29 In 1402 new built : John Bukke, pellipar (i.e. a tanner). In 1597 William Watts, tailor, John Standen, yeoman (1608), Giles Sherrier in 1649, when it had kitchen, wash house, 2 chambers and garret over and a malting floor,

11m x 5m. Approval to encroach on street in 1704. 1851 – Fogden, corn dealer.[16] Present building 18th century.

29A, 30, 31, 32, 33. More Dean and Chapter properties. In 1533 Richard Gardner, William Dowlinge and John Cook (alias Sympson) were occupiers. Repairs to Dowlinge's shop windows and back door are recorded and Gardner's house had to be underpinned on the west. Subsequent tenants (16th century): Walter Cover – cobbler, John Trydleys – Cathedral sexton, Thomas Billett – vintner, John Pollard – tailor and huxter. In 1649 Michael Austen a tailor, had a shop, hall, buttery, 3 chambers over and 2 garrets above. The property continued as several houses into the 18th century, subsequently being occupied by a succession of brewers. This led to the South Street Brewery, which occupied the bulk of the site by 1856, with a malthouse, chaise house, 3 cellars, 2 gateways, a granary and in the 20th century the brewery site became a garage with front access at 30-33 and has since reverted into separate occupations at 29 and 30-31 and 32-33.[17]

34-36 Until recently the site of the United Reform (previously Congregational) Chapel. Site of 3 tenements leased by Owen Benyon from Dean and Chapter in 1562. In 1649 there were 3 shops each with chambers over, a kitchen, woodhouse and gardens behind and they continued as 3 houses into the 19th century.[18]

37-40 The remaining property to the south wall was originally a garden belonging to the City Council and is recorded in 1416 as a quitclaim to Geoffrey Prykelove (the City received the plot by grant from Prykelove and he obtained a clear title by quitclaim from John Dautrye). In 1573 it was leased to John Diggons, alderman, when it was described as a messuage, stable and garden. His heir William Bullaker conveyed it for 100 marks to Richard Stanney. In 1670 the building was substantial – 10 hearths – its occupier Mrs. Powley. In 1743 it had a coach house and had been recently occupied by John and Elizabeth Farrington; subsequent owners were the Rev. William Wareing, Robert Bull and Richard Smith. 37-38 are a pair of early 19th-century houses and 39-41 18th century.[19]

Southgate was demolished in 1773.

East Side

43-45 This site now comprises the old theatre, a bank and the Regnum Club.

Because of its earlier history this site is dealt with as one entry. The earliest record covering the whole site is of 1587: a sale for £110 by Walter Edmonds to John and William Michelbourne of a 'messuage or tenement with gardens, orchards, backsides and stables' in South Street and the Pallant. John Michelbourne's inventory of 1620 describes the house: kitchen, hall, coach house, little back room, 2 upper rooms, pantry, chamber over hall, and 2 other chambers, maid's chamber, study, buttery and brewhouse. The kitchen contained 23 silver spoons, beer bowls and wine bowls; the hall – fowling pieces and muskets.

In 1669 the site contained a great messuage, new stable, gatehouse, barns and orchards, with 12 hearths. By 1745 a Dean and Chapter property to the

Fig. 11-6 Regnum Club, Bank and Theatre before modern development

north had been absorbed into the site. 1764 saw the first sub-division of the site.[20]

45 (C on plan) Regnum Club. Sir John Miller's 18th-century house was sold in 1776 to Philadelphia Russell who kept a dame's school in the house and was there up to 1815. The house had a garden which ran through to the South Pallant. In 1880 the property came to the Chichester Literary and Mechanics' Institute.[21]

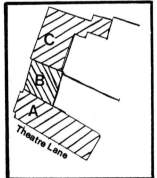

Fig. 11-7 Plan of Regnum/Bank/Theatre

In 1764 the malthouse, storehouse and granary at the southern end of the site (A) had been adapted as a theatre; in 1791 the buildings were taken down and rebuilt as a purpose-built theatre or playhouse, which lasted as such until 1850 when it was sold to E. Combes for £335 and used as a brewhouse. Sale particulars of what was 'Lot 5' show that scenery and props were included in the sale in 1850.[22]

46 and 47 Now separate were, for part of the 19th century, occupied as one, but before that they were again 2 properties. The southernmost (46) was a Dean and Chapter property (St Augustine's Chantry). In 1533 it had a detached kitchen and bakehouse and one of its 2 occupants was Sir Robert

Christmas. In 1649 when Nicholas Collins, a tailor, was the tenant, it had a shop, hall, kitchen and buttery and 4 chambers over. It was newly rebuilt before 1727 when it had a coach house, brewhouse and bakehouse. In 1779 the coach house became a schoolroom. In 1812 Henry Silverlock took the lease and combined it with 47, which had been a tenement of the Chantry of St Cross (dissolved in the 16th century). By the 19th century a large garden was attached and a cottage in South Pallant.[23]

48-49 At the rear was South Street Court, one of the relatively small number of infills of the late 18th century in Chichester. The Court consisted of 5 tiny dwellings with a common pump and privy.[24]

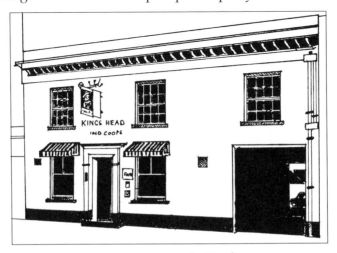

Fig. 11-8 *King's Head*

50	*King's Head* public house. An alehouse was recorded in the mid-18th century. The site belonged to the Dean and Chapter and had a succession of buildings recorded from 1402. In 1649 it was a large house with 7 ground floor rooms and 5 chambers over, a stable and garden. In 1724 the timber frame was enclosed and encroached into the street. In 1804 the publican, Fogden, was also a watch and clockmaker.

51	Dean and Chapter property, new built about 1640 and had a little hall and a wainscotted parlour, kitchen, cellar, 2 butteries and 5 chambers above – one a 'fayre dining room'.[26]

52-53 Was converted in 1891 for use as a Post Office. An old building on this site was pulled down in 1797. Sir Charles Ashburnham lived here in 1750.[27]

54	A Dean and Chapter site, previously of the Canongate Manor, with records from 1361 when it was inherited by John de Offham from his father. In the 16th century successively occupied by 3 singingmen and a verger; John Little, an apothecary, had it in 1649. In the late 18th century it had become 2 stables and was rebuilt in the early 19th century.[28]

55	Farrington House. The first mention of the Farrington family on this

site is in 1563 in a quit rent to the Dean and Chapter for his 'great house'.
Earlier records mention Walter Maryng in 1493 and Sir John Maryng in 1534.
When Thomas Farrington died in 1576 he willed the house to his son John.
In 1609 the house was recorded with another house and a garden in West
Pallant; in 1670 the house had 15 hearths and is described as a capital messuage.
The occupant was now Sir John, who settled it on his second son, Richard,
who became a baronet in 1692. The date of the present building can be
established from a marriage settlement of 20th February 1696, which refers
to 'the messuage lately new built'. When his wife, Dame Elizabeth, died, the
property descended (as part of the estate of Sir Richard) to a distant relative,
Cowley Palmer, the couple having outlived their progeny. It was then described as a capital messuage with coach house, stable, etc. Palmer sold it
to Thomas Baker, chandler and grocer and Thomas Bennett, a blacksmith,

Fig. 11-9 *White Horse Inn*

jointly. Misfortune struck. This bright pair, ahead of their time, decided to demolish this fine building for its materials and only stopped when the bay on the north side had gone. At this time the house was set back, and in the late 19th century shops were built in the forecourt so that the original doorway has now disappeared.[29]

56-56A, This group of 18th- and early 19th-century properties has varied **57-59,** in its number of units. In the 16th century it was a tenement of the **60** Earl of Arundel; in the 17th century it was several small tenements. In the 18th and 19th centuries it was shops with a cider manufactory and workshop with stables at the rear. There was the encroachment into the street in 1724, 24m long and 1m deep, of a new front brick wall.[30]

61 *White Horse Inn.* The first reference to the inn, by name, is in 1533.

The Sussex County Coroner's Inquest for 10th September 1533 refers to a William Skynner, alias Hobson, who had been drinking and making trouble in the *White Horse Inn* and eventually went on to be killed by Edward Holland. In 1574 John Colpat was the innholder, whilst Thomas Suter was presented to court for holding unlawful games at the cellar against the *White Horse*. The resignation of Robert Williamson of his rectory at Graffham took place at the inn on 21st February 1576/77 which suggests some use of the place for ecclesiastical purposes. The will of Thomas Farnden in 1577 gave the lease to his son Henry (soon to be known as 'Farrington'). The innkeeper in 1599 was James Brisenden. In 1604 it was reported to Court that 'the sign of the White Horse is very much decayed and not well to be discerned by reason of the weather ... which hath washed away the colour of him.' The landlord in 1641 was John Combes who was brought to Court for allowing unlawful games and for suffering 'his dung to be layed against the Pallant Church.' In 1660 the building was described as 'a hall, great and small parlour, kitchen, paved yard and well, with the yard leading into 2 stables with hay rooms over them.' Upstairs the main building had 5 wainscotted chambers and it had 11 hearths. The Vicars' Choral owned the site.[31]

Cooper Street to the Cross.[32] This area was in the ownership of the Hospital of St Mary from the 13th to the 19th centuries. The Church of St Mary in Foro was the precursor of the present Hospital in St Martin's Square (see Chapter 13).

St Mary in Foro operated from the reign of Henry II to about 1290.

There were, at one time, 13 inmates, so when the poor and other officials are counted in, the building could not have been tiny, unless it was over-crowded. The map (Fig. 11-10) shows the property mentioned which accrued to the original foundation and which survived into modern times. The income was used for the upkeep of subsequent inmates.

The Church of St Peter in the Market must have been in the corner of the streets in view of the following entry on the Chartulary of the Hospital:
'Grant by Clarice of "all that moiety of the messuage ...
in the South Street of Chichester which moiety is
adjoining the Church of St Peter in the Market Place
on its south side" '

1   Grant by Christiana and Clarissa
    daus. of Richard the Robbur
    c.1230. Property.

2   Grant by John Sturm to William
    of Arundel 1210-36. Property

3   Grant by Thomas Scute 2 shops

4   Shop of Daniel son of Adam

5   Grant by Martin of plot held by
    David the Goldsmith

6   Grant by Daniel. 2 shops

7   Grant by Alice, heir of Ralf
    Sefare. Tenement & buildings

8   Tenement of William the parson

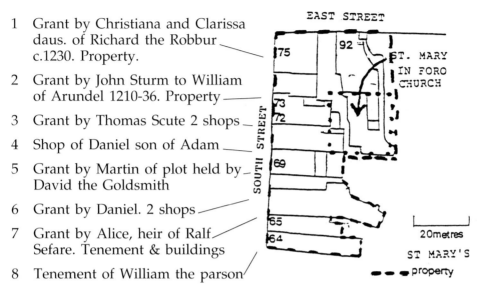

Fig. 11-10 13th-century buildings[32]

However, W.D. Peckham suggests that there was only one church, originally
St Peter, renamed St Mary.

From the same Chartulary a number of grants of property to St Mary's
in the 13th century make it possible to reconstruct the list of occupiers of what
were called shops at that time. In accordance with custom each plot was
probably about 20 feet wide and up to 100 feet deep; initially the 'shops' would
have been little more than stalls, which gradually encroached and became
permanent.

What now appears in this stretch is a series of 17th-and 18th-century
buildings with an early granary behind 65. The street frontage was complete
until 1807 when two houses were demolished and Charles Cooper built 16
houses off the main street. The house demolished was freehold and in 1664
Thomas North, gentleman, had lived there. He had a great chamber, hall,
parlour, malthouse and kitchen.[33]

69   Occupants included: Costelow, maltster (1683), Stokes, butcher (1765),
       Blagden, watchmaker (1779), Wells, grocer (1793) and Newman, grocer
(1821).[34]

72-73 Occupants: McBrair, cabinetmaker (1765), Hardham, baker and Chalkley,
       fishmonger (1804), Wells, draper and Harris, grocer (1851).[35]

74-75 There is a plaque on this building $\begin{smallmatrix} W \\ J \ J \end{smallmatrix}$ 1709.

They were John and Jane Williams and the memorial relates to the
rebuilding. Previously occupied by Henry Peckham (father of Jane). Other
occupants – Richard Drinkwater, surgeon (1737), McFarland, draper (1793),
Gatehouse, grocer (1821), Charge, draper (1851).[36]

CHAPTER 12

THE NORTH WEST QUADRANT
The Empty Quarter

A city as closely circumscribed by its walls as Chichester is might be expected to have always been filled to capacity with people and buildings.

This was not so: whilst the south west had the Cathedral, the south east the Pallants and Blackfriars, the north east the markets and churches, the north west – behind North and West Streets – had no churches, few fine buildings, few shops, no civic buildings.

The street pattern has remained unchanged (until a year or two ago) from the 12th century – Tower Street, Chapel Street, Crane Street and North Walls.

For hundreds of years the quarter consisted mainly of pasture, small-holdings, gardens, barns, granaries and a few cottages. Visually it must have resembled a large modern allotments site.

The few buildings were mainly of ribbon development edging in from the main streets. The maps of 1595 and 1610[A], however, give a false impression, exaggerating the emptiness which was there and ignoring, as will be shown, the small number of interesting buildings.

Individual property boundaries between Tower and Chapel Streets have remained constant for many centuries. Much of the land in this area belonged to the Dean and Chapter, St Mary's Hospital, Vicars' Choral, the Chantry of Bishop Arundel and the Guild of St George. Whatever changes were made *within* these boundaries – buildings erected, enlarged, demolished – the outer shapes, however inconvenient, remained through to the 20th century.

This quadrant has been devastated by the redevelopment of the last 20 years. Fig. 12-1 shows the quadrant at something approaching its most developed stage in 1898. It had rows of terraced houses, some industry, several public houses. By 1992 it has almost all gone.

Consequently the gazetteer which follows cannot, in this case, copy the course used through most of this book of tracing the history of standing buildings and the precursors of those buildings on the same plots. A sequential numbering system has therefore been used (Fig. 12-1) and this relates to source references also. The few buildings which have survived from 1898 are blocked in.

Tower Street and Chapel Street have been known as the lanes or West Lanes of West Street. They were included in the 'upper ward' of West Street for tax purposes in the cases where the main street was subdivided.

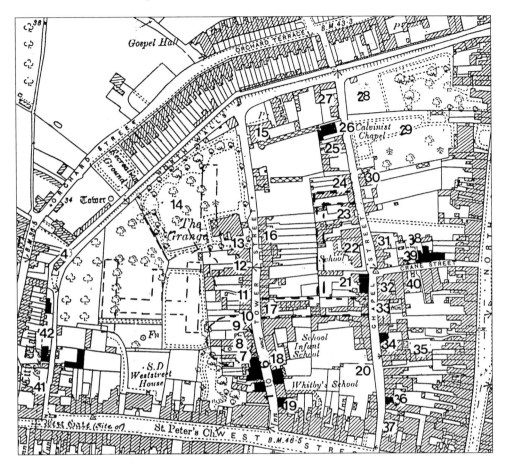

Fig. 12-1 1898 O. S. map of the north west quadrant with a few key modern buildings and Woolstaplers road dotted in (numbers refer to the text)

TOWER STREET
West side

Lower West Lane until the 19th century; in the 13th century known as 'Backeslane'. Now named after the Bell Tower which is clearly in line with the south end of the street.

The area behind the west of the street remained in cultivation, or as gardens, until it was developed for the first County Hall buildings.

By the 1851 census the occupants were predominantly of the lowest socio-economic groups – there were 3 laundresses, 10 labourers, 3 chars and 2 chimney sweeps, as heads of households.

In the 13th century there are a number of records in the Chapter chartularies[B] of land and buildings, including houses. Development, however, was not intensive. There are few records for the 14th and 15th centuries. A will of 1527 (John Cresweller) refers to 'My shop with a close adjoining to the common barns', and to a mill house. The 16th century provides many sources showing that the street consisted mainly of gardens. The development shown in Fig. 12-1 in 1898 was well under way in 1769[c] but along the street frontage only.

Ref. on Fig. 12-1 & sources

1   Public convenience: stables for *Eagle Inn* (opposite) 1900. House in 1527.

2   1: Now a printer. *Prince of Wales* public house 1842. 18th-century building.

3   2: House occupied by a weaver (Chitty) in 1610. House rebuilt and used as 2, with a malthouse in 1786 (William Cobden, maltster).

4   3-4: Vicars' Choral site: records from 1603. Parliamentary survey records one house with 4 low rooms, a cellar and 5 chambers over. In 1785 fire insurance was provided for the property as '2 houses of brick and tile', but separate leases are only found from 1830. Timber framed inside.

5   6: Formerly 5 and 6. 18th century. Records from 1534; house with malthouse at rear in 1605 (Edmund Sargeant, maltster); 2 hearths in 1670 and malthouse still recorded in 1686 (Robert Sargeant, cordwainer).

6   Vicars' Choral property. Records from 1534; 4 rooms up and down in 1649.

7   This well-documented property has disappeared under the non-fiction section of the Library. Records from about 1200 (Chapter rentals from 1521). Known as 'St Richard's House' (from Bishop Richard). Stairs repaired in 1533, so two-storeyed then, also the roof was tiled, and in 1649 had 4 ground floor rooms and 2 chambers over. Plot measured 29m long by 8m. In 1678 divided into 2 plots. Rebuilt in 1787 as one house and converted by Humphrey, brewer, into a storehouse by 1825.

8   Garden of the Chantry of Bishop Arundel which was appropriated by the Crown in 1550 and subsequently sold, remaining a garden in the 17th century. In 1832 a close of 8 houses.

9   *Ship Inn* (under fiction section of the Library) pre-1766 probably 1734 – when purchased by William Wackford, victualler. Rebuilt 1880.

10   Garden in 16th century; with stable 1649; in 1680 used as stable for *Sun Inn* in West Street; by 1763 two houses.

11   House recorded in 1611. In 1856 site included a public house called *The Olive Branch*. In 1887 4 cottages (2 at rear).

12 Dean and Chapter site. Garden in 16th century; small new house in 1618; 3 small houses in 1661; storehouse and warehouse mid-18th century (Richard West, fellmonger). In 1869 described as 'now freehold'. Nos. 20 and 21 were demolished in 1976 to make way for the new County Council Offices. In 1851 Thomas Henley, a fellmonger, lived in the house; subsequently Ebenezer Prior had his house, offices and yard there.

13 Garden of Subdean. In 1246 described as 'next to the gate of the Dean and Chapter's barn.'

14 Common Barns: The Grange. This was an area of barns, cottages and stables in the ownership of the Dean and Chapter and St Mary's Hospital (the latter's being described as 'a close called Longcroft'). Records start from 1246; in 1481 Thomas Cresweller leased the 'communebarne' for 7 years for £16 a year and in 1533 the barn and a tenement adjoining called Blackhurst, with all outhouses and the tithes of hay and grain, for 31 years for £20 a year (the tenant to do all repairs and the Dean and Chapter to provide rough timber). And so the leases go on every few years over the centuries. Large buildings are shown in the middle of a large open area in the Norden Map, 1595.

On the night of 29th-30th March 1654 there was a disastrous fire with losses totalling some £1,050 for 12 people – about £50,000 today. These included:

	£	s	d	
Richard Hildrup	12	5	0	barley, fodder
George Butterly	7	1	4	hay, calf, stable and shed
" "	40	0	0	Parsonage house
Henry Bullock	3	14	8	mead, tools
Edward Long	20	16	7	household goods, clothes
Henry Perrin	47	6	6	barley, fodder, pig, tools, household goods
Edward Morey	33	5	2	household goods, bees
Richard Tanner } Nicholas Edwards }	76	0	0	barley wheat
Thomas Lower } William Louff }	54	15	0	carts, ploughs, cattle horses, hens
John Whicher	178	11	1	contents and buildings – malthouse and candlehouse
Richard Goodman	575	0	0	2 houses, 2 storehouses, 1 barn, 2 stables, carthouse, cowhouse, household goods, cattle, carts

The fire must have destroyed all the buildings and contents in an area now covered by the Library northwards to the wall. The individuals claimed at Quarter Sessions for their losses but it is doubtful, from the smallness of their final inventories on death, whether any help was given.

The predominance of this area as a granary was perpetuated when the house called The Grange (see Fig. 12-2) was built near to the site of the old granaries in 1837 by W.C. Rhoades replacing an earlier house.

East side

Ref. on Fig. 12-1

15   Only in the last hundred years has there been any significant development on this site at the north end of the street. Before the Reformation it was a garden of the Chantry of Bishop Arundel and even in the 19th century much of it was nursery ground, with the only development – Elm House and 6 Elm Grove cottages – at the north side.

16   The whole of this plot was owned by the Dean and Chapter, certainly from the beginning of the 16th century, at which time it was 3 separate garden plots. The northern half was developed with several houses by 1649 and during the next century a continuous stretch of 14 small houses was built.

17   The Woolstaplers road is a modern phenomenon. It runs through what had been the Culverhouse ('a pigeon house') garden from 1566 if not earlier, and a house and shops in the early 17th century used by a dyer. There was a saffron plot here in that century. In the 18th century a number of houses under one roof were built behind the frontage in the form of a court. They were called 1-6 Spring Gardens and 1-5 Rose Court and were among the few back-to-back houses in Chichester.

From Woolstaplers to No. 52

18   The next site to the south – at present mainly a car park has had a chequered history.

a   St Mary's site. Garden in 1562. First house on site 1678. Poor House of St Peter the Great parish to 1755. Royal Lancastrian School in 1811 – archaeological excavations produced a large number of scholars' slates. Prior's wool store in 1911 (pits found in excavations). *Fighting Cocks Inn*, 1766. Tankards and mugs found in excavations (see Figs. 12-5 and 12-7).

b   Dean and Chapter site. Storehouse for building repairs. Materials: tiles, slates, lime, up to about 1570. Bell founding carried out before 15th century. Storehouse was timber framed and thatched. House in 1570. National School 1870. Demolished 1958. (See also Chapter 7.)

c   House and garden in 1534. School 1870.

Fig. 12-2 Tower Street, the Grange – 19th century

Fig. 12-3 Cottages at north end of Tower Street

d   Pair of 18th-century houses (c.1786) in flemish bond brickwork. No. 51 previously owned by Elizabeth Gubbett in 1617 – she provided, in her will, for a perpetual rent of £1 on the property for her charity. Here lived Nicholas Drinkwater, a cook, in 1607, who appeared before the Court Leet for disruption of the King's Peace, in that he had put the Petty Constable in bodily harm. His inventory (1619) describes a hall, buttery, 2 chambers over, a backside with wood and coal. He kept pigs and poultry and had a silver bowl, 2 china dishes and a looking glass.

19 Nos. 53-56 are now part of the Army and Navy Stores and were originally partly used as a schoolroom of the Oliver Whitby School and as its infirmary. What is left is a facade of the late 18th century.

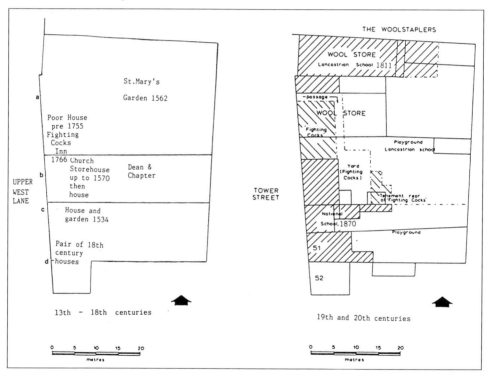

Fig. 12-4 Plans of Woolstaplers' site

CHAPEL STREET

The name of the street is recent: it derives from the Independent Chapel which was founded in 1774. Before that it was variously East Lane, Upper West Lane and Paris Lane (in the 13th century). The name 'Paris' may be derived from OE *pearr*: an enclosure, corresponding to a parcel or district.

Like Tower Street it was an area of gardens until the 18th century and even as late as this century the upper east side had gardens running right

Fig. 12-5 Tower Street, school and Prior's woolstore 1960's

Fig. 12-6 Tower Street, archaeological excavations 1970's

back from the houses in North Street and had few buildings fronting the street, other than coach houses.

In the last 200 years there have been a number of slaughterhouses, malthouses, tallow manufactories, corn stores and stables which must have made 19th-century Chapel Street an unpleasant and odiferous place in which to reside.

West side

Ref. on Fig. 12-1

20   Post Office site. Up to about 1780 the southern part was an open space, a garden belonging to the house in West Street. The northern part was industrial from the early 18th century: in 1739 a slaughterhouse and stable, 1755 workhouse and store; 1786 3 slaughterhouses, a wool loft and a stable; 1799 corn store; 1808 a malthouse; 1823 2 candle manufacturies; 1848 spirit store, piggeries and coach houses. These burned down in 1856 – a contemporary report says 'fortunately several cases of brandy were removed in time'; 1878 a cart house, cattle pens, dung pits and workhouse.

21   Nos. 1-3 Chapel Street and Providence Place. The small alley opposite Crane Street led in 1851 to 5 tiny brick houses at the rear, which was then called Mellisher Court after Mr. Mellish, a blacksmith, who lived on the street frontage. The Chapel Street houses, which still survive, date from the 18th century. In the 17th century there was a slaughterhouse occupied by the Cox family.

22   This site has recently been redeveloped. Previously it was the Central Girls School. The land was granted by John de Beauchamp and his wife Matilda to St Mary's Hospital on 27th May 1250. There were buildings on that and the sites to the north and south at that date. The site remained unchanged, in the hands of the Hospital, through to 1882 when it was conveyed to the Bishop for the erection of a school. Hospital leases give: 1625 tenement and garden plot; 1677 court and garden plot (William Williams, a gardener). An estate plan of 1763 shows four houses and gardens and thereafter there is continuous occupation by small town houses in a terrace until the demolition to make way for the school.

23   There was a tenement here in 1250, but the site was a garden for several centuries prior to 1798 with a barn around 1600. In 1820 there was a wheelwright's shop, with outhouses and a smithy. To the rear was the Coronation Hall and to the north the old Gospel Hall.

24   Here were several small houses in the 19th century on a site occupied by a slaughterhouse in 1786 and a malthouse in 1780 onwards.

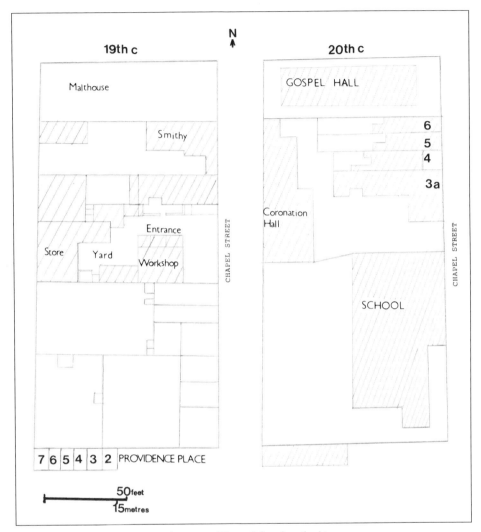

Fig. 12-7 The old school site

25-7   From here northwards to the wall an unusual series of Chartulary records lists 10 occupiers of a row of small houses in the 13th century.

25   *The Woolpack Inn* (a beerhouse) occupied the site in 1843 and was still recorded up to 1890.

26   Providence Chapel site. Built 1809 and still standing. No record of buildings in the 16th – 18th centuries.
There is a plaque to two Protestant martyrs, Thomas Iveson and Richard Hook (1555).

27   There were cottages, a slaughterhouse, piggeries and sheds in 1855 and, in the 18th century, houses, stables and a barn are recorded.

East side

The frontage down to Crane Street was largely undeveloped until the 20th century, being often gardens of North Street houses.

28   This plot of land had the evocative name of The Cherry Garden and had been a close of undeveloped land right through until the 20th century. It was owned by St Mary's Hospital.

29   St Cyriac's Chapel. Probably founded by Earl Roger. First mention is in 1155. In 1250 described as 'area with buildings' when it had become the habitation of a recluse. It was re-endowed 1269. Repairs are mentioned in 1405. In 1588 it is referred to as 'edifice called St Cyriacs'.

30   Occupied by Taplin family of pipe makers (see also Chapter 9) in the 18th century.

31   *Butchers' Arms* public house (15 Chapel Street). Was a freehold inn in the possession of Lambert and Norris in 1898. A house is recorded of the St Cross family in 1277 with a house of Osilia next door.

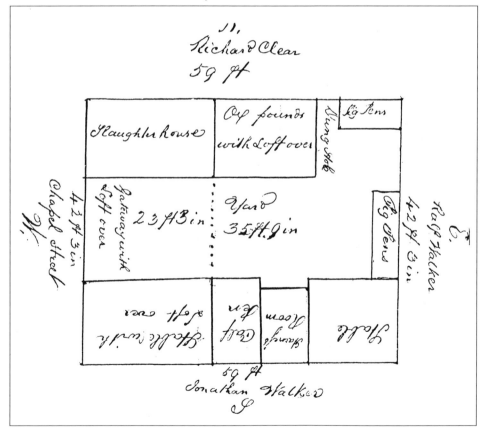

Fig. 12-8 Plan of 1838

32   Owned by St Mary's Hospital (records from 1250, when it was granted by John de Beauchamp to the Hospital, and had buildings on it). By 1623 it had only a stable; in 1670 a house with 2 hearths and continually occupied by buildings thereafter; 1759 3 tenements and a storehouse, malthouse and cellar. In 1973 the *Chichester Observer* carried a photograph of a six-and-a-half ton bulldozer which had crashed through the roof of the old cellar during rebuilding, despite the warnings of the Documentary Research Group of the presence of the cellar. In 1774 Lady Huntington attended the opening service of the New Independent Chapel converted from the previous stone building. A new chapel was built on the site in 1796 and burnt down in 1820. In 1903 became a store for Arthur Purchase (wine and spirit merchants). Now Trustee Savings Bank.

33   No. 23 Chapel Street. Rear of M & S. Another St Mary's site from 1250 and with a cottage as early as 1253; 2 hearths in 1670. It was an inn before 1683. *The Three Tuns* inn from about 1800.

34   Land of the Brotherhood of St George until it was sequestered in 1550 and granted to the City. It then had a house and dovecote on it and for the next 200 years stables and a garden. Slaughterhouse in 1755 and still so in 1881.

35   Six small houses were built in a court behind the previous slaughterhouse, half way between North and Chapel Streets, between 1738 and 1745. They were approached through a tiny alley. Whilst the properties continued right through the 19th century, even by 1787 their occupants were too poor to be assessed for Land Tax. In 1851 known as Walker's Alley after an early owner who developed the site and by the custom of the time gave his name to it.

36   The brickwork at the rear of the *Dolphin and Anchor* is largely the facade of 18th-century buildings (e.g. No. 30) used as a workhouse in 1716. Before that it had been a stable and also was known as The Cockpit.

37   Corner of West Street. Dean and Chapter records indicate that there was an inn called *The George* here in 1521 (see Chapter 8).

CRANE STREET

The earliest documentary reference to Crane Street is July 1277. The buildings on the south side are all new; on the north side, whilst there has been modernisation, some 19th-century and earlier structures remain.

North side

Ref. on Fig. 12-1

38   The early reference noted above was for a grant by Simon Curte to John de St Cross of a house with curtilage on the north side of the

lane; on either side were the house of John Lude and a yard of St Cross, who obviously had an agricultural use, for a record of 1282/3 refers to Godfrey de Bebitone granting to John de St Cross a plot at the gate leading to the latter's barn.

39   To the west of No. 6 was a new built house in 1754, with a malthouse. Nos. 5 and 6 are also described as 'new built' in 1754; this is on land which had belonged to Shulbrede Priory in the 16th century. Part of the lane was blocked with rubbish and the malting apparatus of the Prior of Shulbrede in the 16th century.
In 1665 Thomas Trevatt, a tobacco-cutter was here. His landlord was Thomas Miller of the Pallant.
The corner plot (at Chapel Street) was a garden in 1534.
The Victoria Arms was at No. 3 in 1861.

South side

40   Had a malthouse in the 19th century with a cellar and 2 floors; there was an earlier one in the 16th century and the City Sessions recorded foul water coming from one in 1754.

NORTH WALLS

Nos. 8-10 are today the sole remnants of what, in the early years of the 19th century, was an almost continuous row of small terraced cottages, with their backs against the city wall. Over the years there was much division, amalgamation and rebuilding. The earliest reference to the lane itself is in 1330 – 'a certain lane leading from Westgate by the walls to Northgate' (CapI/37/1). There were tenements on the east side of the lane at that date.

All the land on the west side was in the ownership of the City Council at least from the 18th century.

West side

Ref. on Fig. 12-1

41   Nos. 1-7 The rear of Westgate House and some small cottages demolished when Westgate roundabout was formed in 1963 (see Chapter 8).

42   Nos. 8-10 The first houses probably date from about 1700 and were rebuilt by Thomas Barnard, the City Crier, in 1745, on the site of the earlier buildings. Three had become unfit and were pulled down in 1880 and the site sold to Robert Raper. In 1799 two others, south of No. 10, were 'ruinous'. By 1880 the south end of the row 1-10 was a wash house. Where No. 10 is now there was originally one tenement converted into 3 and reconverted by 1885 into one.

43   3 cottages were built on City land on the rampier. They were built of brick and stone around 1753, and were pulled down in 1899. The road through the North Walls was made in 1846.

Fig. 12-9 Old print: from Tower Street looking south

Fig. 12-10 Old houses formerly in North Walls

CHAPTER 13

THE NORTH EAST QUADRANT
Alms and the Pigs

The quadrant divides into 5 areas of interest:

A Shambles and
   Hogmarket of
   St Martin's

B St Martin's
   Square to
   Guildhall St.

C Priory Park

D St Mary's

E Little London
   (east) with
   East Row and
   East Walls

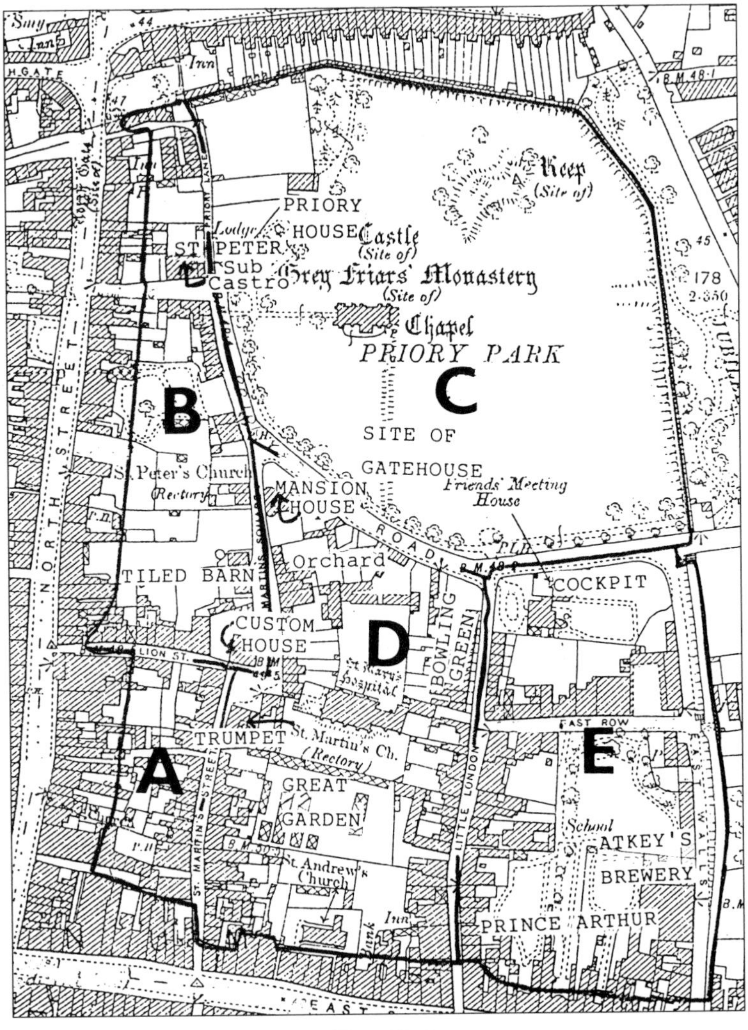

Fig. 13-1
1898 O.S. map of north east quadrant
with features mentioned in text added

A   The Hogmarket
This area has been known as The Shambles, The Pig Market, Hog Lane, Vintry, La Swynchperinge.[1] In 1604 nine butchers lived in the parish of St Martin's. St Martin's Street is of medieval origin. During the Roman period a building occupied the East Street frontage where the street starts.[2]

ST MARTIN'S STREET
West side
1   *Hole in the Wall* (St Martin's Brewery, Inn). New built house and malthouse in 1746.[3]
2-3   18th-century house under one roof span, with a malthouse in 1794.[4]
The area next to the north and before 1A St Martin's Square, was recently a car park and had been bombed in 1943. The site which had been 4-5 was a barn and garden in 1653, a house and malthouse in 1703, and a new house and beerhouse in 1785.[5]

Next was St George's Row – the Poor House – in 1492 when a bequest was made, and bequests continued through the 16th and 17th centuries. The Mayor inspected the building in 1744 and found it 'to be very ruinous, likely to fall down and dangerous to passengers'. The lease was then auctioned at the *Swan Inn* 'during the duration of an inch of candle'. A storehouse and shop were then erected. The northern boundary of this property was the southern side of Crooked S Lane.[6]

The remainder, to the north of the old Crooked S Lane was, before 1550, a tenement, garden and stable of St George's Brotherhood, granted to the City on the Dissolution. Eusabius Grevatt had a common alehouse here in 1640. His inventory describes a parlour, hall, kitchen, brewhouse, mill house, cellar, 2 upstairs chambers, a shovel-board

Fig. 13-2 Shamble Alley before demolition

room, closets and a stable with an old horse. In 1697 it was the *Trumpet Inn* and by 1755 a house called The Old Trumpet.[7]

ST MARTIN'S SQUARE

1A, 1 and **2** Dean and Chapter site. Probably land of the Abbot and Convent of Jumièges (gift by Ralph de Montfort for 'his salvation') who sold it to the Archdeacon. He granted it to the Dean and Chapter in 1254. In 1522 a barn and garden plot; 1534: three tenements, one occupied by Thomas Hardham a butcher. He and his wife were brought before the Court Leet in 1574 for 'disturbance of neighbours in the night time with chiding and brallinge'; the next lessee, John Farrington left the lease in 1608 to Hillary Billet, a vintner. In 1649 consisted of three properties (southernmost two, each with 2 tenements) and described as 1A (William Billet): 8 low rooms 4 chambers over; 1 (William Broman junior, butcher): 6 low rooms, 4 chambers over, 4 garrets above, 2 cellars, woodyard, garden; 2 (Thomas Wheeler, citizen and merchant): hall, parlour, 3 chambers, 2 garrets, wash house, kitchen, cellar, yard. 1A was described as new built in 1697. Later occupiers included Mrs. Painbleau (charity) 1786; Richard Dally 1803; Edward Fuller (surveyor) 1830.[8]

CROOKED S LANE *(Shamble Alley, Trumpet Lane) (See Fig. 13-2)*

Originally where the butchers' shambles or stalls stood. Was for foot-passengers only, with flagstones. There were 2 distinct kinks in the short lane as it ran west-east from North Street to St Martin's Street. The land was mainly owned by the City and in the 18th and 19th centuries contained cottages, stables, dung holes and workshops.[9]

LION STREET

Originally Custom House Lane (from the house used as such at 3 St Martin's Square), Council House Lane (from the Council House at the North Street end) and Market House Lane. The word LION derives from the animal on the Assembly Rooms. The south side of the street was in the parish of St Olav.
South side

There was one house on the south side in 1670. To the west – now under the Assembly Rooms – was a stone cutter's yard.

B   St Martin's Square to Guildhall Street

LION STREET

North side

This side is 18th century or earlier.

2-3   In 1579 was the house of John Hardham, with a slaughterhouse. Occupied by the Knott family, also butchers, in the 17th century.[10]

5   In 1692 divided into several tenements.[11]

6   A substantial, originally timber-framed house with 6 hearths in 1670, occupied by Richard Greenfield, butcher. Present house 18th century.[12]

ST MARTIN'S SQUARE

West side

3   Land of the Priors of Boxgrove in 1266. In 1608 described as 'the land late of Johann Cowper of Dycham sometime of the Priors of Boxgrove

late in the occupation of Robert Bennett butcher' (he had his own slaughterhouse). The Priory lands had passed at the Dissolution in 1550 to the Crown,
then to the de la Warres, then the Morleys. John Cowper married Magdalen,
daughter of Sir John Morley. Agnes Bennett married John Greenfield in 1603
(her surety at baptism was John Cowper her godfather) in St Martin's church.
There was a timber-framed house on the plot, which forms the core of the
present house, in the 17th century. John and his wife had no children and
it went to their nephew John (son of Richard of 6 Lion Street, next door).
He died in 1663 and his widow, Martha, was still there in 1670 (5 hearths).
The property was sold after her death to the Farrington family who refronted
the house in brick, giving it its present appearance. Subsequently the property
passed to Thomas Till (mayor in 1738) and then to Till Hollier (his nephew)
in 1763. He leased it to the Controller of Customs and occupied the house
as Collector.

Fig. 13-3 3 St Martin's Square

It then passed to the Cobby family in 1788, still used as a Custom House.
In 1764 described as 'messuage, offices, yard, garden, several warehouses,
storerooms, vaults, cellar, stable, now used as a Custom House of the Port
of Chichester.'[13]

4-6 Site acquired by St Mary's in 1232/41. Southern part was timber-
framed, 'the barn lately built' in 1608; a candlehouse in 1810 and a stable
later in the 19th century. There were buildings on the site in 1250. To the
north 4 houses were built by 1745 and these have gone through several stages
of conversion.[14]

GUILDHALL STREET

Priory House The site of the Church of St Peter Sub Castro (built 1260, last
in use 1521, demolished 1574). Much of the stone was used for paving
the city streets.[15] Present building 18th century.

3 18th-century front. Robert Glasyer, butcher, 1491. Called The Rose in 1676.[16]

4   18th-century front but core is timber-framed, newly built in 1676, with
       hall, chambers over and garrets above, 'old kitchen', suggesting current
rebuilding, buttery and 2 gardens.[17]

PRIORY ROAD
Rear of Greyfriars in North Street. There were cottages on this frontage facing
       Priory Park from the 16th century. From the corner of Guildhall Street
there was a row of between 2 and 5 cottages in the period 1784-1935 and
in the next stretch to the *Park Tavern* there was a site of the Vicars' Choral
with one house in 1521; in 1649 this had 3 low rooms, 3 chambers over and
a small yard and garden with a well. By 1756 there was a group of small
houses and a lime house. Occupants included a bricklayer, carpenter, plumber,
glazier, shoemakers, cooper, dressmaker, grocer, whitesmith and washer-
woman over the next century. The houses were demolished to provide rear
facilities at Greyfriars around 1880 and these in turn have been recently
replaced.[18]
11   *Park Tavern*. This was a barn and garden in 1521. By 1877 was the *Ritz
       Inn*.[19]
C   Priory Park
       The castle was built by Roger, Earl of Montgomery. It had a motte and
bailey. A chapel was built in 1142 and a gaol in 1198.
       The Greyfriars (Franciscans) moved in 1269 to the site of the castle
(which had been destroyed by 1225). The Friars built a church (1270-80), guest
house, parlour, library, frater and brewhouse.
       With the Dissolution the site passed to the City and the church became
the new Guildhall in 1541. The remainder of the site was leased in 1543 to
John Knott, who built a house next to the church, and later to Sir Richard
May (1674) and eventually to Sir Hutchins Williams and Henry Cromwell
(who took the name of Frankland).

Fig. 13-4 The 18th-century House of Sir Hutchins Williams

Eventually the 5th Duke of Richmond purchased the freehold in 1824 and a successor presented it to the City as a war memorial in 1918.[20]

Before the drill hall in East Row was built in 1912 a small room in the Guildhall was used as an armoury.

Fig. 13-5 Greyfriars Chapel

In 1778 the City took consideration of the danger to which the inhabitants were exposed from great quantities of gunpowder for the use of His Majesty and forces being frequently lodged in private dwellinghouses and other buildings in the populous part of the city for want of a proper place to secure the same. To prevent the fatal effects of an explosion as far as possible a building for a guardhouse and powder magazine was to be built at the expense of the city in the angle formed by the east wall of the city and the Friary wall (subsequently the guard-house was considered unnecessary).[21]

D **St Mary's Development**

The rough triangle embracing St Martin's Lane, Priory Road, Little London and the rear of East Street, delineates the home estate of St Mary's Hospital.

In 1242 the Franciscans occupied the site. When they moved to the castle (Priory Park) in 1269 St Mary's Hospital moved from its cramped site at the corner of East and South Streets. A footpath which ran from the end of Crooked S Lane to East Row was blocked up in 1290 and the Hospital built thereon.[22]

The land to the north was rented out as a part of St Mary's Farm and a mansion house was built in the north west apex. The land was largely used as orchards.

By the 17th century a bowling green had been made on the Little London frontage. (Bowling greens and alleys were quite common in the Stuart period. There was a bowling green in the Spring Gardens at Charing Cross in 1634 and one in Southampton in 1299.) In 1543 John Grygorye was admonished by the Chichester Chapter for bowling in public.[23] The land to the south of the Hospital – the Great Garden – was rented out to add to the Hospital's income. The mansion house was burnt down by 1678.[24]

From about the early part of the 18th century frontage strips on the streets began to be leased for building houses, ownership of the sites being retained by St Mary's.

St Mary's Hospital

The buildings included the gatehouse, at the west end, and an aisled hall (of which one-third no longer remains). There is a chapel at the east end. Originally the hall was 31m by 13m. The huge brick chimneys within the hall are 17th century (one is marked '1680'). The internal almshouses are relatively modern.[25]

ST MARTIN'S SQUARE

East side

Virtually the whole frontage was land of St Mary's Hospital and had been the orchard of the farm, the only buildings in this stretch being barns, stables, outhouses and the farm mansion house. Street frontage building started soon after 1700.

8   After the early mansion house was destroyed by fire the site was described as 'a croft of land'. Another house was recorded by 1712. In 1829 a malthouse was mentioned and in 1845, a weighbridge.[26]

9-10   In 1755 a coach house, garden, limehouse, stable, workshop and granary. Stable burnt down in 1785 and 12 small dwelling houses (15 by 1822) erected on the frontage and in a court behind (St Martin's Court). In 1878 a report of the Medical Officer of Health expressed opinion that the houses in the Court 'are in consequence of want of outlets, bad aspect, looking directly into narrow court where it opens out containing a cesspool, large privy and ash tip, quite unfit to be occupied.' He recommended pulling down as a benefit to the sanitary condition of the neighbourhood.[27]

11-12 Department of the Environment describe as '17th century cottage refaced'

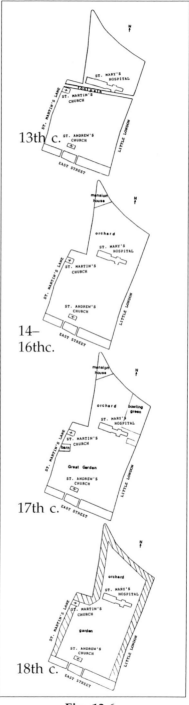

Fig. 13-6
Development of St Mary's site

12 was *Crab and Lobster*, a beer shop, in the 1861 census and which closed about 1900.[28]

St Martin's Hall. Before 1741 was a stable and carthouse; 1755 storehouse; 1828 a warehouse. By 1833 converted into Ebenezer Chapel. Sunday School 1857.[29]

Fig. 13-7 St Mary's Hospital

Almshouses. 6 new houses with carthouses and stables in 1731. Part candle manufactory in 1834. Rebuilt 1905 as almshouses.[30]

20   A house on site in 1623. An entry in St Mary's accounts refers to a ruin in 1757. It had been recently occupied by Mr. Fosbrook a gentleman and a lunatic, and for four years the property was in multiple occupation. It was rebuilt in 1758.[31]

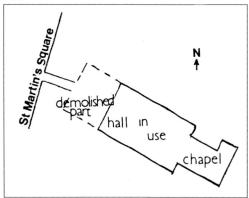

Fig. 13-8 Plan of St Mary's Hospital

21   Plot of ground used as Pound. House built thereon by 1766. City owned
the land.[32] The common well was to the north.

Fig. 13-9 St Martin's church in the 19th century

St Martin's Church[33] In 1260 described as 'in the Pigmarket'. Demolished
     1906.
Public conveniences. Barn in 17th century with a gateroom. New house 1670.
ST MARTIN'S STREET
East side
     The remainder of the street is now occupied by one owner Marks &
Spencer.[34] The present store plan is superimposed (thick outline) on
Fig. 13-10, which is taken from the 1875 Ordnance Survey (scale 1:500). The
irregular ground plan is a common phenomena of ancient towns, and is
particularly relevant in Chichester which had considerable areas of land
originally owned in perpetuity by the Dean and Chapter of the Cathedral,
St Mary's and similar bodies.
EAST STREET frontage
16-18 The earliest records are of 1644. John Dunstall, a stationer, sold the
     eastern part which was divided by the long entry still shown in 1875
in the map. This entry ran from East Street into the back of the site. Here,
in 1644, were two newly set out gardens and a spring of water which was
available 'for washing clothes and other things'. The purchaser of 17-18 was
James Penton, a hosier. The building was pulled down and rebuilt, the

occupants (in 1647) being Daniel Barker, a blacksmith, and William Lipper, a cooper. Subsequent trades carried out on the frontage properties up to the time of Marks & Spencer were: glazier, painter, tailor, basket-maker, barber, pork butcher, perukemaker, grocer, attorney, cooper, tea-dealer and grocer, boot and shoe stores and tobacconist. The trade of a cooper was carried out right up to the late 19th century.

Behind the East Street frontage was a jungle of gardens, brick walls, wells, passages, brewhouses, kitchens and workshops.

ST MARTIN'S STREET
South to north

16-18 were small dwelling houses feeding into the jungle mentioned above. The properties were linked into 16 East Street and shared the right to use the passageway between 16 and 17 East Street.

15A was the *Black Horse Inn* in 1689 and had become disused by 1730. As an inn it had stables and a yard on the north side. By 1811 it had become a blacksmith's shop with stables and by 1848 it was used partly as a smith's shop and partly as a printing office linked by a passage to 21 East Street. In 1850 it was described as a new building with an arched cellar and three tiers of workshops, a two-stalled stable and a coach house. To the rear was a building used as a cooper's shop in conjunction with 18 East Street until 1823, when it was described as ruinous (marked 'C' on map).

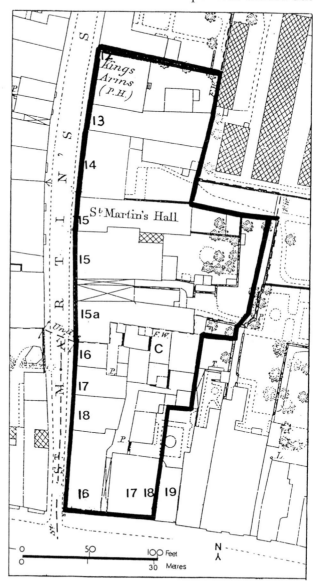

Fig. 13-10 Marks & Spencer's site (1875 O.S.)

12-15 Leasehold of St Mary's, whose lands stretched through to the street
       up to 1700. Before 1633 the site contained a barn and gateroom. The
Hearth Tax of 1670 records that William Fletcher had a new house with 4
hearths. Around 1700 the frontage land was leased to individuals and houses
were erected all along the frontage.
15   had a cottage on the site until Mr. Edney, a furniture dealer, bought
       the freehold in 1869 and subsequently erected St Martin's Hall. Previous
occupants had been a glover, cabinet maker, perukemaker and carpenter.
14   had a range of buildings and stables in the 18th century, including an
       iron warehouse and two dwelling houses. One occupant was Mr.
Tapner, a clay pipe maker. In 1804 there was a young gentlemen's preparatory
school on the site.
12   was the *King's Arms* public house in the 19th century up to 1905. The
       garden wall can still be seen in the bottom part of the store wall.
       Not surprisingly, Marks & Spencer is carrying on in modern form many
of the retail services which have been provided on its site over several
centuries. The shape of the overall building, including the non-retail area at
the rear, derives directly from the site history: the original garden of St Mary's
Hospital and the subsequent street development dictated the shape of the
boundary at the rear; the 'kink' in the south-east corner of the food department
follows an old property boundary, as does the bend by the stairs at the east
side. The East Street frontage itself equated to that of the properties of 1644.
       The moral might be that we are prisoners of our history.

LITTLE LONDON
West side
       Because the land ownership was almost exclusively of St Mary's,
virtually no building on this side of the street is earlier than 18th century.
1   This was a Dean and Chapter property. It lines up with the rear of the
       East Street frontage and therefore was not part of St Mary's Great
Garden. The southern part was a plumbery in 1755 and the rest was a
brewhouse and storehouse; by 1877 there was a house also.[35]
2-2A Car park entrance: malthouse and stable 1695; by 1716 a religious meet-
       ing house; by 1750 *King of Prussia* (1829 *Golden Cross*).[36]
3   6 stables in 18th century; in 1822, 2 counting houses and stables and
       cellar with a vault underneath.[37]
4-6A Group of 6 houses built in 1813. In 1683 there were 2 houses on this
       site. From here northwards was the bowling green in the 17th century
which was not built upon (except for one small house) until the 18th century.[38]
7-8   18th-century houses built before 1745.[39]
9   Stable, then a new built house in 1731.[40]
10   Little house in 1595 map. In 1706 so described in a lease of St Mary's
       farm. Also wool warehouse and other buildings erected by 1831.[41]
11-12 Pair of 18th-century houses (earliest lease is 1788). Beerhouse mid-19th
       century.[42]

13-16 2 pairs of 18th-century houses (earliest lease is 1745) 14 has a bronze
    fire insurance mark which was issued to Captain Robert Sandy in 1758.
15 has a firemark of 1771 issued to John Price, silversmith and merchant.[43]
17-20 Land, stable and outhouses in 1737. Range of houses built around 1800.[44]
PRIORY ROAD
6   Built about 1740.[45]
LITTLE LONDON
East side
    For too long the whimsy has been untiringly repeated, particularly in
guide books, that Queen Elizabeth I said, on a visit to Chichester and seeing
the street in question 'Verily 'tis a little London' and that the street thereafter
became named 'Little London'.
    The earliest document seen wherein the name Little London is used
is a will of 1487 of Richard Myldewe,[46] but it also appears as such in the
Escheators accounts of 1254. There is also a grant of a corner garden in Little
London in 1529.[47]
    The most important record is the Crown Grant to the Mayor and
Citizens, of the same garden on 14th May 1549. This grant, which is in Latin,
comprises the sale for £100 of much of the expropriated property at the
Dissolution. The relevant section says 'illus gardinum vicatum le corner
garden ... in Lytle London'.[48] Queen Elizabeth succeeded to the throne on
17th November 1558. So it seems likely that Her Majesty, if she saw the street
at all, merely *confirmed* 'verily '*tis* a Little London'. Why she should think
so I cannot imagine.
    In some documents it is the area which is described as Little or Pety
London, and the street as Savory or Saffron Lane. Perhaps the Great Garden
of St Mary's was used for growing saffron to be used in the local industry
of dyeing cloth.
    Spershott comments that Little London 'now so gay' (approximately
1780) was very dirty when he was a boy (approximately 1720) with a few
old houses, partly underground.
    The east side had a very different history from the west side, which
had been dominated by St Mary's and was late to develop. On the east there
are houses recorded:

    1451 Land and tenements late of Richard Swetapple[49]
    1456 Croft and buildings opposite East Walls[50]
    1492 Barn and 6 cottages; land and 2 tenements[51]
    1487 House nigh Little London[46]
    1541 House in Little London[52]
    1552 Divers free tenements[53]
    1568 2 houses[54]

21   Friars Gate (1793) Previous building known as Cockpit House and had
    4 hearths in 1670.[55]

22-25 7 cottages built between 1803 and 1805 on site of an older property which had a stable, yard and garden. [56] Now 4 houses.

28 House on site in 1595.[56] Present house erected 1794.

29 Museum. Was Sadler's corn store. In 1510 corner garden of Brotherhood of St George. Bought by City upon Dissolution (1549). Subsequently stables, malthouse, currier's workshop, storehouse, coach house, corn store and now City Museum.[57] Building is 18th century.

30 Early 19th century. Previous building had 6 hearths in 1670.[58]

31-32 Pair of 18th-century houses. Part of a garden plot in 1598. Building in 1640. Described as '2 new dwelling houses' in 1813.[59]

33-34 18th-century house. In 1849 Lancastrian Girls School in purpose built building at rear. Adjoining house for mistress.[60]

35-38 Timber yard of Henry Peckham pre-1738 when the house was built. 2 new courts of 5 cottages built by 1755 at rear. Southernmost at rear of 38 called Mulberry Court.[61] See Fig. 10-5 for a plan of this site.

41 18th century. Was *Prince Arthur* public house (previously *Mason's Arms*).

Fig. 13-11 Prince Arthur

EAST ROW
South side

There was a stable and garden in 1598,[63] and land of the Queen which had been in the ownership of St John of Jerusalem up to 1552 and then was granted to the City.

To the east, in the corner of East Walls, a croft with buildings is recorded in 1456.[64]

North side

3 Suffolk House. Dwelling house built on the site of stables and other outbuildings in about 1736.[65]

West of 2. In 1824 a storehouse previously part of a malthouse, counting house, stable and yard with a garden behind. Partly leasehold and partly freehold. In the 18th century was 4 small houses. The leasehold site had been held of the Hospital of St Mary Magdalen and St James the Apostle, and had 2 cottages in 1540.[66]

EAST WALLS[67]

The western section of the street frontage is now firmly buried under Shippams. Part was the garden of 43-44 East Street in the 18th century. East Walls Brewery had a malthouse 29m x 6m up to 1889.

There was also a timber yard by 1782 and subsequently cottages. Also on the frontage was the Wesleyan Methodist Chapel in 1814 which moved here from North Pallant.

On the north corner of East Row in 1781 there was a malthouse, stables, barns and a coach house. The northern part became the Lancastrian Girls School 1812-1849,[68] which then moved to Little London.

On 5th January 1857 upon representation of the Duke of Richmond the Quarter Sessions ruled, under the Militia Law Amendment Act of 1854, that the place provided in Chichester was insecure and insufficient for keeping arms and accoutrements and that for £500 (subsequently £800) the property in East Walls should be purchased. The Royal Sussex Light Infantry Militia occupied the site until 1879 with a Militia Depot, a capital residence, cells, coach house, dunghole and a parade ground.

PRIORY ROAD

South side (remainder)

Friends Meeting House erected 1698, rebuilt 1968. The sum of £40 was provided in the will of James Lucas[69] 'to allow or pay at any time as opportunity shall offer to buy or build a meeting house for my friends called "Quakers".'

CHAPTER 14

THE SOUTH EAST QUADRANT
A Place Apart

This portion of Chichester has always been a place apart – an anomaly within. One part of it – The Pallant – was extra-parochial, i.e. the Bishop (and often the Mayor and Corporation) had little jurisdiction; the other part was for 300 years the sole preserve of the Blackfriars.

The quadrant has moved through 3 phases, shown in 3 maps.

Map I shows the position before the coming of the Black Friars.

Map II When the Black Friars acquired their walled site the lane under the walls was closed, also a street on the line of the present New Town Street.

Map III After the Dissolution the Black-friars site passed into private owner-ship and remained as the garden of a large mansion house, until it was sold as building plots. The Black Friars thus left a permanent large foot-print on the map of Chichester.

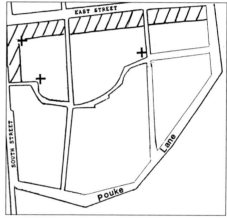

I – before 1289

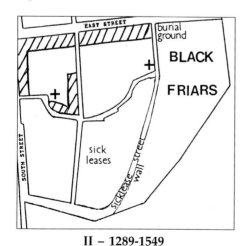

II – 1289-1549

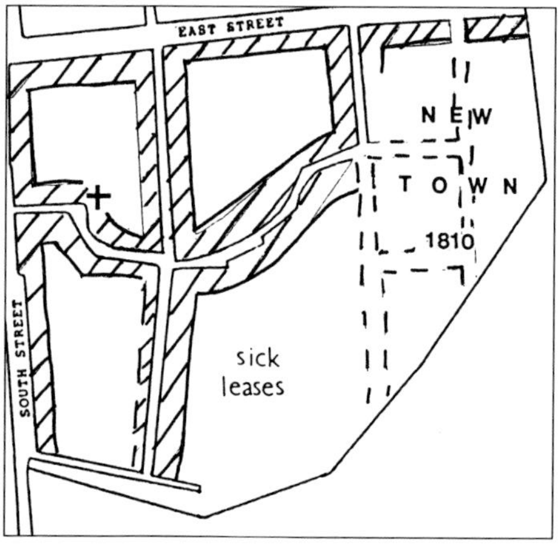

III – 1549 onwards

Fig. 14-1 Development of south east quadrant

The Pallant passed through a phase of malthouses and gardens, followed by affluent houses, and finally largely offices, which at least preserve the Georgian facade.

PALLANT
The name is mentioned as early as 1193 and is supposed to mean 'a fenced place', but this may have been more symbolic than real. It was, however, a separate area, being part of the Archbishop of Canterbury's Peculiar, and it was appended to his Manor of Pagham until it was severed from the See in 1552. The chartularies of Pagham account for the income.[1] The Cathedral chartularies record houses, plots and buildings in the 12th and 13th centuries, with grants to the Dean and Chapter.

Boxgrove chartulary, too, records a number of plots from 1224 to 1250, often with houses and other buildings. So whilst the Archbishop had jurisdiction, ownership of individual plots was expanding and, despite a manorial type of organisation, properties could pass by will.

Some examples from chartularies and other sources are:

Late 13th century – grant by John de Coruleto to Dean and Chapter[2] of 2 messuages
1239-56 Holding with buildings. Gervase and his wife grant to Dean and Chapter, with houses abutting on either side[3]
1241 Plot and house granted by Boxgrove to Richard de Merston[3]

Problems of jurisdiction arose periodically, e.g. the Mayor, Richard Exton, arrested a man within the Pallant in 1595 on suspicion of felony and was reported to the Archbishop for unlawful arrest.[4]

In the 15th century the Pallants contained tallow chandlers, huxters of bread, tanners and butchers; in the 16th century there were 2 inns, huxters, brewers and tipplers; in the 17th century tanners, butchers, tiplers and huxters: in this time there were many complaints about leaving heaps of dung in the streets and against stable-doors (10 complaints in 1628 alone) and for scalding porkers in the street; in 1641 complaints about leaving wagons in the street.[5]

Because the Pallant is a town-within-a-town, with a repetition of the city's pattern of four streets crossing in the middle, it has been thought helpful to divide the area into four quadrants (see Fig. 14-2).

North west quadrant
The gardens of the properties fronting East and South Streets ran back well into the quadrant even in the 13th century. The west side of North Pallant is accounted for by:

Land of Emma Ludeny 1246
Messuage of Bernduis 1249
Land of Ralph Sefare 1246

The Dean and Chapter owned much of West Pallant (north) and several properties in North Pallant (west). The present frontage is mainly 18th century.

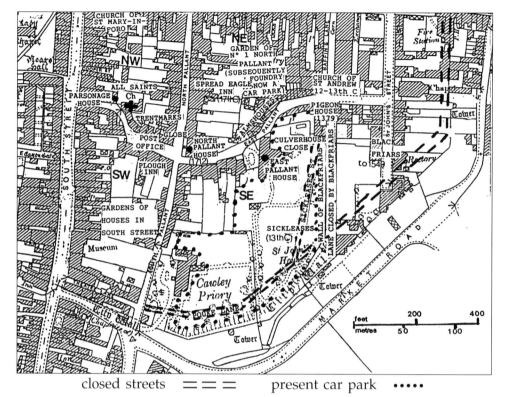

closed streets ═ ═ ═ present car park •••••

**Fig. 14-2 South east quadrant – 1878 Ordnance Survey map
with features mentioned in the text overlaid**

WEST PALLANT
North side

Behind the *White Horse Inn* was the parsonage house of All Saints Church recorded in 1635 (see Fig. 14-3) and demolished in this century. It was a hall house, only 7m by 3m with a little court (or trippett) and ¼ rood of land [6] – approximately 15 square metres.

All Saints Church

The present building is 13th century, built on the site of an earlier church (probably 1086).[7] A small burial ground to the north of the church was used from 1783 for less than a century. To the south of the church is a passage which is described as 'a procession way' in 1534.[8]

The property immediately south and east of the passage was described as 'a garden plot and tenement of the parson' and was demolished by 1669. It was used as a stable by him from the 18th century.

1-4   Dean and Chapter property.[9] Newly built as 4 houses about 1750. In 1670, 3 houses each with 2 hearths, one house being occupied by Nicholas Breades, a tailor. His father's inventory of 1650 describes the property as having a hall, parlour, shop, chambers over, a copploft, buttery and

Fig. 14-3 All Saints Parsonage House and *White Horse Inn*

washroom, which suggests more than 2 hearths and successful avoidance of tax by the son (who inherited also a musket, sword, bandoliers and fowling piece). In 1534 repair records include 320 tiles, 100 laths, 100 four foot boards and refers to studding, breding and daubing the north and street sides, and mentions boards for shop windows.[10]

Fig. 14-4 All Saints Church in the 19th century

5   One freehold property in the middle of a series of Dean and Chapter leaseholds. Circa 1767. Had been 2 messuages built under 1 roof. 5 hearths 1670. Post Office 1834 (John Attree Fuller, postmaster).[11]

6-8   Dean and Chapter site. Corner house – 1580 John Hilles (fuller), 1608 John Hide (butcher). The latter's widow willed it in 2 halves to her sons, the easternmost being a shop, the two brothers, Henry (tailor) and John (butcher), not to hinder each other in the use of one common passage for the whole house. In the rear was a well and quince trees. Described in 1777 as 'some years since new built and now used as 3 houses'.[12]

NORTH PALLANT

West side

10-11 18th-century Dean and Chapter property, with records from 1435. Occupier in 1517 was Denys Hicks, bricklayer. He was given a life tenancy and required to do every sort of work on behalf of the Dean and Chapter. When on the work of the Church he received 6d. a day. He had to ensure that the weeds did not grow about the church walls and to cast snow from the leads and clean the gutters and when there were great rains he had to be in the vaults of the church. In 1649 it had 6 low rooms, a cellar, kitchen and 3 rooms above. It was known as The Globe in 1683. First recorded as 2 houses in the late 18th century.[13]

12-13 18th century. Another Dean and Chapter property recorded from 1435 and known as Trentmarks. In 1649 it had 6 low rooms and a malting floor 12m by 6m and 6 chambers above the low rooms. Then occupied by Thomas Diggons, a wealthy merchant and in 1663 by Thomas Miller, another merchant. 8 hearths in 1670. Held in 2 parts from 1708. 13 became the City Club.[14]

14-15 In 1649 was the stable of the *Spread Eagle Inn* (opposite). During excavations at the rear, a 17th-century wine bottle seal was found with a representation of a two-headed eagle on it. The seal is almost certainly that

of Thomas Bury and his wife Elizabeth who lived in North Pallant (east side) in 1670. He was mayor in 1671. New built house and stable on the site in 1713 when it was sold for £172. Charles Cooper erected two houses on the site of the stable in 1798. Present building has a 19th-century front.[15]

Fig. 14-5
17th century bottle seal

16 Built 1814 by Charles Cooper (who created Cooper Street) on the site of a previous house of 1707, stables and granary.[16]

17 New built in 1713 and rebuilt 1824.[17]

18-20 18th century. Thomas Taylor and then George Coombes had a malthouse here by 1780. *The Brewers Arms* public house was here in 1762, also a salt storehouse.[18]

To the north a little passage and court led to 83 East Street in the 16th century and onwards.[19]

North east quadrant

Wealthy merchants found the east side of North Pallant palatable from the 16th century. By 1670 Hearth Tax records show an exceptionally high average of 8 hearths each over 6 houses.[20] Three of the houses also dominated East Pallant: between them their gardens and coach houses formed the majority of its north frontage. Part of these gardens, following Victorian trends, became an iron and brass foundry in 1845; and still following fashion, a car park in the 1980s.

NORTH PALLANT

East side

1-1A 3 houses in 1647, with stables, barns and malting rooms. One house in 1730 with a malt and brew house. Enjoyed gardens through to East Pallant until sold to Halstead for the foundry.[21]

2-4   Records go back to 1561. 2 houses in 1637. Lambert Barnard lived here
        in 1632. Refronted in 1752 when alterations and additions also made.
The refronting involved building into the street up to 1m (north end) and
0.5m (south end). The City's view was that to grant any more than this would
be prejudicial and 'desight' to the street, the same already being 'full narrow'
but the amount requested would not be a convenience, rather an ornament.
The Wesleyans had their first chapel in a loft above stabling at the rear before
1814 and there was a schoolroom here in this period too.[22]

5   *Spread Eagle Inn* before 1597 and certainly up to 1682. By the 18th
        century the lawns and gardens ran through to East Pallant (stable and
coach house).[23] Present building 18th century.

6   18th-century home of Johnson family (he was Town Clerk in 1804).[24]

7   Thomas Hayley's house 1721-37. North part briefly used as a Custom
        House. Also briefly occupied by the Literary Society and St Margaret's
school in the 19th century. Present house 19th-century frontage (18th-century
core).[25]

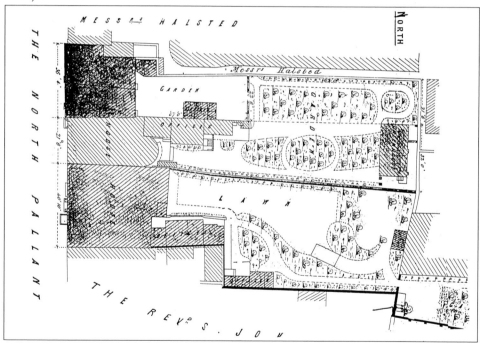

Fig. 14-6 Plan of 7 North Pallant (19th century)

8   Earlier house contained a 15th-century groined cellar and an 18th-
        century staircase. One room on the south-east was joined on to 9. Capital
messuage in 1653.[26]

9   Present house 1712, built by Henry Peckham, was one of the first new
        brick houses in the city. Known as Pallant House. Ostriches on gate
posts. Additional storey on north west corner added later, as a look-out. There

Fig. 14-7 9 North Pallant

was an earlier house (1653) with a malthouse, cellar and garden.[27] Pallant Market Cross stood outside and Peckham was given permission to take it down and use the materials – he was to provide a shed in St Martin's in lieu. (See Fig. 14-7.)

EAST PALLANT
North side
6 almshouses known as Heather's Charity Building recorded from 1790 was previously a store; next, to the east, was a coachhouse, stables and a garden belonging to 5 North Pallant and used as such in 1875.[28]
BAFFINS LANE
West side
Baffins Hall Now auction rooms. Was a Presbyterian chapel from 1721 when the tenement was purchased from George Carver for £90. Known as the Meeting House in 1707.[29]

The Church of St Andrew in the Pallant (or St Andrew Twainchurch) was probably on this corner. In the Cathedral Chartulary Thomas Blome granted to Robert Cobbe, for 10 shillings, his lands in Palenta of the Bishop's fee, between the Church of St Andrew on the west and the lands of the fee of Sir William de John. The date is not known. In 1199 there is a reference to land held next to the same church.

Another entry in the same chartulary, for 1229-54, refers to the Parish of 'St Andrew Twain Churche'. There are no records after 1254. Probably the church became redundant as a result of the enclosure of the whole area to the east by the Black Friars in the 13th century. The jurisdiction of the parish seems to be perpetuated by the enclave of Sub-deanery which can be clearly seen in Fig. 1-7.

Fig. 14-8 Baffins Hall

South east quadrant

The frontage of South and East Pallants had some buildings from the 13th century, but the back land was gardens and meadow.

FRIARY LANE

Previously George Street, dates only from the early 19th century. There was an earlier lane, roughly on this alignment in the 13th century prior to the occupation by the Black Friars, but they closed it and it then lay within their walls.[30]

Sicklease Lane/Street (so called in 1379) replaced the above closed lane (see map Fig. 14-2); on the west side there was an orchard which had a cottage in 1660/1. The road was taken into Robert Bull's property in 1763.[31]

Also on the west side were 4 garden plots recorded from the 13th century and called the Sickleases[32] totalling some $1\frac{1}{2}$ acres and owned by the Dean and Chapter. Not until the 18th century was there any regular record of buildings on this land.

The name 'Sicklease' is probably Old English, meaning meadow or grassland beside a stream (the nearest stream was the Lavant outside the wall).[33] There was a Robert de Sicklease in the 13th century with property near the South Walls. In accordance with the contemporary custom he must have taken his name from the land.

EAST PALLANT

South side

East Pallant House and car park.[34] The nucleus of the house was probably built about 1750 by Robert Bull. He was the son of Nathaniel Bull of Aldingbourne, and had been apprenticed to a Gray's Inn attorney. He inherited considerable wealth from the estate of Sir Richard Farrington in 1743 and moved to Chichester where he became a member of the Merchant Guild and of the City Council, Bailiff and then Mayor. During his occupation of East Pallant House he developed the lands to the south as pleasure grounds; there were kitchen gardens, stables, a coach house and a chaise house. This was, at the time, one of the largest properties within the walls. Recent excavations, prior to the building of the new Council Chamber, produced a six-sided tea bowl of Chinese blue and white porcelain with the name 'Bull' painted under the glaze. This would have been part of a service made to order and was only affordable by the rich. A brick and tile kiln was also found during the excavations, the products of which were used for the 18th-century buildings.

Fig. 14-9 East Pallant House before use as offices

In the north east corner of the car park there was a pigeon house in 1379; in 1402/4 there were various new built tenements with an adjoining croft and a dovecote. It was still described as a Culverhouse Close (i.e. Pigeon House Close) in 1529. In 1755 there was a slaughterhouse here.[35]

2   There was a house, garden and thatched barn here in 1533; it was occupied in 1555 by William Marcant, a cordwainer, and in 1628 by

James Pilbeam, a merchant. This house had recently been built by Laurence Alcock.[36]

3   18th century. Houses recorded from 1533; 1556 Robert Exton; later occupiers include Captain Dilke (1755), a relative of Charles Wentworth Dilke.[37]

4   Occupiers include John Marsh, junior; James Tutte M.P.; John W. Prior, woolstapler, 1851.[38] Present building early 18th century.

Fig. 14-10 East Pallant

5   Described as 'ground of William Royce' in 1534 and still undeveloped in 1660. By 1680 was a messuage with malthouse and garden. Purchased by George Bayley and new house built about 1760, subsequently occupied by his son John.[39]

6   Dean and Chapter property with a house recorded in 1534 and thereafter continuously.[40] Present building early 18th century.

7   Mentioned in will of Thomas Colbrooke the elder in 1579 – given to his son John.[41] 18th century.

SOUTH PALLANT

East side

South Pallant was previously 'Plough Lane' from the inn at West Pallant corner.

1   'Lately erected' 1788.[42]

2-4 This building now includes 3 houses. Earliest record is 1605, referring to one messuage and in 1698 it had been divided into three. In the Hearth Tax records for 1670 there are 3 adjoining properties, each with 2 hearths. In 1776 there were 5 separate dwellinghouses and this is confirmed in the

Land Tax records for 1780-1810 when the numbers vary from 3 to 4 and to 5. This all suggests an early building, 16th century, which has been considerably altered over the years.[43] To the north of Cawley Priory was a currier's shop around 1700.[44]

Fig. 14-11 Cottages in South Pallant

Cawley Priory Home of the Sanden family (alderman, doctor) with records of a house from 1726. In 1599 there is a record of a previous freehold house (lately built) occupied by John Brown, a coalburner (a collier). William Cawley rented the sickleases, to the rear, from the Dean and Chapter up to 1660.[45] Building 18th-19th century.

Pouke Lane (south of Cawley Priory). Excavations have revealed the old road.
It was of flint and was 17 feet wide and 1 inch thick. The road sealed a culvert and a Roman ditch. The road had been thickened in Tudor times; the lowest course contained only 13th-century pottery. This is the road which was taken into Robert Bull's garden and was partly hacked away in the period 1763-1822 and a wall and flint courtyard built over it.[46]

South west quadrant

SOUTH PALLANT

West side
The lower part was the garden, stables, malthouses, coach houses and gardens of houses in South Street.

10 There was a small house on the corner in the 17th century, otherwise the area north-westwards was the garden of the great house in South Street, where the bank and Regnum Club now are.[47]

11-12 Pair of early 19th-century houses (1804). Previously a storehouse and wine vaults (18th century) and in the 17th century a garden.[48]

13-16 5 houses mid-18th century.[49]

18-19 *The Plough Inn* recorded in 1604 and up to 1684; had stables, outhouses and a gateroom. By 1714 it was a malthouse.[50]

WEST PALLANT
South side

In the 19th century there was a predominance, as today, of doctors and lawyers: then it was mainly the Gruggen family and the difference was that they lived over the shop.

9   Core of 17th-century house, probably late 16th. There is a feoffment of 1587 from Mrs. Butterwycke to Dr. Johnson of a house. In 1627 described as a corner house facing Pallant Cross. 8 hearths in 1670. In 1687 Robert Edmond's inventory (£401 5s. 4d.) lists kitchen, little parlour, hall, great parlour, study, three chambers and garret over, cellars, brewhouse. County Court house in the 19th century.[51]

10   House on site before 1587. 7 hearths in 1670. John Braman M.P. occupier in 1678.[52] 18th century.

12   18th century. House of the Drinkwater family.[53]

To the west was a passage leading into the Mulberry Garden taken into the original house in 1869, and outbuildings and stables partly in the ownership of St Mary's Hospital; also a cider house in the 18th century.

BLACKFRIARS AND NEW TOWN[54]

The remainder of the south east quadrant was enclosed by the Black Friars until the Dissolution.

In 1228 Edmund, Earl of Cornwall, founded the house of Dominican or Black Friars. Initially the friars lived in temporary buildings. In 1284 Edmund quit-claimed the whole of their plot, with all services, giving them leave to acquire other adjoining sites so that they could have a suitable area to enclose with a hedge. In 1285 when she was in Chichester with King Edward I, Queen Eleanor bought a plot of land from John Blel, 32m by 13m, which was held of the Earl of Cornwall and gave it to the Friars; she added another plot from Sir John the Chaplain (this was 'for her soul's sake'). By 1297 there were at least 34 friars.

When they laid out their grounds they enclosed 2 public ways (see maps I and II, Fig. 14-1). A new road was acquired by Royal Writ to run southwards from St Andrew's in the Pallant to the city wall.

In 1337, as they had not sufficient land for the church, churchyard and cloister, they were allowed to purchase 5 more plots (123m by 92m) contiguous to their site and were enabled to enlarge their burial ground and cloister.

By the Dissolution the friars had diminished to 7 brethren, in great poverty. On 8th October 1538 the house was taken by the King and, after a year, was purchased by Edward Mylett ('site and houses with church, belfry and churchyard and all buildings, gardens and land within and without the precinct of the same'). By 1550 nearly all the buildings had gone.

The site remained the estate of a mansion house in East Street until the early 19th century. While Chichester's population was increasing and the buildings in the suburbs expanding, this sizeable area remained a green enclave free from business, houses and industry. The Georgian revival passed it by.

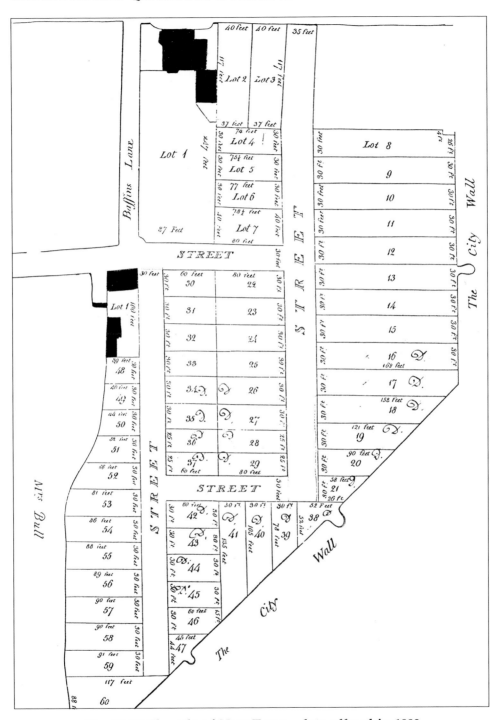

Fig. 14-12 The sale of New Town – lots offered in 1809

In 1809 the land was sold as individual building plots and the affluent middle classes moved in to build the town houses of the day. Covenants were to prohibit the trades of butcher, slaughterman, tallow chandler, soap boiler, innkeeper, brazier, smith and retailer of liquor. St John's and Cross Street were planned in 1808. Friary Street was originally to be called Paternoster Row and for a period was George Street; New Town was to have been Convent Street, and St John's Street, Friday Street. Initially some groups of plots went to builders and speculators, others to individuals.

Of the Lots (or plots) shown on Fig. 14-12, No. 1, which had been the Mansion House, became the Corn Exchange, Nos. 11 and 12 St John's Church (1812-13); No. 13 the Freemasons Lodge; Nos. 20 and 21 Ivy Bank.

Many of the plots were not developed until after 1820. In 1822 the City had to provide chains down both sides of St John's Street to prevent the beasts from the market getting on the new pavements.

By 1851 the Census reveals a doctor, rector, minister, house proprietor, annuitants, retired Lt. Colonel, dentist, timber merchant and a brewer among the occupants.

CHAPTER 15

THE SOUTH WEST QUADRANT
Cloistered Calm

Fig. 15-1 Drawing of the Cathedral in 1790

In 1147/8 Pope Eugenius III confirmed to the Bishop of Chichester all the property already held or to be acquired in the south west quarter of the city. It encompassed the whole area within the old Roman walls from West Street to South Street. In 1163 Pope Alexander III confirmed this and also his protection. In 1261-64 Pope Urban IV again confirmed, and forbade, within the closes, rape, theft, arson, bloodshedding, imprisonment, killing or violence.

In 1300 the Dean complained that the buildings within the close were dilapidated. In 1616 the Chapter had to decide to purge the churchyard of 'hogges and dogges and lewde persons that playe or doe worse within'.

The above and many other items are to be found in the chartularies and Chapter Acts published in *SRS* Vols. 46 and 58.

In 1649 a useful list of all the property in the quadrant was made by the treasurers constituted, at the Commonwealth, 'for abolishing Deans, Deans and Chapters, Canons, Prebends and other offices and tithes belonging to any Cathedral or Collegiate Church or Chapel in England or Wales.' It resides in the WSRO (CapI/30/6) and is reproduced in full:

Manor of Canon Gate, gatehouse and gateroom on W. side of South Street, Chichester, messuage or mansion house called the Dean's house in the Close, two capital messuages heretofore used as general dwelling houses for two of the canons residentiary, capital messuage or mansion house heretofore belonging to the Treasurer in the Close, capital messuage or mansion house sometimes belonging to one of the canons residentiary in the Close, messuage heretofore the house of four prebends and non resident, messuage sometimes the mansion house of the Precentor in the Close, little low-built house on a small parcel of waste ground near Canon Gate in the Close, plot of ground called Paradise in the Close, capital messuage called the Vicars Common Hall in the Close, messuage in the Close at N. side of W. end of the Little Cloisters, messuage in the Close on W. side of said Cloisters, messuage on S. side of that last-mentioned, messuage on W. side of said Cloisters next to that last-mentioned, rooms and chambers called the Cloisters School, chambers used for the Register Office at S. end of the little Cloisters, room called the Common Bread Binge [Bin Room] in the Close, messuage on S. end and E. angle of the little Cloisters, messuage on E. side of said Cloisters next to the house of Thomas Betsworth, messuage between the Common Hall of the Little Cloisters and E. end of the Great Cloisters, messuage on E. side of entrance into the Great Cloisters mentioned in the particular of the said manor and premises to be heretofore demised by the late Dean and Chapter to William Royman, and all messuages, houses, gardens, orchard, yard, backside and curtilages with appurtenances mentioned in the said particular to be respectively heretofore demised by the late Dean and Chapter to John Bereman, Edward Osborne, William Ems, and all other messuages, houses and tenements with appurtenances to be heretofore respectively demised by the late Principal and Commonalty of the Vicars Choral to Richard Brigham, John Newman and Sarah Cox, widow.

The various buildings are now dealt with separately. The identification number refers to the map (Fig. 15-2) and also to the source references for this Chapter.

1 Cathedral

There are the remains of a Roman building under the present cathedral and within Paradise. It is not known whether the South Saxon see cathedral was built within or upon the Norman building; as some of the Roman building has survived it suggests that there was not exact conjunction of the two

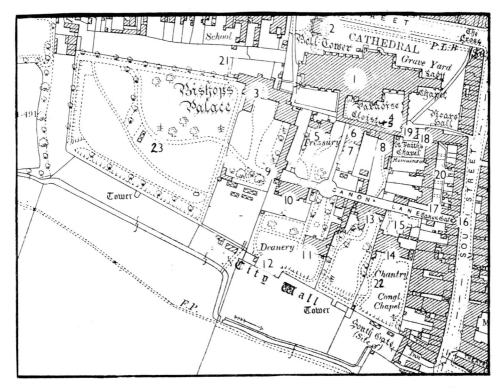

Fig. 15-2 Identification Map (based on Ordnance Survey map, 1898)

cathedrals. The 11th-century cathedral was severely damaged by fire in 1114 and again, after rebuilding, in 1187. In the 16th century there are records of repairs to the building. Some examples give a picture of the materials and depradation of the time, all taken from one year 1533:

> 4,000 blue-slates spent upon the cloister and church.
> Glazing work – library windows, Lady Chapel windows, north and south windows on either side of the high altar, 2 windows in St George's Chapel, 3 windows on north side of body of Church – in all 25 days work for glazing.
> Lead casting for archbutment.
> New doors in vaults; locks and key for door in great belfry.
> Mending the 3 bells in the great belfry.
> $6\frac{1}{2}$ days helying on west side after 'last great wynd'.

The north west tower of the Cathedral fell in 1636 and was rebuilt. The following account, quoted verbatim, shows the materials used and the condition of the tower previously:

> An Estimate of the new building of the Tower that is now fallen downe at the West end of the Cathedrall Church of Chichester 1636.

	£	s
Inprimis for 12000 Foote of Portland stone Ashler delivered ready wrought at this Church at 14d the Foote	740	0
Item there is conteined in this worke 674 Perches which at 10s the perch for ye workemanship accompting 18 Foote [in breadth and 1 Fo. high] to the perch cometh to	337	0
Item for the workeing and setting the windowes and Batlements	100	0
Item for pulling downe of that part of this Tower now standing and clensing the stuffe and layeing it severall and cleareing ye Foundacon	150	0
Item for 200 loads of large filling stones to be spent amonge the smale stone that is now there for the makeing of the worke stronge and substantiall which I am certified will coast 5s. the Loade delivered there, which cometh to	50	0
Item every Perch of this worke will take halfe a loade of lyme and twoe loads of sande, the which will come to 12s. the Perch accompting for the sand 5s. and 7s. for the lyme, 20 bushelles being the halfe loade	404	8
Item for the shoreing of the wall adioyning to the Tower and centring the vault and reping of it	150	0
Item for 20 Squares of Carpenters worke conteined in the twoe towers and the Roofe at £4 the Square	80	0
Some totall	2011	8

The spire was rebuilt after a collapse in 1861.

2 Bell Tower (see Chapter 8)

3 Bishop's Palace, Kitchen and Chapel

Originally the Bishop of Chichester had 4 residences: Chancery Lane in London (lost in 1535), Amberley Castle (lost in 1588), Aldingbourne, and the Palace in Chichester. Refurbishment was carried out at Chichester in 1606-9. Much of it was basic and essential: repairs to guttering, floors, leaking roofs, underpinning and pointing, tiling, and involved plumbers, bricklayers, glaziers and masons.

The Palace had 25 hearths in 1670, the largest number of any building in the city.

The chapel was not under the control of the Dean and Chapter and was used as a Chapel of Ease for country incumbents living in Chichester.

The Chapel and walls of the Great Kitchen date from the 13th century, otherwise largely rebuilt 1724-31.

4 Paradise

This is the open space within the Great Cloister. The name derived from the Garden of Eden and has come to mean a walled garden where rare plants are grown. It was originally a burial ground and the leases of 1607 to Francis Nevill says 'on special occasions of mortality' burials may take place there; however by 1635 it had been leased as a private garden and in 1687 the lessee was required to use it 'only as a garden, orchard or green plot, to prevent all nuisances there and … shall allow such persons to be interred and buried there as the Dean and Chapter shall grant licence for'.

5-5A Treasurer's House

The present building dates from 1834 and is partly on the site of the old Treasury which faced St Richard's Walk. The cloister wall and the west wall of St Richard's Walk are of the old building. In 1686 this building was described as 'of long time been ruinated and dilapidated and such dilapi-dations happened chiefly in the time of the Great Rebellion in the years 1644, 1645 and 1646 or therea-bouts and that amongst other things the great hall belonging to the said house was made wholly useless so that it was in-deed a burthen only and a charge to keep up same … and that the said hall was so ruinated by Collonell Downes and by him converted to a stable and the wall and roof likely to fall And further allegedeth that the … Treasurer … hath at his own great charge caused to be well repaired the said

Fig. 15-3 The Old Treasury

house and edifice saveing the said Hall which for the reasons aforesaid he desires that he may be permitted to take down.'

6 No. 1 St Richard's Walk

The House of the Wiccamical Prebendaries. An early 14th-century building, altered in the 16th and 18th centuries. Has a 14th-century undercroft. It was allotted by the Bishop in 1523 as rooms for the 4 newly created prebendaries. In 1649 it had a decayed large hall and great and little cellar, large dining room over the hall, a great kitchen, little parlour, 2 lodging chambers and garrets, a stable and a gate into Canongate.

7 No. 2 St Richard's Walk

18th-century building.

8 House of the Royal Chantry Priests (or Royal Chaplains) A 13th-century building assigned to the priests of Mortimer's Chantry in the 15th

Fig. 15-4 Canon Gate and Bin Room, from Canon Lane

century. Passed into private hands at the Reformation and altered in the 18th century.

9 Entrance Gate to Bishop's Palace. Built in 1327 and is mentioned in an indenture 30th September 1327 as the 'new gate'.

Prison. The Bishop's Prison is also mentioned in 1327 as being 5m to the south of the gatehouse. It was used for persons convicted of heresy and other crimes at the Bishop's court.

10 Residentiary next to the Bishop's Palace

This was rebuilt in the 19th century but retains a 12th-century doorway and a 14th-century window.

11 The Deanery (present) Canon Lane

Was built in 1725 to the north of the old building.

12 The Old Deanery

The earliest Deanery lay against the city wall with a part on the south side. In 1178 Henry II

Fig. 15-5 Entrance Gate to Bishop's Palace

permitted the Dean to make a postern in the city wall to enable him to go out to his orchards and fields and houses. This grant was destined to provide the seeds of the Deanery's destruction, for the weak point created in the city's defences was taken advantage of in the Civil War and led to its damage in the siege of 1642. The old Deanery had been large: it had a hall 14m x 6m, 2 parlours – one summer, one winter – buttery, a kitchen and dining room, lodging chambers, garrets, a study, courtyard and had a one-acre garden and a well. It was stone built and covered with tile. In 1649 the glass of the hall windows and much of the brick had been taken away and by then the house was much dilapidated in many parts. The stone gatehouse was converted into a coach house in 1674.

13 The Residentiary, Canon Lane (the Precentor's House)

Probably 15th century. In 1431 the Bishop granted the ruins of Mr. Northbury's old house to the Dean and Chapter to be rebuilt for the next canon to make residence, and who was willing to build on it. It was ruinous due to having stood empty for a long time. By 1649 it had the status of a mansion house with an old high hall, 2 parlours, wainscotted, a buttery, 2 cellars, kitchen, bake house, wash house and 3 chambers over the parlour, a gatehouse (used as a malthouse), court yard, 4 chambers over the kitchen and a small porter's lodge.

14 The Chantry, Canon Lane

Basically a 13th-century building. In 1649 it was described as a mansion house with great and little parlour, little hall, 4 chambers and 2 closets above, and 4 little chambers on the top floor; also a buttery, pantry, 2 cellars, kitchen, wash house and stable. In 1672 it was 'in great decay' and the lessee Margaret Thomas undertook to repair it and to permit the Dean to dwell there.

15 House on Canon Lane (south)

Recorded from 1595. By 1649 was being used as a stable and hayloft.

16 Canon Gate (see Chapter 11)

Just within the Canongate were 2 little shops in 1616. In 1591 the same building was described as a 'little house called the Almshouse' next to the porter's lodge.

17 Bin Room (see Fig. 15-4)

On the north side of Canon Lane. Until 1831 there were buildings and a gate (the Chain Gate) blocking the southern entrance to the Vicars' Close. To the left of the Chain Gate was the Bin Room, the room for the Common Bread. It is recorded in the 17th century and was still referred to as the Bin Room in 1806. Above were 3 rooms – one a copploft over the stairs.

18 Dark Cloister (or Blind Cloister)

Originally went all round the 4 sides of the Vicars' square. In 1736 it was taken down and the garden laid out.

19 Chapel of St Faith

The origin of the chapel is unknown, but it was in use in 1396 when Mass was said there before the foundation stone of the adjoining Vicars' Hall was laid. By 1402 it was being used as a lumber room and as a through way from Canon Lane to the Cathedral. The cloisters were built in the 15th century and the chapel then lost over 3m at the west end to make way for the cloister, and nearly 6m at the east end forms the courtyard for the residence which is now a private house.

20 Vicars' Close

Foundation stones for the Vicars' Close were laid in 1396/7 and the close was built to house the Vicars, but was let commercially by the 17th century. The central area was known as the 'Little Cloister'.

In 1649 a memorandum refers to the 4 western houses being for the habitation of the Vicars' Choral and 'not to be letten by them so they might gain possession to their successors'.

The central area consisted of gardens used with the surrounding houses, common privies and a common pump yard. The houses belonged to the Principal and Commonality of the Vicars' Choral of the Cathedral. The covenants and conditions of the lease were often strict. One (in 1685) required the lessee to pave the area at the rear (in South Street), not to carry out handicrafts or use as a victualling house, storehouse or wash house, not to disturb the Vicars 'by unlawful assembly of unquiet or unruly persons at unlawful times of night' not 'to keep greyhounds, great hounds, mastiffs, bandogs [ferocious chained dogs] or spaniels'.

Up to 1825 this formed an enclosed square. The southern end was blocked by buildings and the Chain Gate up to 1831. On the east side the houses faced inwards, looking west onto the close with the backs facing South Street. In 1825 they were separated from the rest of the close and a nine-foot wall (which is still there) was built north-south down the close so that the houses could face onto South Street.

21 Chancellor's House and Garden

This was approached from West Street. It had a garden which ran the length of and behind the houses in West Street. The house was ruinous after the siege in 1642, and in 1649 was described as 'a large decayed hall now divided into three parts, an old wainscotted parlour and another also wainscotted, an adjoining closet, buttery, kitchen, pantry, with a large gallery over the hall, 2 further closets, 3 chambers over the parlour and other chambers, a yard, orchard and stable and a garden of 1 acre 2 roods'. The site was sold in 1803 and is now used by the Prebendal School.

22 Choristers Garden

Ran southwards from Canon Lane behind the buildings in South Street (in whose deeds it appears as a west abuttal). In 1569 the Chapter agreed that William Overton, Treasurer, should have a key of the 'Queristers' Garden' with access to it and half the commodities such as herbs, for 2 years, and William Payne a key and the like commodities.

23 Palace Garden

Originally for the exclusive use of the Bishop and now open to the public.

CHAPTER 16

THE EAST SUBURBS
Beyond the Pale

Always the most developed of the four suburbs, over the centuries the east has also suffered many changes in fortune.

There is considerable documentary evidence of occupation in the post-Conquest period. *The Victoria County History* records that 'several houses were held of the Manor of Halnaker, granted at the Conquest to Roger de Montgomery'.[1]

Other early references include:

1225-1250	3 houses outside Eastgate[2]
1241-1256	Plot with building without Eastgate[3]
1249	A manse without Eastgate[3]
13th century	House between gate and church[4]
1225	Land and buildings outside gate, next church[4]
1328	2 new cottages[5]

There were two great common fields: Portfield and Guildenfield, divided into strips until the 19th century. The River Lavant ran through the suburb from east to west.

The Parish suffered in the Civil War siege in 1642. A number of houses outside the gate were destroyed by defenders to create a clear area, whilst the attackers used the church for directing gunfire into the city.

The suburb was the home of many small industries, particularly cottage needlemaking – which declined after the Civil War – parchment making, metal working, brickmaking.

Poverty was endemic until the 19th century. After the siege the suburb became a slum with twice as many poor as previously and the Justices tried to relieve the poverty by levying a special rate on 17 nearby parishes; in every case the parishes found excuses to be left off the levy. Ten years later the situation was still unresolved.[6] By 1670 the Hearth tax records that there were 38 houses with 98 hearths. However 20 of these houses – with 39 of the hearths – were empty or had unpaid tax.[7]

Some rebuilding started fairly quickly, consisting mainly of artisans' dwellings. The poor rate assessments show these as well below the value of those in the city; similarly Land tax assessments are only about half.[8]

It was a parish which had burial grounds, a fever hospital, almshouses and a house of correction. Until it became fashionable to live outside the walls St Pancras was for the un-wealthy.

The original city boundary is shown on map Fig. 1-8.

Market Avenue (previously Snag Lane) came into existence in 1867 to provide a route to the new Cattle Market. Previously there had been a lane and the land by the wall and by the Lavant was largely leased by residents within the city.

Otherwise, prior to the Civil War, there was only the nucleus of the road system. Two roads divided outside the gate, as now: St Pancras went off in a north-easterly direction towards Arundel; the other the Hornet (Newick Street), more easterly to Oving and a road to Rumboldswick went southwards. No side streets fed in or out of these roads before St James on the north and Whyke Road on the south.

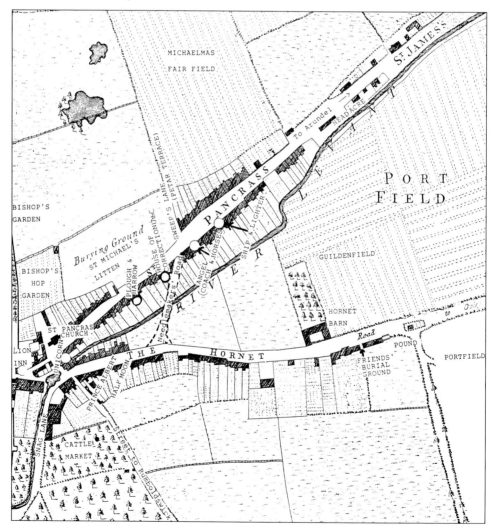

Fig. 16-1 St Pancras – places mentioned in text (1769 map base)

EASTGATE SQUARE

Nothing in the square can be older than 1642 as the whole of the previous buildings were destroyed then.

1   Owned by the City. Croft of Richard Dureman in 1254. In 1571 William Moore, a blacksmith, had a forge, workshops and a house. His will (1582) and inventory show that he was wealthy – he was valued at £360 12s. 6d. His widow, Alice, married Richard Keere and they had an inn, *The Lion*, on the site. The building by now had a great and 2 other chambers, a parlour, hall, 2 kitchens, 4 chambers above, also a brewhouse and stables. Keere died in 1618 and the unfortunate Alice carried on alone at the inn until 1624. Her beneficiary, as laid down in her first husband's will, was her son Thomas Moore who was 'infirm and weak' and had to be provided for. Excavations in 1972 produced some Tudor glass bottle bases, a brass candlestick and the neck of a wine bottle, all of which could be attributed to a large inn. By 1644 the site had become a garden plot and was leased by James Lucas, a carpenter, in 1693. Only by 1737 had it a house and timber yard and by 1752 it was 2 houses. In 1804 William Hardham had a grocer's shop, the predecessor of Sharpe Garland, 1860.[9]

2-3   Partly owned by the Dean and Chapter from the 13th century to 1871. Granted to the Dean and Chapter by Godfrey son of John de Fisseburn, it was used as a house from the 13th century until 1642 when it was demolished. Occupied by a chandler in 1555, blacksmith 1573, wheelwright 1590, glazier 1612. By 1700 it was a timber yard. New built house in 1746 on south east part of the site. Two houses

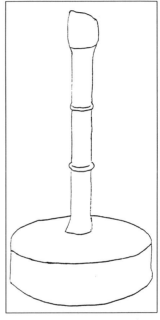

Fig. 16-2 Candlestick excavated at 1 Eastgate

by 1869. 3 was the *Running Horse* beer house in 1880. Meanwhile 2 had been occupied by a succession of butchers from 1801 for much of the 19th century with stables, dunghole, pens and a slaughterhouse at the rear.[10]

4-6   There was a parsonage house with a garden and barn to the west of the access road. After the Civil War it was not rebuilt until 1710 and was again demolished in 1935.[11]

8   The east side of the Square was originally built much further forward. Buildings finally disappeared under road widening in 1938. The Lavant ran east-west at this point and there was a bridge which was certainly there in 1355.

To the east of the bridge was the *Unicorn Inn*. This had been built by 1670 to replace a victualling house occupied by Humphrey Collins. Buildings were constructed, with the permission of the City Council, over the adjacent

Lavant to a width of 2m and a length of 20m: in 1693 there was a brewhouse over the river. The Corporation of St Pancras, a charitable and social organisation, was formed at the inn in 1689. Much of the structure was rebuilt in about 1760 and the inn finally came into the hands of the brewers, Humphreys, in 1807. After the demolition in 1938 a new inn was built on the back of the old site, but it ceased to trade in 1960.[12]

10-12 This site, which measured 24m (frontage) by 37m (west) 49m (east) and 25m (rear), was owned by the City in 1687/8, but this was disputed and after a settlement in about 1747 it clearly became freehold. There was one house in 1681; in 1729 there were 2 houses at 10, the rest of the site consisting of a garden, wood houses, yard and a stable, and granary. In 1781 two westernmost houses (11-12) were built; 10 was rebuilt before 1813. It was 11 which gained immortality by housing Keats for a short period in 1819.[13]

13-17 This site stretched from the city wall on the west to include the Lavant in the east, for the latter was built over by 1800 and became the site of the *Cattle Market Inn*. The first record for the site is the will of Thomas Austin, a maltster, in 1697, in which he describes his millhouse, horse mill, malthouse, outhouses and garden thereon. Austin lived in St Pancras. The area continued to be used for malting until after 1796 when Joseph Figgis bought the property and in 1811 sold it off in lots. A new house was built at 14 about this time. A storehouse and other buildings were erected at 15 in 1819 and it became a house by 1839. On 16 a new house was built in 1813, the date given in the parish rates. It had become a beershop in 1845 and was called the *Market Tavern* in about 1874.[14] It ceased in 1925. 17 lies behind the frontage and against the wall, reached by a passage. The fire engine house occupied a narrow frontage to the street in the 19th century.

Centre of Eastgate Square

Whilst it is clear that St Pancras Street and The Hornet divided at the Eastgate, it is also certain that there was a north-south stone bridge over the Lavant which effectively joined the two streets opposite St Pancras church. This created a block of buildings in the centre of what is now an open area. The block was destroyed in the Civil War – in leases of the City and St Mary's who owned part of the property, the description after the war changes from 'messuage' to 'piece of ground' and one document says 'whereas by reason of the late warr and trouble in and about the city and suburbs all the said messuage and all the buildings thereunto belonging were totally burned and pulled down and carried away'. One of these buildings was *the Dolphin Inn*. When rebuilt, the centre block continued in existence until well into the 19th century – one was even, on sale, described in 1862 as 'a valuable piece of building land in the centre of the square at Eastgate … on the west side of the pump – a most desirable situation for a business house.' This was a sentiment not agreed with by the City Council which eventually acquired and cleared it.

Two early names for the buildings were 'Dardanelles' and 'Crackenhalles'.[15]

Eastgate Hall (Baptist Chapel)
    The records (NC/B1/7/19-29) show a conveyance in 1671 of land on which a meeting house was built in the next year. Rebuilt 1725.

ST PANCRAS
North west side
St Pancras Church
    A building is known from the 13th century. It was destroyed in the Civil War and not rebuilt until 1751; it was altered in the 19th century. In 1685 the churchwardens reported that 'our consecrated ground is put to use of a timber yard.'[16]

Fig. 16-3 St Pancras Church in the 19th century

    Buildings are recorded between the church and what is now New Park Road in the 13th and 16th centuries.
    In the first section, probably 1-3, there were 4 houses in 1618 which were demolished in the war. William Reynolds, who was Paymaster of the Chichester garrison, was ahead of his time as a speculator for he bought the site cheaply, built houses, and sold them by 1652. His inventory in 1664 reveals a value of £396 13s. 0d. (about £20,000 now). By 1749, when a rare plan is available, 1 was a house with a pump, wash house and stables strung out behind and to the west behind the church is shown a hoop shave house and a wheeler's yard. James Pitt, a pipemaker, lived at 2 in 1770.[17]
    The present line of buildings is predominantly 18th century. Occupants of the original properties in the 18th century include a staymaker, clockmaker, maltster, cordwainer, ironmonger, shoemaker, butcher, sadler and currier.
    At the corner of what is now New Park Road there was a stile into St Michael's Churchyard. There was a house here in 1663 owned by the City

Fig. 16-4 *Victoria Inn*, **St Pancras**

and occupied by a needlemaker, John Mounsloe. The house was destroyed by fire in 1880 and the Elizabeth Johnson Girls School was built thereon.[18] This too, has now gone.

16-18 (see Alexandra Terrace)

19-23 A site owned by St Mary's Hospital. Houses recorded from 1606, the easternmost having a malthouse in 1755, which was burnt down.[19]

24-25 *Victoria* Public House (see Fig. 16-4). Richard Deller, a brewer, was recorded in 1845 and William Henry and George Deller, brewers, were at the *Victoria Inn* in 1855.

34 *Hope* Public House. First mentioned in 1837 trade directory. Demolished.

42-45 Four brick and tiled houses were built by William Burcher in 1786 on the garden of an existing house. Valued, for fire insurance, at £150 for the four and £50 for the older house.[20]

Joy's Croft

This piece of land lay from and including Adelaide Road, eastwards to about 78 and covered up to about 8 acres. It is mentioned in 1491/2 as a croft in an enclosure called Joescroft and again in 1497 as 6 acres in one enclosure called Joyscrofte when it was granted by Thomas Tawcke and Margaret his wife to the City. Thereafter it was leased by the City usually for 21 years at a time. There was a cottage on the site by 1751.[21]

Red Lion Inn[22] and Lion Brewery

In 1812 there were 5 houses fronting the street to the west of the Red Lion; 2 were sold in 1814, the others in 1818. By the time the site was reunited in the hands of one owner in 1874 the 2 houses had been split into 4 and the other 3 had been burned down. In 1879 the site was in use as a house,

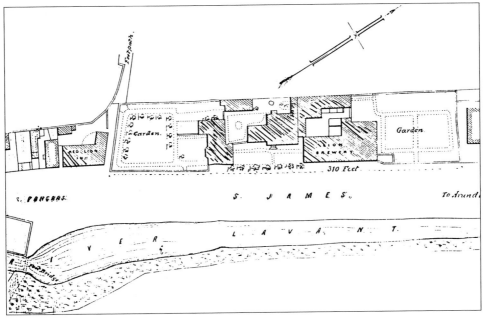

Fig. 16-5 Plan of 1882

stable and timber yard. This area was known as 'no man's land' probably because it was in dispute between St Pancras and St James and was extra-parochial. The Lion House has a date of 1783 and the initials $_J{}^J{}_D$ on its wall.

St James' Hospital

Known as the leper hospital but housed other disabled persons. Dated from 12th century. The building was destroyed by fire in 1781, leaving a small part in the structure of a cottage on the site. The inventory of William Lawrence of St James Hospital in 1701 reveals comfort and possessions: 120 pewter dishes, feather beds, 5 gold rings, corn in the barn, cattle and hogs. There is a considerable burial ground from which 330 burials have recently been removed. The Hospital was maintained by the rents of several cottages in Chichester, land in Portfield, Spitalfield and Oving and by bequests mainly up to about 1600.[23]

NEW PARK ROAD

This area to the north of St Pancras contained the Litten (the burying ground), the Bishop's Garden and Hop Garden. The graveyard dates from 1100 – 1118; land given by King Henry I to the Church. There was an earlier Roman cemetery here, too. The school was built in 1812 by which time the road, first known as Litten Road, had gone through. There was a chapel – St Michaels – on the site by 1216 and a charnel house had to be repaired in 1534.[24]

ALEXANDRA TERRACE and 16-18 St Pancras

The start of the new road is shown on the Gardner Map, 1769. Richard Cooper, a maltster, lived there up to 1678. Following subsequent sales the corner houses and what was to be 1-7 Petars Terrace, Sweeps Lane were built from 1829 onwards. The name Petar derives from John Petar who owned the site up to 1866. The Roman cemetery under these cottages has been excavated and is reported in full in *Chichester Excavations* Vol. 1.[25]

Fig. 16-6 Site of St James' Hospital

ST PANCRAS

South east side

85   There was a water mill called the King's Mill or Lavant Mill with a mill pond and dashing pool, which was reported to the City Council in 1757 as falling into great decay, having for several years been taken down. From now on it was leased as a site only, with a cottage and stables, 2 cottages by 1788, 3 by 1849.[26]

86-88 Owned by the City. One house 1755, four by 1811.[27]

89   *Star and Garter Inn.* City site. Leased by a brewer in 1785.
      First so named in 1801.[28]

      Next came land owned by the City. Several houses in 1757 had 'fallen into great decay for want of repair and the greatest part of the materials so fallen down had been clandestinely taken away by persons unknown'. The houses had been in brick, because 1,500 bricks are mentioned. One building had been used as a spinning house. Four new houses were erected around 1800 and there was a stone mason's yard at the west end.[29]

      A building known as 'The Black Boy' was here in 1627/8 – thus the connotation predates the traditional Black Boy (King Charles II). The Steward of the City was told to clear out sluices because the Lavant could not flow above the Black Boy. The name persisted through City leases, in the way of lawyers, right through to the 19th century. There were 6 cottages here in 1858, and in 1873 a sanitary report referred to open drains and leaking privies.[30]

Church Hall site. Was the National School for boys, girls and infants conveyed to the Minister, Churchwardens and Overseers of St Pancras by the Duke of Richmond in 1843. Previously there were two houses on the site, and in 1733 it was in the will of Isaac Hammond, a needlemaker. He left a very detailed inventory, which shows that the property was mortgaged for £205.

Fig. 16-7 Portfield Windmill

Among trade stock were:

65,000	large needles
35,000	large worsted needles
168,000	small needles
12,500	quilting needles

and some 221,000 other needles, both finished and partly finished. The values seem pathetically small: 2s. 6d. (12½ p) per 1000 for large needles, 6d. (2½ p) per 1000 for quilting needles, etc. The property contained a parlour, kitchen, brewhouse and 3 rooms above.

Isaac Hammond was cited for co-habiting with Ann Deane, a widow, as his wife, for several years, having a wife of his own living (with whom he had several children). He confessed in writing and asked for forgiveness, in 1705.[31]

(Tozer Way) This was known as the Head Acre, the name occurring from 1222 when it went to the Church of Boxgrove as a gift. There were houses on it then and there are continuous records of the use of the site thereafter. In 1604 Edward Manning's will provides for the use of the premises by his son, with sufficient bricks for building a chimney. The words 'head acre' are often found in field names; in Old English it means 'land at the top', probably where the plough turned. Geographically this land forms the head of the Guilden Field, where it reaches the south side of the street.[32]

117   A house and malthouse in 1780.

118   Was *Ship and Lighter Inn*, 1797. Building dates from 1700.[33] At least six needlemakers lived in this section in the 18th century (see Chapter 5).

125A-126 *Angel Inn*, 1754; *Coach and Horses* by 1811.[34]

127-129, rear of (St Pancras Place). In 1866 described as 'approached from the street through a narrow passage. The place contains four houses which have no outlet or windows at the back. The sewage goes into a cesspit which is often quite full and very foul ...' The Council Sanitary Committee visited the court and found the houses to be partly unoccupied, the whole court being foul and the stench intolerable. Even back in 1807 the occupants were recorded as 'poor'.[35]

136-137 Demolished for new road. In 1617 House of Correction (137) At time of demolition seen to have a timber frame.[36]

141-142 Owned by St Mary's. In 1632 occupied by parchment maker, William Richards. Built about 1797. *Black Horse* beer house, 1840.[37]

143-145 *Plough and Harrow* and Farr's Court.[38] Inn known by 1785 (then *The Chequers*). Farr's Court to the east of and the rear of 143-5 was a court of 5 small cottages, running down to the Lavant, and built by 1771. By 1873 were noted in a sanitary report as a previous fever spot, although by this date the water was good and the place improved. The name of the court derives from the family who had the inn in 1851 and founded Farr's Depository.

151 Probably destroyed in the Civil War.

Timber yard from 1675. Coachmakers yard by 1738.[39] See Chapter 6.

152-154 St Mary's property.

Cottage and garden 1445. Buildings demolished in Civil War; garden plot from then to late 17th century, then house, malthouse, barn, stable and gateroom. New built 1788 and divided into three houses.[40]

155-156 Cottage in 1445. Demolished in Civil War. House by 1676/7. In 1805 two houses.[41]

THE HORNET (Newick Street)

North side.

The name Newick Street first appears in 1250; The Hornet is more recent – its earliest reference is in a will of 1563, referring to Hornet in the Parish of Week.

On the north-west corner of the street, now part of the highway, was a house of the Exton family in the 16th century.

19 Dear's Almshouses, which were re-endowed under Martha Dear's will in 1806. The previous almshouses had been in an advanced state of dilapidation and had ceased to be used as such.[42]

21 Was the *Castle Inn.*

Hornet Barn A barn is recorded in the City rate return of 1755 and the Land tax, 1780.[43]

South side

What is now a twitten was until the 18th century described as a highway to Rumboldswick. The site eastwards from the 'highway' for some 62m was owned by the Dean and Chapter. There is record of cottages and crofts in 1302/14 and in 1534 when a shoemaker and baker were residents. There is no sign that this row of properties was destroyed in the Civil War: the relative continuing prosperity of the occupants can thus be accounted for.[44]

FARR'S COURT.
CHICHESTER

Fig. 16-8 Farr's Court 19th century

There have been many inns in this stretch – an indication of some thriving activity. The *Dog and Duck* was a sizeable building in 1670 (11 hearths, William Hudson or Hodgson) and was still active in 1745.[45]

4   *The Eastgate Brewery* (or *Brewery Inn*) was known from about 1780.[46]
           The *Half Moon and Seven Stars* is certainly known from 1714 and had also been known as *The Old Carbiniere* in 1730.[47] It had become dilapidated and was re-built in 1888 on the same site and that of a lodging house and beershop called The *Black Horse*.[48]

The *Bush Inn* was previously called *The Prince Albert*.

One of the houses, occupied by John Smith in 1669, was used as a Quaker Meeting House.

Various other occupations carried out in this short stretch include: blacksmith (Butterly to 1647); miller and horse gelder (John Smith, 1574); carpenter (Oakshott, 1804); staymaker (Paull, 1804); baker (Field, 1782) and gardener (Drewett, 1664).

12   Was rebuilt in 1794.[49]

22   Was burnt down in 1782.[50]

Chapel (now restaurant) moved from Orchard Street in 1865 and closed in 1968.[51]

At 48 was the parish boundary with Rumboldswick and, shortly beyond that, the parish ditch.

Near the junction with Whyke Road was the Quaker burial ground acquired in 1673 and shown on the Tithe Map[52]; next door was the small thatched meeting house.

The cattle pound mentioned in 1604 and on the Tithe Map was a short distance to the east of the burial ground.[53]

Portfield and Guildenfield

The development of this large area of land between St Pancras and the Hornet and to the south, is dealt with in Chapter 1. Portfield was mentioned in the 12th century. Before the Enclosure Award the land was held by a large number of owners in inconvenient plots.[54]

Guildenfield was also mentioned in the 12th century. It seems to have been named after the Guild merchants of the city. The Guild of St George had lands up to 1548/9 when they were bought by the City.[55]

Cattle Market[56]

The new cattle market outside Eastgate was opened in 1871 to replace the street markets within the city.

CHAPTER 17

OUTSIDE THE SOUTHGATE
The Transport Jungle

A road out of the South Gate is recorded in 930 when it was called 'Fore Street'.[1] The turnpike to Dell Quay was built in 1779 when the road line was straightened. Ribbon development was a feature before 1700.

Stockbridge is referred to in 1376. Old English stocc: land with tree stumps left standing on it; brygg: land by a bridge. This would take the name back to the period around AD 800.

The South Gate was just to the north of the *Cathedral Tavern* (*Fountain Inn*) up to 1773.

As will be seen from Fig. 17-2 the impact of transport on the suburb since 1772 has been traumatic, with canal, railway, tramway, turnpike, buses and various ring roads all carving up the landscape.

SOUTHGATE
West side
29   *Cathedral Tavern*, previously *Fountain Inn* – a late 17th/18th-century building.[2] Building shown on Gardner Map of 1769. Inn recorded from 1804.

27-28 The river Lavant was built over here by the 16th century to the extent of 2.6m width and 11m in length. Building occupied by fellmonger and glover Anthony West, 1706, and a tallow chandler, 1740.[3]

Immediately to the south was a lane which ran in to Deanery farm at the rear of the frontage properties.

16-26 There had been a row of cottages here from the 16th century. 24 has timber framing.

19-23 (Waitrose site up to 1992) cottages were demolished and a garage built. The original plaque in the shop entrance related to Richard Bassett, a wheelwright, and Margaret, his wife. He left the house to her in his will of 1702.[4]

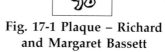

Fig. 17-1 Plaque – Richard and Margaret Bassett

Behind **6-18** was Newman's nursery in the 19th century, and where Avenue de Chartres now is stood the *Railway Inn*. The Middle Class School was just to the north of the *Globe Inn* and was demolished in 1974.

Globe Inn. A site owned by the Vicars' Choral. Before 1649 it was known as Stubber's garden and was an orchard. In 1813 there was a sawing house, stable and workshop and in 1819 an iron foundry was erected. *The Globe Inn*, with brewery, stables, sheds, offices, yards and a Tap had developed on the site by 1851.[5]

The Railway Station opened in 1846 (see Fig. 17-3)

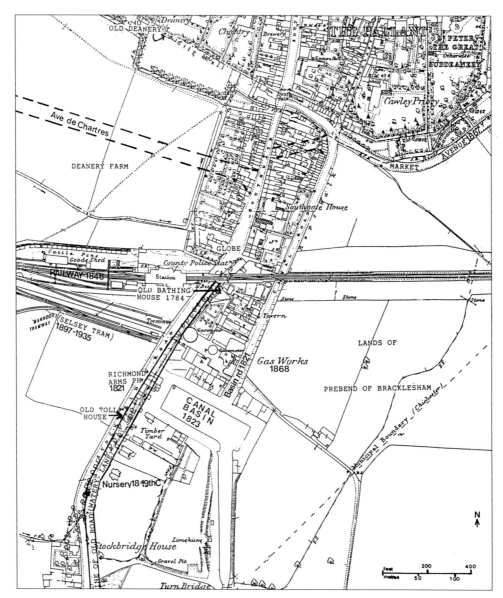

**Fig. 17-2 Map showing development outside Southgate
based on 1875 Ordnance Survey**

Stockbridge House. There was an earlier house on the site (John Buck, 1617)
and Paul Burrard paid £50 in 1678 for it. In 1698 Francis Sone, a tanner
from Havant, completed an agreement for John Lilliott, a carpenter, to erect
a new dwellinghouse for £150 plus the materials from the old house. The
new house was to be 14m long and 8m wide. The walls were to be 0.3m thick
and the building 6m high. It was to have 9 transom windows in front,

3 pediments in the roof, 8 windows at the rear and other windows for closets, 6 chimneys, 1 large staircase and a little stair to the garrets and a handsome cornice under the roof. The kitchen of the old house was to be left standing to be used as a brewhouse. The house was completed in 1699. In 1747 the property was described as 'messuage, called Stockbridge House with all its barns, buildings, tanyards, tan pits', which confirms that the Southgate tannery was close to Stockbridge House. The tannery was still shown as operative in the Land tax in 1789.[6]

Deanery Farm[7] (see Fig. 17-2). Except for the narrow ribbon development on the west side of Southgate all the back land westwards round to Westgate was the Dean's farm with access through the postern in the wall. In the Civil War the mansion house of Deanery farm, barns, stables and other outhouses were demolished. At various times the farm has contained pasture, orchards, meadows, barns, arable, stables, a pigeon house and hop gardens.

Fig. 17-3 Railway Station before modernisation

East side

30   The City owned the land immediately south of the wall to just south of the Lavant. Permission was given to build over the river as long as this did not obstruct its course, leaving a footway on the north side leading to Kingsham, 2m wide. It was leased in 1688 to Daniel Lucas and there follows a series of leases by the City of the waste ground on either side of the Lavant, and ultimately 2 messuages built over it by 1816. To the north there were 2 new-built tenements in 1766.[8]

The remainder of the site north west of the new road.

This is part of a 1-acre plot of the Dean and Chapter which stretched southwards along the east side of the Southgate road. History has repeated itself because the ancient road which led in to the meadow of the Prebend of Bracklesham from the 17th century (if not earlier) has become part of the new road.

The earliest documentary source is of 1402 which refers to 2 tenements which were demolished in 1534. The site was cultivated ground – a garden – up to 1649. In the late 17th century it was still basically a garden but a shop had now been built on the road frontage (31-32). This can be seen on the Gardner Map of 1769. During the 19th century the whole site was intensively developed and with the opening of Basin Road in 1821 the ancient road was no longer required and was partially built over. The 2 properties still standing at 31 and 32 show signs of timber framing. Building continued behind these properties primarily for commercial and industrial use – cordwaining, carpentry, brewing, upholstery, stables, carthouses, workshops.

The Old Southgate Methodist Chapel was built in 1877 and was damaged by bombs in the Second World War. The site was sold and became freehold in 1864.[9]

Under the new road were plots owned by St Mary's and the Dean and Chapter.

33 Cottage, recorded from 1402. *Woodman* inn, 1875.[10]

34-35 There were 3 cottages here in 1402, in 1530 there was a barn, and a smith's forge in 1596, by 1607 a house – demolished by 1660, a shop by 1745; and by 1827 it had become a complex with blacksmith's shop, stables, carthouses, and, shortly after, cottages again.[11]

39-42 Richmond Terrace: Although this was largely an area of garden and

Fig. 17-4 Old Southgate Police Station

orchards in the 17th century, there was a house and backside here in 1687, but by the time of the Gardner map, 1769, this was devoid of buildings. The present terrace was built by 1812 by James Farrenden, a timber and coal merchant.[12]

Law Courts Site of Southgate House, a house with stables, greenhouse and a large pleasure ground. Probably mid-19th century.[13]

Bus Station. This site contained in the 19th century a large house, Southgate Villa, and 3 houses, Southgate Terrace, all certainly there in 1812.

Immediately north of the railway was the Police Station, which was on a site owned by the Vicars' Choral and known as the Common Hall Garden and Our Lady's Garden. In 1649 it was an orchard and by 1843 it was still a nursery. There is a record of a house in 1579 and two houses, which were there in 1642, were demolished 'when the city was a garrison'.[14]
The old Gas Works site and the Canal basin[15]

The site has been curiously affected by the transport and industrial expansion of the last 200 years. Firstly the line of the old lane to Stockbridge was lost when the turnpike road was built in 1784; next the Canal Company cut through a road down the east side in 1823; then the railway came on the north in 1846; finally the gas works was built in 1868. Before all this happened the gas works site had been an orchard on land owned by the Vicars' Choral.

The Prebends of Bracklesham owned all the meadow land to the east. There were 2 cottages on the road frontage in 1769. At the north end of the site there was a greenhouse and pigsty in 1843.

At the extreme southern end of the site were coal yards and the canal basin in the 19th century and the *Richmond Arms Inn*, which is still extant. This was occupied by Clement Sayers who was also a coal merchant in 1851.

With the coming of the new turnpike a tollgate cottage was built on the road. The turnpike straightened the old cart road and left a watercourse and a bathing house, erected in about 1784, by the side of the road. The old road was called Watery Lane, probably with good reason.
BASIN ROAD
Canal. The cutting through of the road from Southgate to the canal basin after 1818 opened up the opportunity to build a row of small houses on the west side of the road. On the other hand it was necessary to demolish 12 houses facing south from the city wall.[16] Also, at the rear of what is now the Bus Station, a group of 10 small units called Smith's Buildings were erected on a timber yard site. The occupants in 1851 included labourers, mariners, chars, porters. All the houses from the railway northwards have now gone. The canal was opened in 1824.
A public house called the *New Inn*, subsequently the *Railway Tavern*, then the *Railway Arms*, was provided by 1841 and survives as Tavern House (see Chapter 4 for a note on the canal).
MARKET AVENUE

Up to the early 19th century the land directly outside the south and east walls was pasture, orchard and gardens owned by the Prebends of Bracklesham and Somerley and the City and leased by them to various tenants. The land was cut through by the Lavant running round from Eastgate.

In 1867 land was bought under the Chichester Cattle Market Act for a new road from Basin Road to Eastgate, turning what had been a lane, Snag Lane, into a full road and requiring a diversion of the Lavant.[17]

CHAPTER 18

WESTERN SUBURBS
Tanning and Orchards

Until 1773 there was a gate at the end of West Street where the wall met the street. A porter's lodge was on the south side, the *Castle* inn (now *The Chichester*) inside, and the *White Horse* inn just outside. When the turnpike from Cosham to Chichester was built in 1762 the toll house stood alongside the *White Horse* inn.

The older road to Fishbourne took almost the same route as the turnpike and the modern road. Scuttery Lane – now superseded by Orchard Street – ran from West gate to North gate through the fields.

There was a settlement – a suburb – in the 13th century and a few buildings are recorded in the Cathedral Chartulary.[1] The suburb suffered in the Civil War. In December 1642 the church was destroyed as was the *White Horse* inn and other buildings nearby. The area was occupied after a fierce struggle but the defenders burned 'with wild fire' certain houses and forced a retreat.[2] Destruction was considerable from the gate to the church. Some rebuilding commenced in the next 20 years. Two houses next to the West gate were given by 1670 in a will of Jane Hodgson[3] and are referred to in her husband's inventory of 1662.

Along what is now Orchard Street there was never much building until the 19th century: the area was in cultivation. To the south west of the city was the Dean's farm, with just a few farm buildings and all building here has been very recent.

In 1888 there was a plan which pre-dated the Avenue de Chartres by 90 years, to take a road through Mount Lane to the railway station.[4]
WESTGATE
South side
Toll house site[5] There were houses and other buildings immediately outside
the gate in the 13th century and a forge of Roger la Dal. One of the houses was sold to the Church of the Holy Trinity to provide a chaplain to celebrate the soul of Dean Thomas at the altar of St Augustine. This appears again in the Valor Ecclesiasticus in 1535; between 1772 and 1808 a blacksmith's shop, 2 stables and a coach house were erected on the land behind.

An ancient cartway led under the walls to the old Deanery.
Under the Avenue de Chartres. The Parliamentary Survey of 1649 refers to
'a piece of ground where lately was the house of the White Horse inn'.
It had been re-established before 1673 and it is described in detail in the inventory of John Scott in 1677 – it had a little parlour, kitchen, hall, Bull

Chamber, Sun Chamber, shuffleboard room, lodging chamber, Half Moon, garret loft, other little rooms and two more garrets, a cellar and a brewhouse.[6] The inn survived through to the late 19th century.

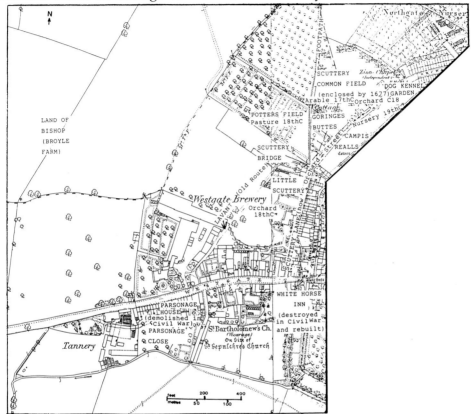

Fig. 18-1 West gate – based on O.S. Map 1878

To the south were 5 houses built in 1825 by the Guardians of the Poor. Theological College (7, formerly 3) The site was originally the waste of the Manor of Deanery and was enclosed. The Tolput family, who were clothiers, had a house here. A large house was occupied by Richard Diggens, 1780, then George Lyon, 1820, W. and E. Humphrey, 1827, and Nicholas Tyacke, 1863. It was bought for the College in 1919.[7]

13 18th-century house. Records from 1720. To Charles Collins of Kensington in 1720. Left to William Collins and sold to William Milton in 1746.[8]

15-17 (formerly 6-7) New built in 1730, succeeding a house, woodhouse and slaughterhouse. Malthouse added by 1775. 3 houses by 1792 (17 about 1787).[9]

19 (formerly 8) 18th century.

21 (formerly 9) New built house 1755, occupied by Ann, widow of John Greenfield, gent. Earlier property was 'Jolly Johns'.[10]

23-25 House recorded in 1379 and also in 1570. The pair of cottages are recorded in Land tax from 1780, but are shown on Gardner map of 1769.[11]
St Bartholomew's Church and churchyard[12] A will of 1495 leaves 4d. to the 'Round Church of St Bartholomew' (Sancta Bartholomew rotunde ...).

It was destroyed in the Civil War in 1642. The cemetery was first mentioned in 1379 and the church in 1227. A petition for an Act for a new church claimed that the population had grown. The new church was built on ground adjoining the old cemetery. At the time of building, 1832, there was a shortfall of £600. It was decided to raise £200 by selling pews, the largest subscribers having first choice; the remaining £400 was covered by a loan to be repaid by a rate.

The church was united with St Paul's in 1959 and was then used as a chapel by the Theological College.

Fig. 18-2 The round church from an old print

The original name for the church was 'St Sepulchre's'.

West of church (from 27 to end of the row). In 1227/41 the Dean gave to the perpetual Chaplaincy of the Altar of Our Lady 1 acre of land in Cherchescroft next to the Chapel of St Sepulchre on the east, which he bought of Eua de Keneldewerde for 20 shillings. In 1535 the Valor Ecclesiasticus recorded a mansion and 2 acres of ground of St Sepulchre's. There are continual references to the land of St Bartholomew's parsonage house and garden – the abuttals fit – from 1603. The east abuttal is the churchyard. In 1622 the Dean and Chapter leased the parsonage house and garden (abuttal as above); the Dean's leases give similar entries for 1670-1736. There is also one building on this frontage on the Gardner map of 1769.

In the Land tax, initially, there were 3 houses here owned by Richard Heath in 1780. In 1783 there were 5 houses, a timber yard and stables. In 1786 Charles Shippam had a storehouse and there were 8 houses; by 1803, 10; and by 1810, 12, occupied by labourers at the tannery. The plan of 1846 (Fig. 18-3) shows the large house of Shippam, the row of cottages, and the open Lavant watercourse. The easternmost house was demolished in 1888 to enable Church (Mount) Lane to be widened. The site layout had changed again by 1874 when the property of E.W. Johnson, deceased, was sold[13] (see Fig. 18-4).

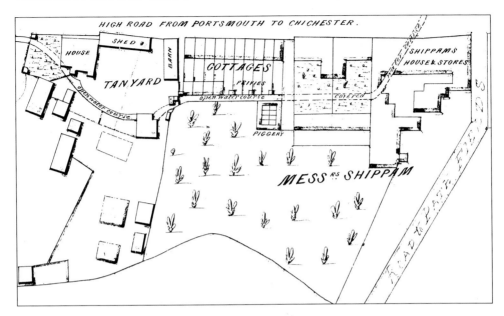

Fig. 18-3 Map of 1846

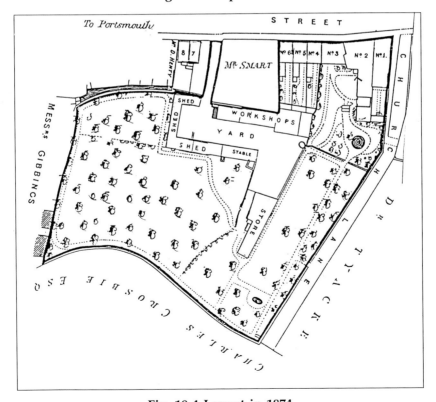

Fig. 18-4 Layout in 1874

Tannery.[14] The earliest reference to tanning in St Bartholomew's is:

1549   Will of John Parker refers to John Undershill, witness, tanner. This
         is followed by -
1570   Will of Thomas Undershill, St Barts. Executors to have the putting
         and letting of my 2 tenements with my tanner house ... until son
         Samuel is 21.

The Undershill family are recorded in the parish in 1526 when they share in a lease of 20 acres of land, with a house.

1596   Will of Simon Undershill, St Barts, tanner. To wife Johane for life
         'messuage and tenements wherein I now dwell and all singular
         gates, gateroom, backsides, gardens, orchards, vatts, chesernes,
         lyme pytts, cases ... and then to son Edward.'
1612   Will of John Payne of St Barts, tanner. To Simon Undershill, my
         landlord, 10s. in gold.
1624/5   Inventory of Henry Woolgar, St Barts, tanner. Hall, kitchen,
         buttery, chamber over hall and kitchen, tan house and vault; also
         a detailed list of various leathers, valued at £96 5s. 4d.
1639   Will of Thomas Bridger, St Barts, tanner.
1640   A will refers to Thomas Sandham, tanner.
1649   Will of Simon Undershill, St Barts, tanner. To elder son Edmond,
         after decease of wife, tan yard, vats, etc. This suggests that the
         tanyard was not destroyed in the Civil War (1642) or was quickly
         re-established.

Through the 18th-19th centuries the references are consistent:

1703   John Woolvin, a knacker, mortgaged his tan yard on south side
         of the highway.
1795   William Penny, tanner – brick and thatched dwelling house,
         millhouse, weather boarded, tiled and thatched.
1803   Richard Philpott, house and tanyard.
1831/5   William Norman, house and tanyard.

The present tanning house was built in 1910. It is now used for offices. The ground behind is honeycombed with 120 pits each roughly 2m cubes.

The site had an available water supply from the Lavant which ran through it. It is not known whether all the above listed tanners operated on this site, but it is known that the Undershill family were on the south side of the road out of Westgate in the 17th century and they would have to be near to the water supply, the nearest of which is shown in Fig. 18-3.

North side

2-10 Now demolished (roundabout). A forge in the 13th century. The Lavant
ran northwards through the middle of the site. Site mainly owned by the City who gave permission in 1698 for the section of the city wall next to the westgate to be taken down and allowed a door to be opened into the street. When they renewed permission for the door in 1708 the 'fine' was to be a bottle of wine for everyone present at the sealing of the lease. A subsequent house built in 1782.[15]

From **16** to **48**.[16] A row of mainly 18th-century houses which replaced the 17th-century houses destroyed in the Civil War.

Included in this stretch were four inns: *The Swan*, which replaced an earlier beerhouse in the 19th century; The Ship, recorded 1672; the *Three Tuns*, 1688, and the *Waggon and Lamb* at 34, previously *The Mitre*, 1780-1939. See Fig. 18-6 for *Waggon and Lamb*.

Brewery (Westgate House).[17] Employed 22 men and boys in 1851. The site in 1855 was described as a dwelling house, brewhouse, malthouse, malt kilns, warehouses, storehouses, granaries, stables, coach house, wood house, gardens, orchards and lands. It had been owned by John Dearling, then William Humphrey and, in 1855, by Henty.

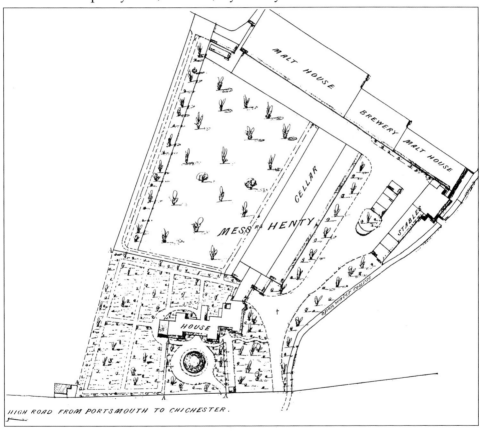

Fig. 18-5 Westgate Brewery site in 1846

ORCHARD STREET

There was a lane from Westgate to Northgate from the 12th century or earlier. Until the 19th century it was known as Scuttery Lane. In documents it appears as Squittery, Scuttereith, Scutterreridere. The origin of the name is uncertain. The OE sceat refers to a block of arable land in strips;[18] there was land in strips in the great common fields on the west and north-west side of the lane westwards until they came up against the great fields of the Bishop's Broyle Farm. (See Map Fig. 18-1.)

Records of ownership and occupation of land go back to the 13th century:

1254   19 Croft of Richard le Conyer, held of the Dean
1254[19]   Holding of Clement de Porcestre, which goes as far as the west gate and which was 9m wide at the gate.
1275[20]   1½ acres lying in field called Scutterreridere – grant by Roger, son and heir of Gilbert Ketelbern to William called le Despensyr.

Except for the area immediately outside the West gate virtually no houses are recorded on either side of what was later Orchard Street, until the late 18th century.

Fig. 18-6 *Waggon and Lamb*, **Westgate**

East/south east side

Car Park[21] (south end) This was an orchard in the 18th century and a row of cottages owned by the City in the 19th. There were also stables, a blacksmith's shop and a carthouse. The Lavant course ran between the street and the houses.

14-152 This land under the wall was known as 'Campis' or 'Realls' – it was a close with barns and a stable in the 18th century and part of Silverlock's nursery up to 1874. As early as 1741 the scholars of the Free Grammar School had access to it to 'sport themselves'. The northern end was known as 'Dog Kennel Garden'. There had been one house on the site before 1723. The present row of houses date from the 1880s.[22]

154-208 (154-168 have now been demolished) Known as Orchard Terrace in the 19th century, this row was built by 1840. It contained at various times the *Nursery Arms* public house (188). and the *Jolly Sawyer* (*Sawyers' Arms*; *Beehive*; *White Hart*) at 202.[23]

West and north west side

Southern part up to **19**. The River Lavant, which had run north along the other side of the lane crossed at Squitry Bridge and ran back southwards through this site, eventually crossing the Fishbourne Road. Before the Civil War Simon Maxse had a house and lands here. There were orchards which survived to the 19th century.[24] In 1769 there was a single building and in the 19th century a house and yard belonging to the Westgate brewery.

The area in the bend of the Lavant[25] was known as Little Scuttery field – an area of pasture belonging to the Dean and Chapter and described in 1402 and 1534. In 1806 it was meadow with fruit and willow trees. By 1840 there was a house and offices. (9)

The bridge was wooden. In 1535 there is a record of 12 feet of timber for its repair.[26]

To the north of 19 is a chapel building established about 1835 by the Bible Christians who abandoned it in 1865.[27]

School site and rear. To the west of the footpath which leads from Orchard Street to Parchment Street (where Hawthorn Close now is) was called Potter's Field.[28] It is known as such in the Tithe Apportionment of 1846. Prior to 1430 the site with a messuage and a chamber was held by John Potter and his father William before him.

The land where the school now is was part of the Scuttery common field for which the Dean and Chapter received rents and which had been enclosed by 1677. The school occupied the site in 1910.[29]

From here to St Paul's Road[30] was the North Gate nursery of Henry Silverlock in 1846. There were houses on the frontage about this time.

CHAPTER 19

OUTSIDE THE NORTH GATE
The Old Forest

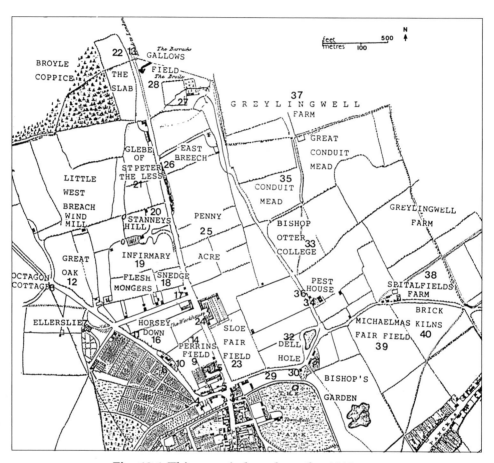

Fig. 19-1 This map is based on the 1812 map
The numbers relate to the text

This area has always been different from the areas outside the other three gates. Whilst they had suburbs in the 13th century, which were well established by the Civil War – and consequently suffered in the siege, the northern flank started life as a forest. Much of it was The Broyle in the 13th century – a word meaning a forest enclosure, which contained animals for hunting and was enclosed by a wall or a hedge.

190

The Broyles were granted by Henry III in 1229 to the Bishop of Chichester.[1] They could be disafforested and could be enclosed. In his will the Bishop gave his own lands at Greylingwell to the Church at Chichester and directed that the Broyles should go to the Church and his successors.

The land subsequently was divided into farming units and leased out. Excepting for the immediate area northwards from the wall for about 250m and between St Paul's Road and College Lane, all the land was the Bishop's. The excluded land belonged mainly to the Guild of St George (subsequently the City) and to St Mary's Hospital farm.

Fig. 19-1 is a map showing the very limited development up to 1812. Predictably the City land of Horsey Down became housing, firstly High Street, then Cross Street and George Street. By 1847 the development in Parchment Street, Cavendish Street, Washington Street and Orchard Street was largely completed and by 1851 the census revealed a conventional Victorian suburb with its own church (1836).[2]

The turnpike road to Midhurst (see Chapter 5) was started in 1749 but had no significant effect on development outside the gate.

The various areas, as now described, are identified on Map Fig. 19-1. The later development in the 19th century is shown on Fig. 19-2. The prefix numbers refer both to Fig. 19-1 and to the sources.

NORTHGATE (immediately outside North Walls)

3   Northgate House site. In 1785 building described as 1 messuage and
       garden together with the building thereunto adjoining commonly called
and used as a riding school.

4   Old Granary (Bartholomew's) Newly erected about 1784. Moses Small
       had it and developed the nurseries which eventually went to his grandson Henry Silverlock. Bartholomew took it over in 1918 as a corn merchant and hay and straw dealer.

CORNER OF NEW BROYLE AND NORTHGATE

5   (Metropolitan House) *White Horse Inn*. Originally *Queen's Head*, 1701;
       The Bear and then the *White Horse by* 1763. A large property on City
land with stabling for 35 horses in 1834, when it had 'a very excellent London porter trade'. There was 'a fair spreading elm tree in the garden'. The inn was destroyed by fire in the 1930s.

ST PAUL'S ROAD (Old Broyle Road)

South west side

6   This side of the road as far as Washington Street was the nursery of
       Silverlock in the 19th century; indeed the whole of this side of the road
was undeveloped in 1772 – when a map of the Bishop's farm was produced – as it had long been. The frontage land from Orchard Street to Washington Street was sold by the Silverlock estate in 1902 as building plots.

7   Ellerslie. Described as house and pleasure ground in the Tithe map.

8   Octagon Cottage. The building is on the Tithe map of 1846/7 and is
       described then as Octagon Cottage and garden. There is a building
shown on the plot, too, on the 1772 map of the Bishop's lands.

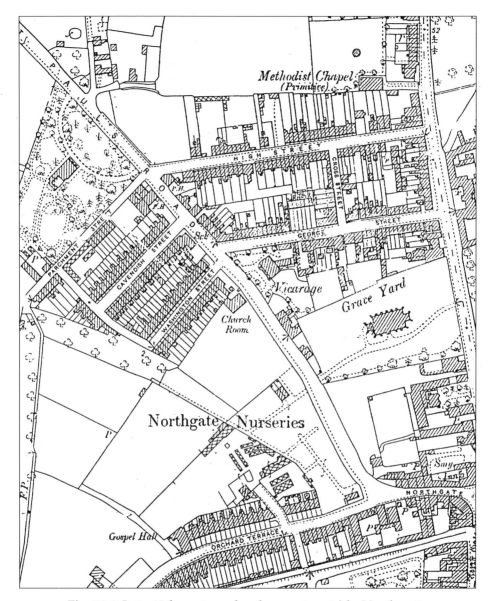

Fig. 19-2 Late 19th-century development outside North gate

North east side

9   Church of St Paul. Built 1836 to accommodate the increasing population of the suburb. The site was Perrins Field, owned by St Mary's.

10   38-42. Cottages erected about 1809.

11   *Rainbow Inn* (north corner of George Street). Built mid-19th century.

12   Great Oak. Two fields of about 8 acres, owned by St Mary's with a road leading through it to a windmill, erected by 1802, and a mill house.

BROYLE ROAD

Fig. l9-3 Octagon Cottage, St Paul's Road before re-roofing

West side

13 The road from Northgate to the New Broyle was in very bad condition in the 18th century. Spershott comments that it was 'deep, dirty, narrow and crooked', and 'footpeople went over stiles into the fields' (see also Chapter 4). A road is recorded in 1249.

14 Perrins Field: the land on which the church is built and southwards almost to Northgate. Owned by St Mary's from 1249 when 5 acres were granted to Adam of Wanstead and Yilaria his wife. Timber yards in 1757. Cottages, stable and coach house, 1785.

15 North Lodge. Built early in the 19th century on Perrins Field.

16 Horsey Down. Piece of land opposite old workhouse. It ran through to St Paul's Road. City land, about 12 acres, which came to the City when the lands of the Brotherhood of St George were dispersed in 1549. Sold by the City 1810 onwards and George and High Streets built thereon.

17 *Star Inn* (15-16). Built 1817. Now demolished.

18 Snedge Field 1½ acres (City land) to the north of High Street.

19 Royal West Sussex Hospital (Infirmary). Began as Dispensary for Sick Poor in 1784. Present building started in 1825. Hospital functions now transferred to St Richard's.

Fig. 19-4 North Lodge

20   Stanney's Hill. Land to north of the Infirmary. 7$^{1}/_{2}$ acres in two fields, the glebe land of All Saints' church. Had a cottage on it by 1827.
21   Glebe of St Peter the Less. Next to the north.
22   *Green Dragon*, opposite to the barracks. With 3 tenements. Pre 1854.

Fig. 19-5 Infirmary

East side
23   Car Park (Sloe Fair Field). Land owned by St Mary's having been granted thereto in 1249 by Adam de Wanstead and his wife. The right to grant a fair between 5th and 13th October annually was first made to the Bishop by Henry I (1107-8). The name is supposed to be derived from a sloe tree on the site.
24   Workhouse. Cawley's Almshouses (Hospital of St Bartholomew). Built 1625 by William Cawley, the regicide, 'for the maintenance of 12 decayed tradesmen of Chichester'. After the Restoration Cawley's goods were seized and the City took possession. It was converted into a workhouse in 1681. In 1753 it became a poor house for 8 united parishes. In the 1851 census 124 paupers were registered.
25   Penny Acre 'Land on which a penny was paid' (OE). City acquired it in 1549 from the disposal of St George's property. Consisted of about 10 acres.
26   East Breach (OE: *Brec* – land newly broken) and Mill Post (or Mill Pool). Land owned by St Mary's. A windmill formerly stood on it and is referred to in 1790, with a house. 'Breach' first mentioned 1180-97.
27   The Broyle. House, gateroom, garden and croft immediately south of the barracks. Shown on map of 1772. At this point, in 1772, the turnpike road became a path across the Broyle.
28   The Broyle Gallows. This is where 6 smugglers were hanged in 1749. Gallows Heath is mentioned in 1597.

Fig. 19-6 Almshouses

North East area

29   Franklyn Place. A row of early 19th-century houses. *The Sun* public house with a blacksmith's shop adjoining was then at 1 and is recorded through the century.

30   *Dell Hole* beer house. At the other end of the row. In 1840 it was a malthouse with a gateway.

31   *The Hope* public house. Built on lands of the Baptists.

32   Dell Hole (OE: *Dell* – Valley or Chalk Pit). A natural depression on the south west corner of College Lane (near the roundabout).

COLLEGE LANE

33   Bishop Otter College. Built 1849/50. Architect J. Butler. Built following public subscription.

34   Pest House used until 1920. Date 1665 on front. Was used to isolate smallpox and similar cases. Replaced by Isolation Hospital.

35   Conduit Mead. There was a tank here and water came by conduit to the city. A stone and thatched cottage in 1842. Conduit field is named, as such, in 1330/1. In 1784 described as '2 closes of meadow through which the conduit pipe of the City runs.'

36   Thatched cottage, 18th century.

37   Greylingwell Named in 1244 when Bishop Nevill granted his lands in Greylingwell to the Cathedral. In 1721 house is described as 'a pretty farmhouse with barns and stables in good repair … the ground seems to be in good heart.' However a survey in 1829 found the interior of the dwelling house in a dilapidated state. The lands were purchased in 1897 from the Ecclesiastical Commissioners for £18,900 and the Hospital built on the site. Willis says that 11 million bricks were used.

38   Spitalfields (OE *Spitel* – lands with a Hospital). The Hospital of St James and Mary Magdalene. The site owned by the Dean and Chapter. House erected on the land about 1670.

39   Michaelmas Fair Field. 13 acres on Spittlefield Farm.

40   Brick Kiln Field. 6 acres on Spittlefield Farm. Went out of use in the 18th century.

Fig. 19-7 Cottage, College Lane

SOURCES, REFERENCES AND ADDITIONAL INFORMATION

Most of the material used in preparing this book is in the West Sussex Record Office at Chichester. The references given are those used there, but for reasons of space it has not always been possible, or even necessary, to give the full reference, e.g. Dean and Chapter Accounts 1533/8, which are frequently referred to, is CapI/23/1, but folio numbers have not been quoted. Students who wish to go to the original documents will need to visit the Record Office. There they will eventually find the card index and working papers which have been used in preparing the book and this will provide any link needed from what follows, where references are not in full.

Abbreviations:

WSRO – West Sussex Record Office – and the following sources there:

Cap	Dean and Chapter.
Ep	Episcopal.
STD, STC, STA	Wills.
INV	Inventory (Ep I/29).
Par	Parish records.
C	Chichester City minutes, followed by volume number
CC	Other Chichester City records, with specific reference following. References to CC/AY series can also be seen in SAC 89.
QDD, QDP, QSN, QS	Quarter Sessions records.
LT	Land Tax (in Quarter Sessions records).
Add. Ms(s)	Additional Manuscript(s).
SAS	followed by a reference. These are deeds transferred from the Sussex Archaeological Society in course of being catalogued with the Add Mss series at WSRO.
R	Raper Collection – a vast collection deposited by a local solicitor. This is in the process of final cataloguing. Where permanent numbers have been allocated they are given.
Harris	Harris Mss.
E	Goodwood Archives.
MP	Miscellaneous Papers.
SP	Sale Particulars.
HT	Hearth Tax.
TD	Trade Directory.
PH/PD	Photographs and drawings.
PRO	Public Record Office, Chancery Lane, with specific reference following
'City Deeds'	Documents still held by the Chichester District and City Councils.
OS	Ordnance Survey.
VCH	Victoria County History (Sussex).
SAC	Sussex Archaeological Collection, followed by volume No.
SRS	Sussex Record Society " " " "
CP	Chichester Papers series " " " "
Chichester Excavations	Series of voluminous reports by Alec Down, FSA and published by Phillimore.

Sources listed under chapters are given in the following order: firstly original documents in the West Sussex Record Office; secondly, documents in the Public Record Office; and finally, printed sources.

CHAPTER 1

1   Dawson, Charles *A History of British Earthquakes* (C.U.P. 1924); *SAC* 29 pp. 211-8.
2   Lib 5365. Report on a well at Fishbourne (part of a report to the Local Government Board on enteric fever in 1899 by Thomson and Marsh, HMSO).
3   I am indebted to Mr. T.R. Holland MA, for this information in *Heritage of Chichester*, on a report of a boring in South Street in 1844 at the site of Gatehouse's brewery (Nos. 30-33).
4   *SRS* 36.
5   See Chapter 14.
6   QDD/6/W15. 17 owner groupings owned 188 acres before enclosure in 93 strips. The owners were:

	Plots
Rev. Billingley (Lord of the Manor of Shopwick)	10
Bett Boniface	1
James Cosens	6
The City and Cosens	8
The City and Teesdale	6
The City and J.L. Williams	2
The City and Ewens trustees	2
J.B. Freeland and Ewens Trustees	3
John Osborne	1
Railway Company	1
Duke of Richmond	16
W.C. Rhoades	1
General Webber Smith	24
St James Hospital	4
St Mary's and Ewens Trustees	5
St Pancras glebe	1
J.L. Williams	2

7   Add. Ms. 1239; *VCH* Vol. 3 p. 71.
8   MP 940; Add Ms 1931.
9   Add Ms 11257; OC/CC8/273; CC J4.

CHAPTER 2

1   1086 – Domesday. I have used the calculations suggested in Darby, H.C. and Canpell E. (eds.) *The Domesday Geography of South East England* (CUP 1971) which was first expounded in Ballard, A. *The Domesday Boroughs* (Oxford 1904) pp. 13 and 56. This takes the number of hagae ($97\frac{1}{2}$) and crofts (3) previously in the city, adds the increase in houses to 1086 (60) and the number of hagae in the city of nearby manors (135), and the burgesses (9), producing a grand total of $304\frac{1}{2}$. A multiplier of 5 persons per household gives a tentative population of 1500 (say 1200-1500).
2   1377. An estimate of 1300 in *SAC* 114, p. 15.
3   1524. Estimate 1600 plus (*SAC* 114 p. 15) Based on 330 assessments (householders) and includes those outside the gates. With a multiplier of 5 (suggested by W.G. Hoskins for Lay Subsidy Rolls) this gives 1600 plus.
4   1610. Speed's map reveals a house count of about 370. A multiplier of 5 would give a population of 1800.
5   1625. Fletcher, Anthony *A County Community in Peace and War* (Longman 1975) estimate 2300.

6   1641-2. Protestation Return. A census of all male inhabitants over 18 years. An oath required them to defend the Protestant religion, the King and Parliament. Those who refused are also listed. Using a multiplier of 3.25 suggested in Bradley, Leslie *A Glossary for Local Government Population Studies* (Local Population Studies, 1978) this produces a population of 2400. Approximately 710 persons took the oath and 25 refused – *SRS* 5 pp. 45 – 57.

7   1670. Hearth Tax lists all taxed and untaxed houses in Chichester and includes Westgate and St Pancras (PRO: E179/191/410). A multiplier of 4 or 5 is suggested by Bradley and Hoskins. 602 x 4 = 2408.

8   1676. Based on the Compton Census – the number of communicants, non-conformists and recusants – a total of 1233. Chalklin, C.W. in *Provincial Towns of Georgian England* (Edward Arnold, 1974) p. 18, calculates 2400 therefrom.

9   1740 and 1762. The Duke of Richmond commissioned a census which produced a total of 783 houses and a population of 3711 giving a useful multiplier of 4.7 for 1740 and a population of 3636 for 1762.

10   The 1755 Poor rate covered every house in the city, with suburbs, and listed the poor. With 900 houses (EPI/16/2) this suggests a slightly higher population than 9 above.

11   1801 Census: 4752; 1831: 8270.

12   *SAC* 24 pp. 70-75.

13   *SAC* 114 p. 16.

14   Darby, H.C. *New Historic Geography of England* (CUP 1973) p. 134. Table is the ranking of provincial towns. Also Hoskins, W.G. *Local History in England* (Longmans 1974) p. 239 which places Chichester at No. 36 in 1523/7.

15   PRO: E179/258/11.

16   Burnett, John *History of the Cost of Living* (Pelican 1969) pp. 61 and 71.

17   West, J. *Village Records* (Phillimore 1982). The purpose of Hearth tax was to raise £1.2 million a year for the monarch.

18   Latham, Robert (ed.) *Shorter Pepys* (Bell and Hyman 1985) p. 210.

19   PRO: E179/191/410.

20   From the listing for St Pancras in PRO E179/191/410 must be deducted 3 properties which are in East Street within the gate but nevertheless in St Pancras parish. It is more meaningful for these properties to be listed in East Street.

21   50% of the Hearth tax return for Westgate (at PRO) is illegible. Total hearths and number of assessments however can be extracted and used.

22   Thesis: Cowley, G.O. *Sussex Market Towns 1500-1750* (1964).

23   EpI/16/2.

24   MP 998.

25   Lib 6564. *Report of Commissioners to enquire concerning Charities and Education of the Poor 1815-1836* (Vol. XXIV Sussex); Oving Tithe Map 1848.

26   Par 162/9/1-4.

27   CapI/26/5.

28   *SRS* 54 p. 174 (Quarter Sessions Order Book); St Pancras parish registers.

29   CapI/24/3 and 10; CapI/28/270 and 272; *SRS* 52 No. 337; *SRS* 46 No. 186. The Bin Room was on the ground floor at the west end of the former gateway to the Vicars' Close; CP 14.

30   Study based on the 1851 Census. The 5 classes listed in *Census 1951 – occupation table* (HMSO 1956) are: I Professional, etc. II Intermediate III Skilled IV Partly Skilled V Unskilled.

CHAPTER 3

1   The Parish Registers are at WSRO.

2   QSN/14A.

3   CC K2.

4   CC K3.
5   CC K6.
6   CC K7.
7   CC K7.
8   Warren, J.L. *Chichester Past and Present* (1901 Pub. J.W. Moore, East Street, Chichester).
9   Aldridge, N.J. *Mortality Patterns of Infectious Diseases in Chichester 1720-1812* (MP 1674).
10   Spershott's Memoirs, see CP 30, pp. 10-12.
11   CC El (12.11.1794).
12   CC El (28.2.1803).
13   CC E2 (19.3.1819).
14   CC E4 (11.10.1859).
15   C9 (30.6.1859).
16   C10 (4.11.1865).
17   Longmate, Norman *King Cholera* (H. Hamilton, 1966).
18   Leaflet issued 7.11.1834 and reproduced by kind permission of Avon County Library.
19   *Report on the Sanitary Condition of the Labouring Population of Great Britain*, presented to Parliament, July 1842.
20   *Public Health in Mid-Victorian Bristol* (Historical Association, 1974).
21   *Norwich – the Growth of a City* (Norwich Museum).
22   C8 (March 1852).
23   C8 (November 1855).
24   Report to Sanitary Committee 24.1.1866 by John Lawson (C10).
25   C10 (4.9.1866).
26   C10 (13.4.1866).
27   C10 (8.12.1866).
28   Report by Arnold Taylor 1867 (C10).
29   Registrar General's Annual Reports. This then dropped steadily to 11.8 in 1946-50.
30   *West Sussex Gazette* 24.1.1889.
31   MP 1208-9.
32   Mr. Prior, quoting the Registrar General; C16.
33   R : *Report to Local Government Board on Enteric Fever in Chichester* (HMS0 1899).
34   R 351 : Report of M.O.H. 1896.
35   *VCH* Vol. 3 p. 82
36   Willis *Records of Chichester* p. 269
37   Willis ibid p. 271.
38   The calculation is intended to be illustrative, not scientific. Assuming 1000 years of urban life, an average population of 2000, and an average expectation of life of 35 years, this produces about 60,000 bodies. To this can be added Roman and Dark Age residents. The higher population of later years is only partly matched by a longer expectation of life.
39   Par 42/4/15.
40   Cawley Almshouses – burials seen as 'a mass of bones' – PH 132/3.
41   Chichester Excavation Committee Report 1966 – the bodies were both friars and lay people.

CHAPTER 4

1   Hill, Christopher *A Century of Revolution 1603-1714* (Edinburgh, Nelson 1980).
2   2 & 3 Philip and Mary Ch 8.
3   MP 970.
4   Albert, William *The Turnpike Road System in England* (CUP 1972).
5   MP 867.
6   Yeakell & Gardner map 1778.
7   10 Geo. III 1770.

8   *SAC* 92 p. 93.
9   PR0 Port Books, Class E190.
10   27 Eliz. Ch 22, 1585. The route would have probably used the Lavant and come in through the West Gate.
11   10 Geo. III, 1770.
12   55 & 56 Vict. Ch 138, 1892.
13   *VCH* Vol. 3, p. 104 quoting L. and P. Hen. VIII, vii No. 1677.
14   *VCH* Vol. 3, p. 86 quoting Landsd. Mss (BM) 81 No. 44.
15   *SAC* 90 Street Administration p. 27; reinforced by Act of Parliament 1575.
16   C1.
17   CC E1-4.
18   QDP. W 95 and W 248: Chichester to Bognor; QDP W 96: Guildford to Chichester and Itchenor; QDD W191: Selsey; QDP W 139: Chichester – Midhurst.
19   QDP W248; QDD W191; Griffiths, Edward *The Selsey Tramways.*
20   Chichester Posts in CP 47 by G.A. Viner.

CHAPTER 5

1   *VCH* Vol. 3, p. 83.
2   *VCH* Vol. 3, p. 97; *SAC* 10 pp. 70-71.
3   *SAC* 78, pp. 195-210.
4   *SAC* 5, pp. 267-276; *SAC* 84, p. 28; CapI/30/1 and Valor Eccl. *SAC* 92.
5   Darby, H.C. ibid.
6   *VCH* Vol. 2, pp. 255-7.
7   Bowden, Peter J. *The Wool Trade in Tudor and Stuart England* (Cass 1971).
8   Wilson, Charles *England's Apprenticeship 1603-1763* (Longman 1984).
9   CC AH 1-20; *SAC* 87 (reference in will of William Nycholatt 1495 to the Guild of Tanners).
10   Corran H.S. *History of Brewing* (David and Charles 1975).
11   *SAC* 44, p. 173.
12   PR0 Class E 190.
13   Will of William Stamper, STDII Box 4.
14   Price in inventory of Richard Rables 1676 (No. 128).
15   Gregory King's estimate and analysis of the national population for 1688 suggests that about 50% of the population were labourers, cottagers, paupers and vagrants. If this can be applied to Chichester's population of 2,400 this leaves some 1,200 people, with 300 heads of families, who were productively employed. Allowing a working life of 20 years some 1,500 recorded productive heads of household might be expected over 100 years. In addition there will be overlaps at either end of the century and working sons.
16   STCI/35; CP 31; Marriage Licences *SRS* 28; R; The inventory of Isaac Hammond includes also: 12,500 quilting needles, 31,000 small and large happles, 24,000 large and 12,000 small square and 17,000 glovers' needles. Rooms mentioned: kitchen, pantry, brewhouse, parlour, 2 chambers over. Total value £92. 11s. 7^{1}/$_{2}$ d. The house and garden were mortgaged with £205 outstanding.
17   CC AH2; 13th c. *SAC* 51 p. 45; 1327: *SRS* 10.
18   Henry Woolgar: inventory; Simon Undershill: STDI/3; John Payne: STDI/3; Thomas Bridger: STDI/3; others – marriage licence sureties: *SRS* 5, 9 and 12.
19   STAI/7; CC K3.
20   Harris Mss.
21   *SRS* 9 and 11; STDIII/1 f. 61 (Ellis Lewes).
22   EpIV/4/2 (1622); Elphick G. *Sussex Bells and Belfries* (Phillimore 1970); Down A. *Chichester Excavations Vol. 3* (Phillimore 1978) pp. 164-9.
23   CC K6 (Robinson); HT; STDII Box 5; PRO Class E190; *SRS* 5.

24 Thomas 1626/7 STDI/3 p. 199; John 1637 STDI/3 p. 240; Stephen 1639 PROWill 85 Harvey; Edward 1647 STCI/21; Symon 1650 INV 103; Mary 1666 STDII Box 4; George HT; Richard 1693 STDII Exor.; Guild membership 1663: CC AH14, 1686 CC AH18.
25 CC K1-7, N16.

CHAPTER 6

1 Defoe *A Tour through the whole Island of England and Wales* (Penguin English Library 1971) p. 150.
2 Pigot's *directory* lists: Broyle Mill (Charles Adames), St Pancras (Charles Ewens), Dell Quay (Stephen Farndell), Fishbourne (William Goodeve and James and Thomas Hayllor). Budgen's map and the O.S. show salt mills at Appledram. The *Sussex County Magazine* Vol. 11, 1936, pp. 738-803, lists 18th- and 19th-century mills. Dell Quay: Add Ms. 21516; 1851 Census; CapIV (St Mary's terrier 1633), horse mill: Add Ms. 23239.
3 PRO Class E 190; Andrews J.H. *The Port of Chichester and the Grain Trade 1650-1750* (*SAC* 92, 1954).
4 EpI/16/2; James Spershott's Memoirs (CP 30); *VCH* Vol. 2, p. 262.
5 PRO Class E190; Farrant J.H. *The Seaborne Trade of Sussex* (*SAC* 114).
6 Martin, Benjamin in *Natural History of England* (1759) quoted by McCann, T.J. *Restricted Grandeur* (WSCC 1974).
7 R: Preamble to Act of 1807 (47 Geo III).
8 Stockbridge House: Add Ms 7714; EpI/16/2.
9 MP 1371; Down, A. ibid. p. 108.
10 CapI/4/7/30; EpI/16/2 (Spitalfields); QDP W96 (Fishbourne); E. 484 (Westhampnett); Tithe map Westhampnett, 1838.
11 E. 5478-82; for East Pallant see Down, A. *Chichester Excavations Vol. 6* (Phillimore 1988)
12 John Philpot, 1729, comments that 'the buildings of Chichester are mostly brick and covered with tiles'. Spershott (ibid) recalls that in 1720 there were few houses in the main streets which had solid brick fronts except such as had been built within a few years back.
13 Pipemakers. Daniel Gardner: abuttal (R) West Street in 1693 and *SRS* 12; Robert Gardner and William Artwell: *SRS* 12; Mark Briant: 1841 Census; James Harrington: 1862 and 1866 TD's; John Jones: *SRS* 12, surety; Andrew Leggatt: 1861 Census; Stephen Leigh: 1851 Census & TD 1862; Samuel Lucas: *SRS* 12; William Peck: 1871 Census; Pitt family: LT, Add. Ms. 18370, Par42/6/5; Henry Ryle: *SRS* 9 p. 125 (1697); John Russell: EpI/88/35 (1686); Taplin family: Add. Mss. 6146-7 and *SRS* 12. Pipe Clay imports 1661/2 and 1674/5 in PRO Class E190. For information on Samuel Lucas I am indebted to Eric Millington. The only mention of Tapner is in an abuttal to a lease of St Mary's Hospital.
14 Add. Ms. 2606 (1810); Pigot TD (1839).
15 Poll Book 1782; Add. Ms. 13390.
16 MP 1966.
17 CP 47.
18 MP 714; Add. Mss. 2794, 12747 and 23962; R 253/4; TD.

CHAPTER 7

1 CapI/23/1.
2 Taylor, Alec Clifton *The Pattern of English Building* (Faber paper back) p. 392. I am obliged to L.F. Salzman for the basis of Fig. 7-2.
3 Harris, Richard *Discovering Timber Framed Buildings* (Shire Publications) p. 56.
4 Willis, ibid. p. 219, quoting a Pipe Roll.
5 Salzman, L.F. *Building in England down to 1550* (Oxford) p. 175 He quotes *Hist. MSS. Com. Rep., Var. Coll.*, i. 193 'They shall preserve the ancient glass windows (*vitreolas*),

and what has to be washed and cleaned they shall wash and clean, and what has to be repaired they shall repair, at the cost of the church, and what has to be added (*augmentanda*) they shall add, likewise at the cost of the church; and there shall be allowed them for each foot of addition one penny. And as often as they repair the glass windows, in whole or in part, they shall be bound, if so ordered by the keeper of the works, to make one roundel (*roellam*) with an image in each. And if they make a new glass window entirely at their own cost, which is without pictorial decoration (*pictura*) and is 53 ft. in total area (*magnitudinis circumquaque*) they shall receive for it and for their expenses, 12s.'

6   CapI/23/1. See also Chapter 12.

7   Probably South Hams in Devon. Salzman, ibid. p. 233 quotes a record of 1518 of 'blew' stone being used at Warblington, Hampshire – about 8 miles to the west (PR0 E490, 12) and says they were blue schist slates from Cornwall or Devon.

8   CapI/23/1; Parrish, Rev. W.D. *Dictionary of Sussex Dialect* (Farncome and Co. 1875).

9   Braun, Hugh *Old English Houses* (Faber & Faber 1962) p. 69.

10   PR0 Class E190.

11   Hicks: *SRS* 52 No. 352; Lane: CapI/23/1; Crossingham: STDI/3; Kewell: CC K3; Fuggator: CC K5; Austeds: abut. CapI/27/2 p. 358; Allen: STDI/3; Piper: INV. 82; Cooper: Prot. Return; Tracey: STCI/21; Linfield: STCI/21; Chase(l): STDII Box 5; Chase(2) EpI/88/35; Bullock: STDII Box 4; Browne: STDII Box 4; Crossingham: CapI/27/4; John Royle: CapIV/5/1; Grigg: R; Bailey and Allen: Marr. Lic; Henry Royle: E 1269/70; Randall: E 1857/9; Blunden: E 1317; Aylwin: *SRS* 9; Wittman: *SRS* 12; Joy: CapIV/6/39; Souter: EpI/88/35, 1679.

12   CapI/30/1-2.

13   C1 21/11/1687.

14   McCann, T.J. ibid.

15   C1 1705.

16   CapIV/2/4.

17   CP 30.

18   EpI/16/2.

19   C1; C3; CC K5; *VCH* Vol. 3 p. 72.

CHAPTER 8

1   Domesday Survey 1086: *VCH* Vol. 3 p. 83.

2   C3 18/10/1808; *SRS* 62 Nos. 229 and 241.

3   *Dolphin and Anchor*: Par 44/6/3; HT; CP 23; Will of Richard Bragg STDII Box 4; Will of Henry Chitty: PR0, 61 Rivers; Evidence for the George: *SAC* 87, *SAC* 89 (AY 114); CapI/23/1 p. 112a – this refers to a tenement called *The George* on the north side of West Street, giving as an abuttal a tenement of John Cressweller. The name 'George' derives from the Guild which had land here. See also CapI/26/1-D. and C. Rental of 1521 which refers to an inn in East Lane, i.e. Chapel Street, called *The George*.

4   Deeds in possession of Post Office.

5   12: Par 44/6/2-3; HT. 13-14: CapI/23/1, CapI/27, Sub 3-153; HT. 15: HT, *VCH* Vol. 3 p. 74, 1851 Census, INV 9, STDI/3 p. 99b, E 4437/51.

6   Add. Ms. 12570.

7   CapI/23/1.

8   CapI/23/1; CapI/29/27.

9   R; Add. Mss. 9016-7; STCI/2 p. 52.

10   C1; CapI/29/27; *SAC* 51 No. 48.

11   MP 1823; City deeds; Add. Ms. 6151; CC AL46.

12   Add. Mss. 6457-9; CapI/23/1; HT. The drawing is based on various photographs and other illustrations of the period; CP 52.

13   CapI/23/1; STDII Box 4; HT; Census; R.
14   CapI/23/1; Add. Mss. 8292 and 23965-6; STDI/6 p. 247.
15   CapI/37/1; CapI/23/1; CapI/30/1.
16   CapI/23/1; CapI/27; Par 44/6/2; INV 11 (George Lewknor) 30/5/1618, which
      mentions 22 stools, 11 cushions, 12 carpets, aras carpet, books, chessboard and
      tapestry hangings.
17   INV 64 (Thomas Norton) 1624; CapI/30/2; HT; CapI/27/6; *SRS* 46 Nos. 478-9.
18   CapI/23/1; CC AK2 p. 93.
19   *SAS* B497/8; Add. Mss. 12510 and 15138.
20   EpI/16/3; Add. Mss. 23110-1.
21   Chantry Cert. No. 49; Add. Mss. 2585 and 23110-1.
22   CapI/23/1; CapI/27/2; CapI/30/2; HT; Add. Mss. 18508-50.
23   CapI/23/1; Ollerenshaw, *History of the Prebendal School* (Phillimore) 1984; *VCH*
      Vol. 3 p. 74; *SAC* 54.
24   CapI/23/1; CapI/26/1; Par 44/2/2; Valor Eccles. *SAC* 92.
25   CapI/23/1; CapI/27; CapI/30/2; HT.
26   CP 48.
27   C2, 22/8/1770; *SRS* 46 No. 132; *SRS* 62 No. 364; CP 14.
28   INV 115; PRO Will 128 Fines.

CHAPTER 9

1   CapI/23/1; *SRS* 46 Nos 148, 335, 409, 437; *SAC* 51 No. 3.
2   *SRS* 46 Nos 148 and 437.
3   CapI/37/1 f. 3r.
4   CapI/23/1 f. 49v.
5   CC AY 106/7. Bishop Storey purchased the ground from the City for £10 and required
      the building to provide shelter and the ground to be free from tolls; CP 1.
6   CP 30.
7   Work done about the Town Hall CC AF1, K2, 1574.
8   CapI/23/1; CapI/27; CapI/37/1; *SRS* 46 Nos. 409 and 437.
9   *SRS* 62 Nos 229 and 241.
10   EpI/16/2; 1851 Census; R (1716 and 1874); TD 1804.
11   R.
12   Val. Eccles, *SAC* 92.
13   CC AY99 (1493); CapI/23/1; *SRS* 36.
14   CP 46; Censuses.
15   HT.
16   TD 1804.
17   Add. Ms. 12530.
18   Add. Mss. 25188-211; STDII Box 4; STDI/7 p. 248.
19   HT; Par45/8/1; R; TD; PR0 Will 171 Watts.
20   R; CC AY5, 8, 55; CapI/37/1 f 4v and 53; STDI/7.
21   CC E3, 1829 ; CP 46.
22   R.
23   Add. Ms. 6373.
24   Add. Mss. 6146 and 23971; CapI/23/1.
25   CapI/30; CapI/28/210; EpVI/1/3 f84; A. Down, ibid Vol. 3 (note by A. McCann);
      SRS 59 No. 373.
26   EpVI/1/3 f84; CapI/28/210; CapI/17; Par 45/8/1.
27   Par 45/8/1.
28   STDI/3 p. 199 (Butterly); STCI/21 p. 136b (Ann Mellersh, innkeeper, Star); HT; 1851
      Census; Par 45/8/1; R; INV 140 (Simon Dixon); CC K7, N 18; CP 46.
29   Add. Mss. 37574 and 37935.

30   SAS B492; R; Friary Meux deeds.
31   LT; R; St Peter the Less Burial Register 1755-1779.
32   CapI/23/1; CapI/26/1.
33   LT; Add. Mss. 21516 and 37574.
34   Deeds in possession of Mr. Miller.
35   R; STDI/7.
36   Add. Ms. 12527; R; HT.
37   STDI/3 p. 41b; CC AJ5a(2); Add. Ms. 11155. Marjory Wilkinson was imprisoned in
     1683 as a result of her beliefs (QS W17 and Eric Millington); Inventory of Robert Miller
     PRO PROB11/330; *SAC* 52.
38   *VCH* Vol. 3 p. 163.
39   CC AY13 and 116; CapI/17 (abuttal); Add. Mss. 34785-6; *VCH* Vol. 3 p. 93.
40   CC AJ1; R; STDI/3; STDII Box 5; CapI/17; CP 46.
41   CapI/23/1; HT.
42   CC AJ1; CapI/27; STDII Box 5; R.
43   STDI/3 p. 230; HT; C1; *VCH* Vol. 3 p. 78.
44   Add. Mss.24205-22; HT; CapI/23/1 p. 112b; 1851 Census; INV 164 (Hammond);
     PRO 91 (Will of Thomas Ghost).
45   HT; C1, 1723; STDII Box 4 (Howard).
46   R; Phoenix Fire Insurance; CP 46.
47   CC AK1 p. 8.
48   *SAC* 5; *VCH* Vol. 3 p. 162.
49   PRO 62 Nevill: Will of Buckingham; CC AM4(1) and (2), K2; CP 27.
50   City deeds; 1851 Census; CP 46.
51   HT; PRO 81: Will of Young; *SRS* 36, Chantry Cert No. 49.
52   CapIV (site 32); PRO PROB4/18657; *SAC* 51 No. 4.

CHAPTER 10

1   *SRS* 46 (e.g. No. 408); *SAC* 51, St Mary's Chartulary.
2   *VCH* Vol. 3 p. 97; McCann, T.J. ibid.
3   Spershott, ibid.
4   PRO E179/191/410.
5   Spershott, ibid.
6   STDI/6 p. 154; *SRS* 52 No. 350, abuttal.
7   CapI/23/1; STDI/3 p. 167b; STDII Box 5; MP 414; CC K3, AP 1-13; Add. Ms. 10592;
     LT; R60; CC AJ2, Thomas Bird; Phoenix Fire Insurance; *SRS* 36; *SAC* 24; *SRS* 52
     Nos. 192 and 350; Willis, ibid pp. 67 and 109; Portsmouth Borough Sessions Papers
     S3/12/Y, 23/10/1684.
8   Add. Ms. 10862; MP 414; TD; R 601 and 617/9.
9   Add. Mss. 23942-64.
10   SAS E215/223; STCI/21b; STDII Box 5.
11   CapI/23/1; CapI/27/1-2; CapI/30/1; HT; Add. Mss. 5996-6002; EpI/16/3; LT; TD;
     R 606; 1851 Census; Willis ibid. pp. 109 and 296.
12   Par 37/7/2-7; *VCH* Vol. 3 p. 161.
13   *SAC* 51 p. 47; McCann, A. *The History of the Church and Parish of St Andrew Oxmarket*,
     (WSRO).
14   Willis, ibid, p. 109; CP 46.
15   Add. Ms. 23337; C2, 23/9/1763.
16   HT; C1, 14/9/1714; STDI/7 p, 83; STDI/3 p. 220; R; CC K5; *SAC* 24.
17   R 612/3.
18   CapI/29/27 (Plan); CapI/27/20; CapI/30/2; *SRS* 46 Nos. 456, 490, 554-7. The last two
     entries refer to Peter Cook's house in East Street with no identification to side or site.
     However in CapI/23/1f54r an entry for a tenement of Juliana Say which *is* on the north
     side and follows an identifiable property (No. 21 also D. & C.) refers to 'once Peter Cook's.'

19   C2 p. 50.
20   INV 174.
21   Add. Ms. 8497; R.
22   SP 113; CC AJ1; C1 pp. 123 and 125; R; Add. Mss. 2585, 23436-67, 28537.
23   CapIV/6/9; CapIV/5; Add. Ms. 11190; CapI/29/27; EpI/16/2; TD 1804; CP 46; 1851 Census; Willis, ibid, p. 67.
24   CC AK2-5, AL128; INV 137; PRO Will 376; Shippam's deeds; Willis, ibid, p. 391.
25   C2 p. 24; *SRS* 46 No. 791.
26   *SRS* 59 Nos. 151, 152, 234. This also refers to Pouke Lane going to St Andrews in the Pallant.
27   CC AY84 and 108.
28   *SRS* 46 No. 791.
29   STCI/30 p. 440; STDII Box 5; Add. Mss. 999, 2920-39, 5293, 6155, 19804; R; HT; For description of house in sale (1804) see Add. Ms. 19775; *SRS* 4 Nos. 252, 458, 460
30   CapI/27; CapI/30/2.
31   R; STDI/6 p. 25 (Elias Carter, innkeeper 1710); C1 p. 269 (encroachment); CapI/30/2 p. 356; CC N16, K7.
32   STDI/3 p. 242; R.
33   R.
34   R.
35   Add. Mss. 23029-55; HT; CCK5.
36   C1 p. 329.
37   LT.
38   LT,; MP's 414 and 714; R; Add. Ms. 23984; STDII Box 4; EpI/29/541/082; CC K1; CapI/27 (abuttal).
39   CapI/29/27; CapI/27; CapI/30/2; CapI/23/1; CC K4.
40   CapI/27 (abuttal).
41   CapI/23/1; *SRS* 36; C2 p. 70, 1754.
42   CC K2; CapI/23/1; INV 113 (Emme Clarke); R; LT; 'Anchor' referred to in abuttal of CapI/27/1 p. 299, 1583. 'George' 1664 (SPG Bishop's Transcripts: Thomas Willis at ye George, buried); *SAC* 24, LSR 1621.
43   CapI/17; CapI/23/1; CapI/30/2; C1, 8/6/1713.
44   CapI/27/1 (abuttal).
45   LT.
46   Add. Mss. 24747-74.
47   CC K2; CapI/30/2; Add. Ms. 12511; R; *SRS* 58 No 783.
48   CapIV/5; R; CapIV/6/10.
49   CapIV/6/10 (abuttal); R; STCI/21b; *SAC* 68 pp. 263-8; *SAC* 43 p. 59.
50   Willis, ibid, p. 77.

CHAPTER 11

1   CapI/23/1; *SRS* 58 No. 894; *SRS* 46 No. 580-1.
2   CapI/23/1; CapI/27; CapI/30/2; CapI/28/262; E 1897; STDI/6; TD; CC K2; HT; *SRS* 46 No. 607-9.
3   CapI/28/261; CapI/30/2; EpIII/5/1.
4   CapI/23/1; CapI/28/260; *SAC* 51 No. 28.
5   CapI/23/1; CapI/27; CapI/28/259; CapI/30/2; Census 1851; *SRS* 46 Nos. 580-1.
6   Cap IV/6.
7   CapI/23/1; CapI/27; CapI/28/258; CapI/30/2.
8   CapI/23/1; Add. Ms. 24685; STDII Box 4; STDI/3; Blaker & Peters; HT.
9   CapI/23/1; EpI/88/1; CapI/1/2; CapI/30/1; CapIII/6/10; CapIII/11/36; Add. Mss. 235-6; R; CP 12; CP 47; *VCH* Vol. 3 pp. 157/8.
10   Hannah, J.C. *The Vicars' Close and Adjacent Buildings* (*SAC* 56 pp. 56 et seq.).

11   CapI/30/2.
12   CapI/23/1.
13   CapI/23/1; CapI/27; CapI/28/257; CapI/30/2; STDI/3; CC K2-3; Loader Map 1812.
14   CapI/23/1; CapI/27; CapI/30/1; CapI/28/256; HT.
15   CapI/27; CapI/30/2; CapI/8/255; HT.
16   CapI/23/1; CapI/30/2; C1, 1704.
17   CapI/23/1; CapI/27; CapI/28/251-4; CC K4.
18   CapI/27; CapI/28/251.
19   Add. Mss. 237, 255, 8551-5; CC AY40 and 59; HT.
20   SAS B489; STDI/3; INV 32; R 244; CP 9.
21   R 6 and 252-3; CP 9.
22   CP 29.
23   CapI/23/1; CapI/28/249; CapI/30/2; *SAC* 92 p. 171.
24   LT; Censuses.
25   CapI/23/1; CapI/28/248; CapI/30/2; EpI/16/2; C1; CP 46.
26   CapI/28/247; CapI/30/2.
27   CC E1, 29/3/1797.
28   CapI/37/1.
29   CapI/23/1; Add. Mss. 8551-5, 11188; Orig. Will G22; HT; *SAS* P 491; R; *SAC* 39;
      SAC 87; CP 30.
30   Add. Mss. 12516-22 and 37583; R; C1 p. 337.
31   CapI/30/1, CC AA1, K2, K3, K7; City Rentals; STDI/2; *SRS* 74 p. 23 William Skynner
      was keeper of the Bishop's Palace *SAC* 114 p. 9.
32   *SAC* 51 Nos. 29-56; *VCH* Vol. 3 p. 100; *SAC* 68 pp. 266-8.
33   Add. Mss. 7144-99; INV 64.
34   CapIV/5.
35   CapIV/5; TD; 1851 Census.
36   JWJ: CapIV/6/16; CapIV/5; 1851 Census.

CHAPTER 12

A   John Norden 1595, John Speed 1610: see Butler, David, *The Town Plans of Chichester,*
      1595-1898 (WSCC 1972).
B   *SRS* 46 Nos. 341, 430, 451, 487-9, 524, 653.
C   Gardner Map (included in A above).
      The following references agree with those used in Fig. 12-1:
1   STAI/1A p. 52; City deeds.
2   CP 46.
3   Par44/6/2; STDI/3 p. 238; Add. Ms. 17008; LT; TD 1804.
4   Par 44/6/2; CapI/23/1; CapI/30/1; CapIII/6/7.
5   E 1780-1793; STDII Box 5; CapI/23/1 (abuttal).
6   CapI/23/1; CapI/30/1; CapIII/5a.
7   CapI/23/1 (repairs p. 75a and 103b); CapI/26/1; CapI/30/2; CapI/27/5;
      CapI/27/10; CapI/27/20; *SRS* 46 No. 341. St Richard was born in Chichester
      1244/1253. See *SAC* 121 for an article on the cult of St Richard.
8   R.
9   Add. Mss. 26458-77; EpI/16/3; CP 46.
10   CapI/23/1; CapI/27/7; CapI/29/27; SAS H 674; Petworth N22/31.
11   Add. Ms. 6156; Par 44/6/2.
12   CapI/23/1; CapI/27/2; CapI/27/5; WSCC deeds.
13   Par 44/6/5; *SRS* 46 No. 430; *SAC* 92.
14   Add. Mss. 6404 and 8493; CC N18; CapI/23/1; CapI/27; CP 39; *SRS* 46 Nos 26, 337
      and 430; *SRS* 52 Nos. 26 and 368; *SRS* 58 No. 903; For a detailed account of the fire
      of 1654 see *SAC* 123 p. 276 (article by McCann, A.).

15   City deeds; *SAC* 92.

16   CapI/23/1; CapI/26; CapI/29/27; CapI/27.

17   CapI/27/1; Add. Ms. 6156; Par 44/6/2; STDI/3 p. 148; City deeds.

18   Add. Mss. 2216-2232 and 2756; CapI/27; CapI/30/1; CapI/51/10; CapIV/5/1; E35D/5/8; STDI/3 p. 160b; CC K4; INV 23; CP 46 The Tankards and mugs found in rubbish pits of the *Fighting Cocks Inn* include stoneware quart tankards of the 18th century, some with excise stamps 'GR' crowned, creamware tankards and mugs, plain, ribbed and banded, a creamware hand-painted tankard, a buff coloured tankard with applied sprigged decoration, a small red stoneware mug with cream banding around the rim; a green, yellow and brown banded mug with copper lustre rim from the early 19th century, a moulded pint mug, Victorian (from report by S. Morgan to Director of Excavations). See also Down, A. ibid Vol. 3. For material stored in Church's Storehouse see Chapter 7.

19   E35D/5/8; A & N deeds.

20   EpI/16/2; STDI/7 p. 208; SP 758; Add. Mss. 1134-5, 16853-71 and 29710; R; LT; Phoenix Fire Insurance; P0 deeds.

21   Add. Ms. 12575; STDII Box 4; TD 1804.

22   CapIV/6/27; CapI/29/7; *SAC* 51. Re William Williams 'gardener' at this date probably meant market gardener, rather than a jobbing gardner.

23   STDI/9 p. 65; Add. Ms. 17010; R; deeds of Ref. 22 (abuttals); TD.

24   LT; CP 46.

25/7 *SRS* 46 Nos. 280, 450-1, 578; No. 25: CP 46. No. 26: CP19; No. 27: E 3433,; E 1836; LT.

28   CapIV/5.

29   CapIV/6/31; *VCH* Vol. 2 p. 46 and Vol. 3 p. 75; *SAC* 51 No. 71; *SRS* 36 For definitive article by A. McCann see *SAC* 113.

30   EpI/16/2; R.

31   Add. Ms. 2594; CapI/37/1; City deeds.

32   CapI/28; CapIV/5/4; CapI/29/7; Add. Mss. 2458 et seq.; HT; *SAC* 51 No. 71; CP 19.

33   Cap IV/5; Add. Ms. 2804; STDII Box 5; HT; *SRS* 46 No. 451; CP 46; Victoria Wine Co. deeds.

34   Add. Ms. 2585; CC AK2-6; *SRS* 36.

35   Walkers Alley. EpI/16/2; E 1902; LT.

36   Add. Ms. 7688.

37   CapI/26/1.

38   Add. Ms. 2594; CC AY4.

39   STDI/7 p. 179; CapI/23/1; 1861 Census; *VCH* Vol. 3 p. 95 (View of Frankpledge).

40   SP 198; R; *VCH* Vol. 3 p. 95.

41   Add. Ms. 6148.

42   CC AN18; City leases.

43   CC AL 214, AK2-4; City deeds.

CHAPTER 13

1   'Shambles' – an area of butchers' stalls. A lease of 1698 (E1795) refers to 'the highway leading out of Hog Lane to a lane where the butchers' shambles lately stood'. 'Vintry' – a place where wine is stored or sold. Nine butchers are listed in 1604 (CC K3).

2   Down, A. ibid *Vol. 5* p. 13 (Phillimore 1981).

3   Add. Ms. 145; CP 46.

4   R.

5   Add. Mss. 1479 and 12525; City deeds; Fire insurance.

6   STDII Box 4 (Richard Bennett gave to the poor of St George's house 4d. each); C2, 20/5/1744; *SAC* 87 (Richard Dorkyng 1492) p. 9.

7   EpI/16/2; STDI/7 p. 233; CC AA2 and K7; INV 118 (Grevett) The furnishings included: 5 beds, 40 chairs and stools, brewhouse furnace and copper, malting equipment, stone jugs, pewter dishes, flagons, porringers, silver bowls, etc.); C1; *SRS* 36, Chantry Cert No. 49; CP 46.

8   CapI/23/1; CapI/27; CapI/30/2; Add. Ms. 12521; INV 139; *SRS* 46 Nos. 618-9 and 627; *SRS* 51 No. 351.

9   Add. Ms. 22898; R; C1, 30/4/1697.

10 STCI/12 p. 85..

11 Add. Ms. 11191.

12 St Martin's Parish Register; HT.

13 EpI/16/2; CC K2; CapIV/6/4 and 6 (abuttal 1608); HT; St Martin's Parish Reg; *SAC* 50 pp. 57-9; CP 4; *SRS* 59 No. 269.

14 CapIV/6/4 and 6; CapIV/5/2; CapI/29/27; *SAC* 51 Nos. 40 and 69.

15 EpI/88/38; *VCH* Vol. 3 p. 166; *SAC* 74 p. 65.

16 Add. Ms. 19648; *SAC* 87 p. 8.

17 Add. Mss. 19648-50; *SRS* 2 p. 141 – 'Saffron plot'.

18 CapI/26; CapI/30/1; CapIII/6/21; 1851 Census; City deeds.

19 CapI/23/1; CapI/26; CP 46.

20 Par 45/8/1; E 1924 (purchase by Duke of Richmond in 1824 of Grey Friars, with buildings, garden, orchards, 10 acres of meadow adjoining); The consideration was £400 (City min. *SRS* 62 No. 362); CP 2; McCann, A. *A Short History of Chichester Greyfriars and Priory Park* (Chichester District Museum 1983); *SAC* 51 pp. 14-36; *SRS* 46 No. 303; Willis ibid, p. 355.

21 C2 p. 202.

22 *VCH* Vol. 3 p. 78.

23 Boulton, William *Amusements of Old London* (Tabard Press 1970). See also note 38 below; *SRS* 58 No. 943.

24 CapIV/5/1 p. 70; E 1795.

25 *VCH* Vol. 3 pp. 78-9; Booklet by Canon Powey, 1957.

26 CapIV/5; CapIV/6/1; R.

27 CapIV/6/1; EpI/16/2.

28 CapIV/5.

29 CapIV/6/1; EpI/16/2.

30 CapIV/6/1; R.

31 CapIV/6/1; CapIV/2/4; Add. Ms. 12549; STDIII/1f70.

32 CC AL108.

33 *SAC* 74 p. 65.

34 Add. Mss. 2792-7, 2846, 5996-9, 10920-2, 17008, 23970; CapI/27/20; CapI/29/27; CapIV/3/1; CapIV/6/3; EpI/16/2; LT; HT; 1851 Census; STCI/21, 25 and 42; STDI/6 and 7; R 329; CP 46; TD; Willis ibid. p. 109.

35 EpI/16/2; CapI/28/220; Add. Ms. 8515; LT.

36 CapIV/5; C1, 1698; CP 46.

37 CapIV/5.

38 The earliest record of the Chichester bowling green is 1633 (St Mary's Farm terrier CapIV/6/1).

39 CapIV/5; Add. Mss. 23972-81; R (abuttal).

40 R (abuttal).

41 CapIV/5; R.

42 CapIV/5; Add. Ms. 23766.

43 CapIV/5; EpI/16/2.

44 CapIV/5; LT; CP 4.

45 CapIV/6/1; R.

46 CC AY 89 – will of Richard Myldewe 3/1/1483/4 refers to 'a house nigh Lytyllondon'. See also Mawer & Stenton *Place names of Sussex* (CUP 1929) Vol. VI.

47   CC AY114. Grant by John Cressweller 20/10/1529 of 'my corner garden in Litlelondon.'
48   Add. Ms. 2585. In Warren J.L. *Chichester Past and Present* we even get this gem: 'that portion of the City now known as Little London received its name from the Virgin Queen as she said it appeared to be the busiest part of the town'.
49   CC AY78.
50   CC AY82.
51   *SAC* 87 p. 9.
52   STCI/2 p. 157.
53   *SRS* 36 p. 17.
54   STDI/2 p. 22.
55   HT.
56   John Norden's Map of 1595.
57   Add. Mss. 2585 and 5632-89; EpI/16/2; R; CC AY114; *SRS* 36.
58   HT.
59   Add. Mss. 2254 and 5632-89; R.
60   Add. Ms. 12570; E 35/1/3 et seq; CP 26.
61   Add. Ms. 8497; R.
62   Add. Ms. 23766; 1861 Census.
63   Add. Ms. 2254; *SRS* 26; Cal. Pat. Rolls Vol. 92 Pt. 4 p. 288.
64   CC AY82.
65   Add. Mss. 6127-33.
66   Add. Mss. 5672-9; R; Ballard, A. *History of Chichester* (J.W. Moore, 1898).
67   Add. Ms. 16743; CC AL72 and 124.
68   Add. Mss. 6127-33; CP 26.
69   STDII Box 5.

CHAPTER 14

1   *VCH* Vol. 3 p. 104.
2   CapI/7.
3   *SRS* 46 Nos. 495-6 and 845-8; *SRS* 59 No. 384.
4   *VCH* Vol. 3 p. 104.
5   CC K1-7.
6   EpIV/8/1-10; Par 36/1/1/1. Trippet is a wicket gate in West Sussex (see Parrish, W.D. ibid).
7   CP 5.
8   CapI/23/1.
9   CapI/27/4 No. 4 (abuttal); see terrier EpIV/8/1-10 (1635).
10   CapI/28/239; CapI/29/27; CapI/23/1; HT; INV 104.
11   C2 p. 147; Add. Ms. 23193; R; 1851 Census; HT; private deeds; CP 47.
12   CapI/28/237-8; CapI/27/2; CapI/30/2; STAI/10.
13   CapI/30/2; CapI/3/2; R; LT; *SRS* 52 No. 352.
14   CapI/15; CapI/30/2; CapI/27/4; CapI/28/111; Add. Mss. 21608-30; HT.
15   All Saints Par. Reg: R; LT; Down, A, ibid *Vol.* 2 p. 82 (Phillimore 1974).
16   Add. Mss. 7175 et seq; R.
17   Par 36/8/1-2; R.
18   STCI/42; R; LT.
19   CapI/27/1 of 1583 refers to the gateroom running out of the Pallant.
20   Hearth Tax records show 6, 5, 10, 11, 8 and 10 hearths.
21   R; City deeds.
22   Add. Mss. 5739, 17008 and 24008-14; C2, 1752 ; LT.
23   CC K3, 1604; CapI/26/6, 1597; Add. Mss. 5707-43; Harris Mss.
24   R; TD.
25   E 3746; MP 1439; CP 29.

26   *VCH* Vol. 3 p. 77.
27   C1 p255, 1713-14; Add. Ms. 1479; *VCH* Vol. 3 p. 76.
28   Par 36/8/1-2; Add. Mss. 5707-38; R.
29   STDI/6 p. 37; B1/7/1-3; Add. Ms. 5668; *SAC* 46 Nos. 320, 520 and 850.
30   *VCH* Vol. 3 p. 77.
31   CapI/27/1-2; C2 p 123; *SRS* 59 No. 342.
32   CapI/23/1; CapI/27/2; CapI/30/1; *SAC* 51 Nos. 77 and 80.
33   Field, John *English Field Names* (David and Charles 1972).
34   CapIV/6/13; EpI/16/2; Add. Mss. 8553, 38403-42; CapI/28/2: 243-4; LT; *SAC* 63 p. 145/6; *SRS* 28 p. 30.
35   EpVI/1/3 f85; CapI/23/1; CapIV/6/13; EpI/16/2; Add. Ms. 12543.
36   CapI/23/1; STAI/10.
37   CapI/23/1 (abuttal); STCI/8; EpI/16/2.
38   R; MP 346.
39   CapI/23/1; CapI/27/4; E 3746; Add. Ms. 12529; LT.
40   CapI/23/1; CapI/27/4 No. 241.
41   STCI/12.
42   STAI/3.
43   Add. Ms. 11154; R; Par 36/8/1-2; LT; HT.
44   R.
45   Add. Mss. 2596 and 23193; INV 3A; STAI/7; LT.
46   *SAC* 90 p. 193 et seq.
47   South Street abuttals; HT.
48   Victoria Wine Co. deeds.
49   Par 36/8/1-2; EpI/16/2; R; LT.
50   Plough mentioned 1661 and 1671 as abuttal to 9 West Pallant (R and Add. Mss. 7684, 12516); Add. Ms. 37583; CC K3.
51   R; HT; *VCH* Vol. 3 p. 77.
52   R; HT.
53   R.
54   Blackfriars and New Town: Add. Mss. 999, 2920-39, 6155, 19775; P.M. Inquisitions; *VCH* Vol. 2 p. 94 and Vol. 3 p. 77; Poland, *Friars in Sussex, 1228-1928* (Cambridge, Hove 1928); *SAC* 89; *SAC* 29; Pat. Rolls; *SRS* 62 No. 349.

CHAPTER 15

In this Chapter the source references coincide with the building numbers given in Fig. 15-2.

1   CapI/23/1. The 1636 account is in PR0 State Papers Domestic Chas. I Vol. 342 No. 98 (see also *SAC* 86 pp. 185-6).
2   Bell Tower, see Chapter 8.
3   CapI/18/2; HT; detailed account of repairs in 1607/8 in EpI/75/1 and 3; *SAC* 123 p. 189.
4   CapI/28/269; *SRS* 46 Nos. 1036 and 1268.
5   CapI/4/5/2.
6   CapI/30/2.
8   *VCH* Vol. 3 p. 153.
9   *SRS* 46 No. 851.
12   CapI/7 No. 83; CapI/30/2; *SRS* 46 No. 25.
13   CapI/30/2; *SRS* 46 No. 1.
14   CapI/27; CapI/30/2.
15   CapI/27; CapI/30/2.
16   CapI/26/9; *SRS* 58 No. 513.
17   CapI/27; CapI/28/272; CapI/30/2.

18   CP 30.
19   CapIII/5a; *VCH* Vol. 3 p. 153; *SAC* 56 p. 92.
20   CapIII/6/6; CapI/30/2; *SAC* 56 p. 92 et seq; *SRS* 46 No. 776.
21   CapI/30/2; R.
22   *SRS* 58 No. 727.

CHAPTER 16

1   *VCH* Vol. 3 p. 84 quoting Hay, p. 220.
2   *SRS* 59 No. 387.
3   *SAC* 51 Nos. 18 and 45.
4   *SRS* 46 Nos. 357 and 481.
5   CapI/37/1.
6   *SRS* 54 p. 171; Session Rolls 71/8.
7   PRO E179/191/410.
8   See Chapter 3, Population and Wealth.
9   STCI/12 p. 254; STDIII/1f61; STDI/3 p. 177; STDII Box 5; INV 3 and 17; CC K3-6, AJ 1-3, AK2; C1; TD; R; *SAC* 84; Down, A. ibid *Vol. 2* p. 61 and plate 9 – the bottle fragments found in garderobe Pit A4 are described as 'rim and parts of neck of a green glass bottle etc.' According to Willis, Geoffrey *The Bottle Collectors' Guide* (Bartholomew 1977), bottles were mainly imported around 1600; the use of bottles had not yet become widespread. Imported bottles at this date were thin-walled. Green wine bottles of English manufacture were strong and thick walled and probably no earlier than about 1630. The candlestick illustrated in Fig. 16-2 could be among those referred to in the 1618 inventory of Richard Keere '... Pewter candlesticks and one brass candlestick in the new kitchen'.
10   CapI/23/1f54; CapI/27; Add. Mss. 1511, 14282 and 16741-5; R; *SRS* 46 Nos. 357, 481, 497-8, 500.
11   Par 42/6/1; CP 30.
12   CapI/23/1f54 (Lavant bridge, 1402); HT; R; C1, 20/6/1693 CC AY26, 1355.
13   Add. Mss. 7711-26; R; C1; LT.
14   Add. Mss. 23239-66; Par 42/9/3; PRO Will 133.
15   Add. Mss. 23288 and 24615-7; R; CapIV/6/34; CC AL80 and 229, AJ1 and AY26.
16   *VCH* Vol. 3 p. 166; Churchwardens Presentments, 1685.
17   Add. Mss. 18359-62; CC AY2; CapI/23/1 p. 120a; PRO: PROB4/10979.
18   Add. Mss. 22235-8; CC AN14, AK1-3, AN14, AL22; C1; STDII Box4.
19   CapIV/6/36-7.
20   Add. Ms. 17007; LT; STDI/8 p. 152.
21   EpI/16/2; CC AL41, AK2-4, AY93 and 100.
22   Add. Mss. 6819-35 and 21632-7.
23   INV 155; *VCH* Vol. 2 pp. 99-100; *SAC* 92 p. 177.
24   CapI/23/1 p. 92a; *SRS* 46 Nos. 103, 151, 795 and 903.
25   Add. Mss. 20260-87; STDII Box4.
26   CC AL34, 1757; C2 p. 90.
27   CC AL5 and 153 and AK2.
28   CC AL9 and AK2 p. 354.
29   C2 p. 90; CC AK2-3.
30   CC K3-6, AJ4, AK3-4.
31   STCI/35 p. 260; EpIV/4/2; Par 42/25/1; R.
32   PRO 40 Hart, Will of Manning; *SAC* 59 Nos. 129 and 392; Field, John ibid: OE Hēafod and aecer = head or acre which form a headland. Also see Ekwall *Concise Oxford Dictionary of English Place names* (Oxford, 4th Edition, 1960) p. 229; Mawer and Stanton, ibid.
33   Add. Mss. 17008 (Fire Insurance 1797) and 32896.

34   Add. Ms. 32896.
35   C10; Par 42/9/3.
36   Add. Ms. 12513.
37   Add. Ms. 13867; CapIV/6/38; PRO Will 104 Audley (William Richards) 1632.
38   E 1896; LT; R; C12; CP 46; Newspaper report 14/2/1785 *The Chequers*.
39   EpI/16/2; CapIV (abuttal).
40   Add. Ms. 23239; CapIV; LT.
41   STDII Box4; Arnold, Cooper and Tompkins 332; CapIV (abuttal).
42   Add. Ms. 5646; Par 42/24/3.
43   EpI/16/2.
44   CapI/23/1.
45   CapI/28/233; HT.
46   LT.
47   Add. Mss. 24604-14; R; STDI/7 p. 14.
48   R.
49   CapI/28/233.
50   CapI/27/20.
51   Willis, ibid, p. 292.
52   Tithe No. 19; Shown as abuttal in 1741 (R).
53   Tithe No. 26; PRO Will 40 Harte – Edward Manning.
54   *SRS* 46; *SAC* 51.
55   CapI/17.
56   C12; QDP W157.

CHAPTER 17

1   *VCH* Vol. 3 p. 83.
2   Add. Ms. 17008; LT; TD 1804.
3   Add. Mss. 12523-4 and 12544; C1, 1704; R; Norden Map 1595.
4   Blaker & Peters; LT; EpI/16/2; R; STDI/8; STDIII/5; Waitrose deeds.
5   CapIII/4/1; CapIII/6/37; Census 1851.
6   Harris Mss; Add. Mss. 599 and 7114; Par 44/6/3; EpI/16/2.
7   CapI/30/1; CapII/4/1; *SAC* 84; *SRS* 58 No. 859.
8   C1, 1688; CC AK2 and A1114.
9   CapI/23/1; CapI/27/20; CapI/30/1; Blaker & Peters; *SRS* 58 No. 487.
10   CapIV/5; CapI/23/1 (abuttals).
11   CapI/23/1; CapI/26; CapI/27/2-4; STCI/3; R; *SRS* 52 Nos. 133 and 349.
12   Add. Mss. 6158, 10902-3, 1640 et seq; R.
13   OS 1875.
14   QDP W85; CapIII/4/1; CapI/30/1; STCI/12.
15   R; QDP W85; QDP W38; CapI/29/37; CapIII/4/1, CapII/23/1; CapI/29/28; Add. Ms. 11491; 1851 Census; Chichester Gas Act 1868 (R).
16   R; Add. Ms. 23028; 1851 Census; QDP W85, W95, W38. The demolished houses were mainly owned by George Gatehouse.
17   QDP W157; QDP W38.

CHAPTER 18

1   *SRS* 46 Nos. 442-3 – building of Henry de Lichfeld (1239, 1249), 472 – garden, land and buildings (1227-41), 439 – house of Thomas Ward (1239-56), 594 – Osilia's house (1239-47). All these are described as 'outside the West Gate'.
2   Thomas-Stanford, C. *Sussex in the Great Civil War* (Chiswick Press 1910) p. 53.
3   STCI/24.
4   R.
5   CapII/4/7; *SRS* 46 Nos. 423-5; *SAC* 92 p. 171.

6   CapI/30/1; INV 130; Dean's Rental 1673 CapII/3/1.
7   CapII/4/11; CapI/30/1; Add. Ms. 12566; STDI/3; R; Tithe Map (St Bartholomew)
     No. 34; LT.
8   Add. Mss. 921-35.
9   Add. Mss. 939 and 1515; R; LT; Fire Insurance.
10   STCI/42-3; Add. Mss. 23967-8; R; LT.
11   EpVI/1/3; LT; SAS B646.
12   EpVI/1/3; Par 38/9/1; R; *VCH* Vol. 3 pp. 161-2; *SAC* 87 p. 14 (Round church).
13   CapI/27/2 p. 247; CapII/4/2; LT; R; *SRS* 46 No. 472.
14   STDI/3 p. 57; STCI/21 p. 350; STDI/3 p. 131; STDI/3 p. 249;STCI/7 p. 84b; Add. Mss.
     10812 and 17008; PRO Will 30 Evelyn (Simon Maxse); STDI/2 p. 41 *SRS* 52
     No. 76 (1526).
15   C1 pp. 92 and 203; *SRS* 46 No. 425.
16   CapII/3/5; CapII/4/30; St Bartholomew's Tithe Map and Schedule; LT; R.
17   R; Fig. 18-5 is derived from Add. Ms. 10842.
18   Field, John, ibid.
19   *SAC* 84 pp. 28/30 (1254).
20   CapI/15 No. 5.
21   Add. Mss. 17773-4; CC AK3.
22   E 1801; R; C1; SPG Tithe 243. Campis may derive from OE Camp – enclosed land.
     Realls may mean 'land enclosed with a rail fence'.
23   City deeds 1903 – *White Hart* notice of sale.
24   St Bartholomew's Tithe No. 15 (1847); PRO Will 30 Evelyn (Simon Maxse).
25   CapI/23/1; CapI/27; CapI/4/7/48; R.
26   CapI/23 p. 75b.
27   St Bartholomew's Tithe No. 8.
28   "   "   "   No. 5; CC AY51-2.
29   CapI/23/1; CapI/27/4.
30   St Peter the Great Tithe No. 242.

CHAPTER 19

Excepting for 1 and 2 below the source references also coincide with those on
Fig. 19-1.

1   *SRS* 46 Nos. 137 and 212. The grant includes the King's Broyle and the Broyle called
     Depemers. The Bishop was Ralph II (Neville).
2   Holmes Campbell Ms. 648; R.
3   Add. Mss. 7231 and 21516; R.
4   MP 1241; Add. Mss. 10600-607.
5   Add. Mss. 6149 and 24665-82; SP 79; CP 46.
6   SP 597.
7   St Peter the Great Tithe 1846/7; R.
8   St Peter the Great Tithe.
9   R.
10   R.
11   Friary Meux deeds.
12   CapIV/6/1; CapIV/5; R.
13   CP 30; *SAC* 51 No. 33.
14   STDI/8 p. 84; CapIV/6/11; R; *SAC* 51 No. 33.
15   CapIV/6/1; SP 297A.
16   R; *SRS* 36 p. 15.
17   Add. Mss. 26478-9.
18   CC AK2, AL43 and 92; R.
19   *VCH* Vol. 3 p. 81.

20   Add. Mss. 7200-1 and 24015; R.
21   *SAC* 92 p. 175.
22   R.
23   EpVI/11; *SAC* 51 No. 33.
24   1851 Census; *VCH* Vol. 3 p. 81.
25   R; CC AN4, AL110, AK2 etc; *SRS* 36.
26   R; CapIV/6/1; *SRS* 46 No. 536.
27   CapI/29/24 – plan of Broyle farm.
28   EpIV/l0/3; CP 30.
29   Add. Mss. 23755-66.
30   Add. Ms. 26456.
3l   B1/7/30-6; Friary Meux deeds
32   R.
33   Willis, ibid, p. 275.
34   C2 (1/1742, 1/1754); Willis ibid, p. 354.
35   EpVI/51/2; Add. Mss. 34884-8; *SRS* 31 p. 128.
36   R.
37   CapI/21/6A; CapI/4/7/56; *SRS* 46 No. 212.
38   CapI/27; R; *SRS* 52 No. 133..
39   Par 42/6/1; R.
40   E 1918-9; CapI/4/7/30.

INDEX OF NAMES

People named in the book in respect of occupancy or leasing of property or following a trade. Corporate owners, e.g. Dean and Chapter, St Mary's etc., are in the General Index.

Adam 113
Adames, Charles 202
Addisone, George 23
Alcock, Laurence 152
Allen, James 66
   " John 73
   " Raphe 66
Anderson, Robert 82
Andrews 91
Angell, Joseph 60
Artwell, William 58, 202
Ashburnham, Sir Charles 110
Ashley, Laura 83
Audesbury, William de 104
Austeds, William 66, 202
Austen, Michael 108
Austin, Thomas 168
Aylwin, John 73
   " Thomas 66
Ayres, Edward 75

Bailey, John 66
Baker, Thomas 111
Baldwyn, William 14, 67
Ball, Thomas 83
Barker, Daniel 136
Barnard Lambert 148
   " Thomas 126
Barnes, John 60
Bartholomew (corn merchant) 191
Bartholomew John 44, 104
Bassett, Margaret 177
   " Richard 177
Bastow (chemist) 82
Bayley, George 152
   " John 152
Beauchamp, John de 122, 125
   " Matilda de 122
Bebitone, Godfrey 126
Beeding 92
Belchamber, Thomas 50
Benet, John 22
   " Robert 22
Benham 85
Bennett, Agnes 131
   " George 22
   " Richard 104, 209
   " Robert 131
   " Thomas 111
Benyon, Owen 108
Bereman, John 158
Bernduis 143

Betsworth, Thomas 158
Billet, Hillary 130
   " Thomas 100, 108
   " William 130
Billingley, Rev. 198
Bing, John 14
Binstead 23
Binsted, Henry 70
Bird, Edward 89
   " Thomas 89, 100, 205
Bishop 160
Black Friars 142, 150-51, 154
Blackwell, John 50
Blagden 113
Blel, John 154
Blome, Thomas 149
Blunden, John 66
Bole, Alexander 83
Boniface, Bett 198
Booker 22, 104
   " Thomas 73
Bragge, Henry 22
   " Richard 14, 70, 86, 90, 203
Braman, John, MP 154
Breades, Nicholas 144
Briant, Mark 58, 202
Briday, Joseph 82
Bridger, Thomas 51, 186
Brigham, Richard 158
   " Thomas 84
Brisenden, James 112
Broman, William 130
Brooker, Richard 51
   " William 51
Brown, John 153
Browne, Anthony 66
   " Gyles 23
Buck, John 178
Buckingham, John 86
Budden 94
Bukke, John 107
Bull, Robert 108, 150, 151, 153
Bullaker, William 108
Bullock, Henry 66, 117
Burcher, William 170
Burrard, Paul 178
Bury, Elizabeth 147
Bury, Thomas 90, 147
Butcher, Geoffrey 81
Butler, John 99
Butterly family 83, 176

Butterly Edward 52
   " George 117
   " Harvey 202
   " John 52
   " Mary 202
   " Richard 52
   " Roger 52
   " Simon (Symon) 52
   " Stephen 52
   " Thomas 51
Butterwycke, Mrs. 154

Capel, Thomas 107
Carlton, William 60, 100
Carter, Elias 206
Carver, George 149
Cawley, Robert 91
   " William 83, 91, 153, 194
Chaldecott, John 99
Chalkley 113
Chancellor 164
Chaplains Royal 161
Charge 113
Chase, John 66
Chatfield, Francis 22
Chitty, 116
   " Henry 70
   " Mary 103
Christiana (d. of Richard the Robbur) 113
Christmas, Sir Robert 110
Clarice 112
Clarissa (d. of Richard the Robbur) 113
Clark, Chandler 23
   " Emme 99, 206
Clarke, Thomas 44
   " Thomas Howe 107
Clifford 22
Clinch, Robert 50
Cobbe, Robert 149
Cobby, family 131
Cobden, William 116
Colbrooke, John 152
   " Thomas 152
Colden, Thomas 66
Collicke, Abraham 50
Collins, Charles 183
   " Humphrey 167
   " Nicholas 110
   " Richard 70, 106
   " William 91, 183

Colpat, John 112
Combes, E. 109
  "   John 112
Conyer, Richard 188
Cook (alias Sympson) John
  108
Cooke, Peter 92, 205-6
Coombes, George 147
Cooper, Charles 113, 147
  "   Richard 66, 172
Cornwall, Richard, Earl of 55
Coruleto, John de 143
Cosens, James 198
Costelow 113
Cover, Walter 108
Cowper, Johann (John) 130,
  131
Cox family 122
  "   Sarah 158
Cresweller, John 115, 203, 209
  "   Thomas 117
Cromwell, Henry (see
  Frankland) 132
Crossingham, Charles 66
  "   John 66
Curte, Simon 125
Curtis, Henry 94
Customs, Collector of 131
  "   Controller of 131
Cutten, family 59
Cyriac, Saint 83, 124

Dal, Roger la 182
Dally, Richard 73, 130
Daniel, son of Adam 113
Dautrye, John 108
David, the Goldsmith 113
Dean 162-3
Deane, Ann 174
Dear, Martha 175
Dearling, John 93, 187
Deller, George 170
  "   Richard 170
  "   William Henry 170
Dene, William atte 99
Denecombe, Robert 92
Despensyr, William le 188
Diggens (Diggons) family 100
  "   Francis 60
  "   John 60, 108
  "   Richard 183
  "   Thomas 22, 147
Dilke, Captain 152
  "   Charles Wentworth
  152
Dixon, Simon 204
Dobell, Doctor 14, 71
Dodd, Thomas 60
Dollman, Edward 50
  "   James 50
  "   Thomas 50
  "   William 50
Dorkyng, Richard 209

Dowling, William 108
Drewett 176
Drinkwater family 154
  "   Nicholas 120
  "   Richard 113
Dunstall 94
  "   John 136
Dureman, Richard 167
Durrant, Michael 71
Dyall, John 58

Ede, John 72
Edmond, Robert 154
Edmonds, Walter 108
Edney's 90, 91, 138
Edwards, Nicholas 117
Ems, William 158
English, William 92
Est, John 104
Ewens, trustees 198
Evans, Charles 202
Exton family 84, 175
  "   Richard 143
  "   Robert 152
Eyles, Roger 99
Eyre, Henry 99

Faithful, Richard 85
Farhill 82
Farndell, Stephen 202
Farnden (Farrington) Henry
  112
Farnden Joel 50
  "   Thomas 112
Farr 174
Farrendon, James 180
  "   John 50
Farrington family 110, 131
  "   Dame Elizabeth
  108, 111
Farrington (Farnden) Henry
  112
Farrington John 71, 108, 111,
  130
Farrington Sir Richard 111,
  151
Farrington Thomas 111
Field 176
Figgis, Joseph 168
Fisseburn, John de 167
Fleshmonger, William 83
Fletcher, William 138
Fogden - 108, 110
Fosbrook 135
Foster, Lucy 94
Frank, Thomas 99
Frankland, Henry (see
Cromwell) 132
Freeland, J.B. 198
French, John 71
Frend, William 106
Frye, Doctor 22

Fuggator, John 66
Fuller, Edward 130
  "   John Attree 60, 146

Gardner, Daniel 58, 202
  "   Richard 108
  "   Robert 58, 202
  "   William 73
Garland, Sharpe 167
Gatehouse, Bros. 74, 113
  "   George 213
Gervase 143
Ghost, Thomas 85, 205
Giles, Sir Walter de 104
Glasyer, Robert 131
Godman, Richard 84
Goodeve, William 202
Goodman, Richard 117
Green, Robert 73
Greenfield, Ann 183
  "   Francis 60
  "   John 87, 131 183
  "   Martha 131
  "   Richard 130, 131
Greneliffe, Henry 74
Grevatt, Eusabius 129, 209
Griffiths, Chaldecott, Drew/
  Trew 60, 91
Grigg, John 66
Gruggen family 154

Hack, Dendy and Farenden
  60
Halsted 99, 147
Hammond, Isaac 50, 172, 174,
  201
Hammond, John 50
  "   Thomas 85, 205
Hardham 113
  "   John 130
  "   Thomas 130
  "   William 167
Hargrave 22
Harmwood, Bernard 100
Harrington, James 58, 202
Harris 113
Hayley, Thomas 148
Hayllor, James 202
  "   Thomas 202
Heath, Richard 184
Heather 149
Hence 22
Henley, Thomas 117
Henty 187
Hicks (Hycks) Denys 66, 146
Hide, Henry 146
  "   John 146
Hildrup, Richard 117
Hilles, John 146
Hitchcock, Daniel 50
  "   John 50
  "   Robert 50, 96
  "   Samuel 50

Hobjohn, Edward 14
Hobson, William (see Skynner) 112
Hodgson, Jane 182
    "   William 175
Holland, Edward 112
    "   John 100
    "   William 100
Hollier, Till 131
Holmes, John 99
    "   Richard 99
Hook, Richard 123
Howard, Abraham 85
Hudson, William 14, 175
Humphrey, Stephen 91
    "   W. and E. brewers 116, 168, 183, 187
Huntington, Lady 125
Hurst, Major 14

Ives, George 106
Iveson, Thomas 123

Jacques, Charles 103
Jarrett, Lady 71
Jennings, Henry 44
John the glazier 64
John, Sir William de 149
    "   Sir, the Chaplain 154
Johnson, Dr. 154
    "   Elizabeth 170
    "   E.W. 184
    "   family 148
Jones, Hugh 85
    "   John 58, 202
Joy, James 66

Keats, John (poet) 168
Keere, Alice 167
    "   Richard 167, 212
Kelway, William 107
Kemp 90
Keneldewerde, Eua de 184
Ketelbern, Gilbert 188
    "   Roger 188
Kewell, William 66
Knight, Charles 91
Knott family 130
    "   John 132
Lacklott, Edward 96
Lambert and Norris 124
Lane, William 66
Launder, Henry 58
    "   Thomas 58
Lawrence, William 171
Leberd, Thomas 23
Leggatt, Andrew 58, 202
    "   George 58
Leigh, Henry 58
    "   Stephen 58, 202
Lewis, John 92
Lewkenor, Doctor George 73, 204

Lichfield, Henry de 213
Linfield, Richard 66
Lipper, William 136
Little, John 110
Long, Edward 117
Louff, William 117
Lovent, William 106
Lowe, John 22
Lower, Thomas 117
Lucas, Daniel 179
    "   James 141, 167
    "   Samuel 58, 202
    "   William 50
Lude, John 126
Ludeny, Emma 143
Luffe, Catherine 107
Lumley, Viscount 100
Lyon, George 183
Mann, Richard 104
Manning, Edward 174, 212
    "   Richard 99
Marcant, William 151
Marks & Spencer 91, 96, 136, 137, 138
Marner, Thomas 66
Marsh, John, jnr. 152
Martin 113
Maryng, Sir John 111
    "   Walter 111
Mason 91
Mathew, John 89
Maxse, Simon 189, 214
May, Sir Richard 132
McBrair 113
McCarogher, Dr. Joseph 72
McFarland 113
Mellish 122
Mellersh, Ann 204
Merston, Richard de 143
Michelbourne, John 108
    "   William 108
Miller, Sir John 85, 94, 99, 109
Miller, Mark 85
    "   Robert 44, 85, 205
    "   Thomas 44, 85, 126, 147
Milton, William 183
Montfort, Ralph de 130
Moore, Alice 167
    "   Thomas 167
    "   William 167
Morey, Edward 117
Morley, Sir John 131
    "   Magdalen 131
    "   Sir William 94
Mounsloe, John 50, 170
Murray, Admiral Sir George 84
Myldewe, Richard 139
Mylett, Edward 154

Nevill, Francis 161

Neville, John jnr. 103
Newman 113, 177
    "   John 50, 158
Newsham, John 50
Nightingale, Mary 17
Norman, William 72, 186
Norris, Robert 91
North, Thomas 113
Northbury 163
Norton, Thomas 204
Nycholatt, William 201

Oakshott 176
Offham, John de 110
Ollifer, William 22
Osborne, Edward 158
    "   John 198
Osilia 124, 213
Overton, William 164

Page, Francis 44, 97
    "   William 83
Painbleau, Mrs. 130
Palmer, Cowley 111
Pannell, Mary 82
    "   William 82
Parke, John 75
Parker, John 186
Parsons, Charles 59
    "   George 59
Patching, Thomas 73
Paull 176
Pay, Mary 107
Payne, John 51, 186, 201
    "   William 164
Peachey, John 92
Peck, William 58, 202
Peckham, Henry 14, 71, 113, 140, 148-9
Peckham, Jane 113
Peerman, Amos 90
    "   John 90
    "   Thomas 90
Peirce, Richard 73
Penny, William 186
Penton, James 136
Perrin, Henry 117
Petar, John 172
Phillips, Thomas 70
Phillipson 82
Philpott, Richard 186
Pikkem 22
Pilbeam, James 103, 152
Pile 82
Piper, Edward 66
Pitt, James 58, 169, 202
    "   William 58, 202
Pollard, John 108
    "   Thomas 106
Porcestre, Clement de 188
Potter, John 189
    "   William 103, 189
Powell, William 50

Powley, Mrs. 108
Prebendaries, Wiccamical 161
Precentor 163
Price, John 139
Priests, Royal Chantry 161
Prior, Ebenezer 56, 117, 118
   "   John W. 152
Pryde, Richard 107
Prykelove, Geoffrey 108
Pupet, Nicholas 104
Purchase, Arthur 125

Quennell, Robert 84

Rables, Richard 44, 83, 201
Randoll, John 66
Raper, Robert 73, 126
Rapers, solicitors 75
Ray, Master William le 73
Raymond, Thomas 50
Redman, Joseph 60
Reynolds, William 169
Rhoades, W.C. 118, 198
Richards, William 174, 213
Ridge,William 90
Robbur, Richard the 113
Robinson, James 51
   "   Jasper 51
Roill, Magdalen 50
Royle (Ryle, Roile) Henry 58,
66, 202
Royle (Ryle, Roile) John 57,
66
Roman, Mr. 103
Rowe 59
Royce, William 99, 152
Royman, William 158
Russell, John 58, 202
   "   Philadelphia 109

Sadler 140
St Cross family 124
   "   John de 81, 83, 125
Salloway, Edward 89
   "   Thomas 89
Sanden family 153
   "   Edward 96
Sandham 89
   "   Thomas 51, 186
Sandy, Capt. Robert 139
Sargeant, Edmund 116
   "   Robert 116
Saunders, Thomas 50
Say, Juliana 92, 205
Sayers, Clement 181
Scale family 50
Scott, John 182
Scute, Thomas 113
Seagrave 89, 91
Sefare, Alice 113
   "   Ralf 113, 143
Seymour, George 83

Shayer, William 59, 75
Sherrier, Giles 107
Shippams 96, 104, 141, 206
Shippam, Charles 59, 94, 184
   "   James 107
Shore, Elizabeth 75
Shore, John, Doctor 75
Sicklease, Robert de 150
Silverlock, Henry 110, 189,
191
Skynner, William (see
Hobson) 112, 207
Small, Moses 191
Smith, Alderman 84
   "   Dennis 58
   "   General Webber 198
   "   Henry 58
   "   John 176
   "   Joseph 50
   "   Richard 108
   "   William 99
   "   W.H. 82
Smithers, William 103
Smyth, William 22
Sone, Francis 178
Southcott, Edmund 76
Sowter, John 66
Spershott, James 96
Stamper, George 44, 100
   "   William 44, 93, 201
Standen, John 107
Stanney, Richard 108
Starkie, Rowland 104
Stokes 113
Stonham, Stephen 106
Stradling, Doctor 74
Stubbe, John 73
Sturm, John 113
Suter, Thomas 112
Swanne, Thomas 22
Swetapple, Richard 139
Sympson, John (see Cook)
108

Tanner, Richard 117
Taplin family 58, 124, 202
   "   Henry 58
   "   John 58
   "   William 58
Tapner 58, 138, 202
Tawke, Margaret 170
   "   Thomas 170
Tayer, Robert 60
Taylor, Thomas 147
Teesdale 198
Thomas, Margaret 163
Till, Thomas 131
Tolput family 183
Tracey, Richard 66
Trevett, Nicholas 51
   "   Thomas 126
Triggs, Richard 90 99

Trydleys, John 108
Turner, John 59
Tutte, James, MP 152
Tyacke, Nicholas 183

Undall, Lady 71
Undershill, Edmund 51, 186
   "   Johane 186
   "   John 51, 186
   "   Samuel 186
   "   Simon 51, 186
   "   Thomas 51, 186

Valentine, William 50
Vicars Choral 164
Vicars, Stephen 50
   "   William 50

Wackford, William 116
Wakefield, Thomas 51
Wale, William 22
Walker 125
Wall, Davis 92
Wanstead, Adam of 193-4
   "   Yilaria 193,
194
Ward, Thomas 213
Wareing, Rev. William 108
Warres, de la 131
Watts, John 82
   "   William 107
Wells 113
   "   David 82
West, Anthony 177
   "   Richard 117
Westdean, Ralph 99
Westmyll, Thomas 73
Weston, Henry 58
Wheeler, Thomas 66, 130
Whicher, John 117
Whitby, Oliver 71, 120
Wilkinson, Margery 85, 205
William of Arundel 113
   "   of Keynsham 104
   "   the Parson 113
Williams, Anthony 44
   "   Sir Hutchins 132
   "   Jane 72, 113
   "   J.L. 198
   "   John 72, 113
   "   William 122, 208
Williamson, Robert 112
Willis, Thomas 206
Wilmshurst 91
Winston, William 50
Wisdome, Philip 106
Wise, Stephen 72
Wittman, Thomas 66
Woolgar, Henry 51, 186
Woolvin, John 186
Woolworths 82
Wright, Elizabeth 103
Young, Richard 87

GENERAL INDEX

Aldingbourne 160
Alexander III, Pope 157
Almshouses and Poor Houses:
  Canongate 17, 163
  Cawleys 16, 194
  Dear's, Hornet 17, 175
  Heather's Charity, East
    Pallant 149
  St George's Poor
    House, St Martin's
    Lane 16, 129
  St Martin's Square 135
  St Mary in Foro 16
  St Mary's Hospital 5, 16,
    112, 133-4
  Tower St (St Peter the
    Great) 16, 118
Amberley Castle 160
Banks:
  Capital and Counties 60, 92
  Chichester 60, 99
  Lloyds 91
  London and County 60, 89,
    100
  London and Midland 100
  London and Westminster
    60
  Midland 100
  National and Provincial 60,
    91
  National Westminster 89
  Old Bank House 60, 91
  Sussex and Chichester 60,
    100
Boundaries:
  City 9-10
  Parish 8, 94
  Parliamentary Constituency
    10
  Rumboldswick 10, 176
  Wickham 10
Brick Kilns 57, 196
Bull, Nathaniel 151
Buildings and structures:
  Armoury 133
  Ashley, Laura 83
  Assembly Rooms 80, 85,
    130
  Baffins Hall 149
  Barracks 20, 27
  Bartholomew's Granary 191
  Bathing House 181
  Bell Tower 75, 113, 160
  Bin Room – Common Bread
    158, 163
  Bishop Otter College 23,
    195

Bishop's Palace 160, 162
Bishop's Prison 162
Black Boy 172
Blackfriars 5, 89, 97, 154-6
Blackhurst 117
Bookshop, 24 South Street
  68
Brinkhurst 73
Bus Station 181
Butter Market 86
Canal Basin 181
Canongate 106, 163
Castle, The 4, 132
Cathedral Store and
  workshop 51, 64, 118
Cawley Priory 153
Chain Gate 164
Chancellor's House 164
Chantry 163
Charnel House 172
Cockpit 125
Cockpit House 139
'Collins', North Street 85
Corn Exchange 55, 97, 156
Correction, House of 17,
  165, 174
Council Chamber 85
Council Offices 80, 99
County Hall 72, 115
Court House 154
Court of Guard 73
Crackenhalles 168
Custom House 72, 131, 148
Dardanelles 168
Dark Cloister 163
Deanery 68, 158, 162
Drill Hall 133, 141
Eastgate – Gatehouse 96
East Pallant House 148
East Walls Brewery 141
Ellerslie 191
Farrington House 68, 110-1
Farrs Court 174
Fernleigh, North Street 83
Fire Engine House 168
Fire Rack 83
Freemasons' Lodge 156
Friars Gate 139
Gallows, Broyle 194
Gaol 89, 96, 132
Gas Works 7, 181
Globe, West Pallant 147
Grange 118
Graveyard Wall 102
Greyfriars 6,132-3
Greyfriars, North Street
  84-5

Guildhall 85, 104, 133
Heather's Charity Building
  149
Hornet Barn 175
Horse Entry 100
Ivy Bank 156
John Edes House 68, 72
Jolly Johns 183
Library 72, 116
Lion 130
Lion Brewery 171
Literary and Mechanics'
  Institute 109, 148
Little Tea Pot 96
Lottery Office 91
Market Cross 22, 41, 70, 78,
  81, 100, 102
Market House 79, 85, 86
Marks & Spencer 91, 125,
  136-8
Metropolitan House 191
Middle Gate 75
Militia Depot 141
Millwards 99
Mulberry Court 140
Mulberry Garden 154
Museum 140
North Gate 83
Northgate House 191
North House 67, 85
North-Leigh House 56
North Lodge 193
Octagon Cottage 191
Oriel Lodge 72
Pallant Cross 23, 51, 149,
  154
Pallant House 68, 148-9
Paradise Gate 75
Parsonage House, St
  Bartholomew 184
Parsonage House, St Mary
  in Foro 100
Parsonage House, St Olav
  86
Parsonage House, St
  Pancras 167
Parsonage House, St Peter
  the Great, Tower Street
  116
Police Stations 97, 181
Poor People's Furnishing
  Shop 91
Porter's Lodge, Canon Gate
  106
Porter's Lodge, West Gate
  73, 182
Post Offices 71, 104, 110,
  122, 146

220

Pound 135, 176
Powder Magazine 133
Precentor's House 163
Procession Way 144
Punch House 68
Purchase's 82, 125
Railway Station 177
Regnum Club 109
Residentiary 163
Richmond Terrace 180
Royal Chantry Priest House
  161
Sadler's Corn Store 140
St George, Hall of
  Fraternity 99
St George's Row 129
St Martin's Hall 135
St Richard's house 116
Shambles 129-30
Shippam's Factory 59, 94-5
Smith's Buildings 181
South Gate 108
Southgate House 180
Southgate Terrace 180
Southgate Villa 180
South Lawn, West Street 74
South Street Brewery 108
Squitry Bridge 189
Stockbridge House 51, 178-9
Stockland House 97
Stone Stile 104
Subdean's Place 74
Suffolk House 140
Tannery, Westgate 56,
  185-7
Theatre 109
Theological College 183-4
Toll House, West Gate 182
Tower (Sun, Churchyard)
  Gate 75
Town Hall 85
Treasurer's House 158, 161
Tudor Cafe, East Street 99
Tudor (Tower) Cafe, West
  Street 71
Vicars' Hall and Undercroft
  60, 104, 158, 164
Vinetrow Brick Kiln Farm
  57
Waitrose 177
Walls, City 37, 69, 96
Water Conduit House 100,
  102
West Gate 73, 182
Westgate Brewery 187
Westgate House 126, 187
Whipping Post and Stocks
  80
White Oven 91
Wiccamical Prebendaries
  House 161
Willows, The, West Street
  71

Woolworths 82
Canterbury, Archbishop of
  143
Cemeteries:
  All Saints 32, 144
  Baptist, Rumboldswick, 32
  Blackfriars 33, 97
  Cathedral 32, 75
  Cawley's Almshouses 33
  Cloisters 32
  Eastgate Chapel 33
  Greyfriars 33
  Litten 33, 171
  Paradise 32
  Portfield 33
  Quakers, Rumboldswick
    32, 176
  Quakers, St Andrews 32
  Roman 31, 171
  St Andrew in the Oxmarket
    32, 91
  St Bartholomew 32, 184
  St James 33
  St Martin 33
  St Michael 169
  St Olav 33
  St Paul 33
  St Peter the Less 32
  Unitarian, Baffins Lane 33
  Whyke Lane 33
Churches, Chapels, etc.
  All Saints 4, 32, 112, 144,
    194
  Bible Christians 189
  Blackfriars 154
  Cathedral 1, 32, 64, 70,
    75-6, 157-60
  Chapel (Hornet) 176
  Congregational 102, 108
  Eastgate 33, 169
  Ebenezer 135
  Greyfriars 133
  Independent 120, 125
  Presbyterian 149
  Providence 123
  Religious Meeting House,
    Little London 138
  Quakers, Hornet 176
      "   North Street 85
      "   Priory Road 33,
    141
  Quakers, Rumboldswick 33
  St Andrews Oxmarket 4,
    32, 91-2
  St Andrew Twain Church
    149
  St Bartholomew (St
    Sepulchre) 182, 184
  St Cyriac's 83, 124
  St Faith 163
  St Georges 159
  St John's 5, 156

St Martin's 4, 33, 136
St Mary in Foro 4, 100,
  112-3
St Michaels 169
St Olav 4, 10, 33, 39, 77,
  86
St Pancras 8, 165, 169
St Pauls 33, 184, 192
St Peter in the Market 113
St Peter the Great 72
St Peter the Less 4, 32, 77,
  80, 85, 194
St Peter Sub-Castro 4, 131
Southgate Methodist 180
Unitarian, Baffins Lane 33
United Reform 108
Wesleyan Methodist, North
  Pallant 148
Wesleyan Methodist, East
  Walls 141
Civil War 8, 48-9, 67, 73, 161,
  165-8, 175, 182, 184, 190
Communications,
  Arundel 60
  Birdham 37
  Brighton 39
  Canal 7, 37, 60, 102, 177,
    181
  Coaches 40
  Dell Quay 36-7, 43, 60
  Fishbourne 36
  Midhurst 35, 60
  Oving, 166, 171
  Petworth 36, 60
  Portsmouth 36
  Postal 40, 60
  Pulborough 36
  Railway 7, 38-9, 60, 102,
    177, 179
  Repairs to streets 24, 34, 37
  Romans 34
  Rumboldswick 166
  Selsey Tramway (West
    Sussex Railway) 39, 177
  Stane Street 89
  Toll Houses and Gates 35
  Tolls, Leasing of 36
  Turnpikes 7, 34-40, 60, 77,
    102, 177, 181, 191, 193
  Water transport 34
  West Dean 35
Cornwall, Edmund, Earl of
  154
Downes, Colonel 161
Earthquakes 1
Edward I, King 154
Eleanor, Queen 154
Elizabeth I, Queen 139-40
Enclosures 8-10, 176, 188
Eugenius III, Pope 157
Fiennes, Celia 67
George I, King 82

Gubbett, Elizabeth 120
Guilds 42-3, 50
Health:
  Alleys and Courts 25, 174
  Banbury 29
  Black Death 22
  Bosham, people of 23
  Boards of Health 26
  Bristol – health 26
  Cardiff 29
  Cattle Market within walls
    24-5
  Cholera 25-6
  Chadwick, Edwin, Report of
    26
  Croydon 29
  Dover 29
  Drainage 25-30
  Dysentery 26
  Expectation of Life 26, 28-9
  Ely 29
  Fever spot 174
  Health 22-33
  House survey 28, 30
  Knossos 26
  Lavant, River 27, 29
  Leeds 26
  Leicester 29
  London 28, 30
  Merthyr 29
  Newport 29
  Norwich 26
  Paving Commissioners 23
  Plague 22-3, 33
  Quarter Sessions adjourned
    22
  Roman Baths and Water
    Supply 26
  Rugby 29
  Salisbury 29
  Sanitary Inspector 27, 29
  Smallpox 23
  Somerstown, drainage 28
  Southampton 37
  Street cleansing 22, 24, 37
  Typhoid (enteric fever) 23,
    26, 30
  Typhus 26
  Walpole, Secretary 27
  Warwick 29
  Water supply 1, 23, 25-30,
    100
  Wells, polluted 26-30
Hospitals:
  Dispensary for sick poor
    193
  Fever Hospital, St Pancras
    165
  Greylingwell Hospital 30,
    196
  Infirmary 30, 193
  Isolation Hospital 195
  Pest House 30, 195

St James and Mary
  Magdalen Hospital 30, 33,
    171
St Richards 193
Spitalfields Lane, Infectious
  Diseases Hospital 196
Henry I, King 171, 194
  ″   II   ″   16, 162
  ″   VIII ″   2
Hillary, Bishop 17
Housing:
  Brick bonds 67, 72
  Brick – 16th/17th centuries
    65-68
  Building materials, 16th
    century 61-5
  Building works – Middle
    English 65
  Chimneys – 16th century
    65
  Encroachment 68, 75, 99,
    112, 113, 148
  Fires 43, 78, 117, 134
  Foundations 61, 63
  Jetties 64-5, 68, 85, 99
  Kitchens, 16th century
    detached 61, 107, 109
  Repair records 153-8
  Roofs 61-5
  Rooms 62-3
  Slates 64
  Timber-framing 61, 63-5,
    68, 85, 87, 116, 130-31,
    174, 177
  Window glass 64, 68, 85
  Windows, obstructions 37
Inns, Alehouses, etc:
  Anchor, East Street 99
    ″   West Street 38, 70
  Angel, St Pancras 174
  Bear, Northgate 191
    ″   North Street 80, 87
  Beehive, Orchard Street 189
  Beerhouses 52
  Beerhouses Act 58
  Bell, North Street 38, 83
  Bell Inn, East Street, north
    92
  Bell Inn, East Street, south
    99
  Benham's Beer shop, North
    Street 80, 85
  Black Horse, Hornet 176
    ″   ″   St Martin's
    Street 137
  Black Horse, St Pancras 174
  Blew Anchor, West Street,
    70
  Boot Alehouse, West Street
    71
  Brewers Arms, North
    Pallant 147

Brewery Inn, Hornet 176
Bush, Hornet 176
Butchers Arms, Chapel
  Street 124
Castle, Hornet 175
Castle, West Street 73, 182
Cattle Market, Eastgate
  Square 168
Catherine Wheel, East Street
  99
Chequers, St Pancras 174
City Arms, North Street,
  east 85
City Arms, North Street,
  west 83
Coach, East Street 89
Coach and Horses, East
  Street 99
Coach and Horses, St
  Pancras 174
Coach and Horses, West
  Street 75
Coopers Arms, West Street
  74
Crab and Lobster, St
  Martin's Square 135
Cross Keys, East Street 94
Crown, North Street 52, 80,
  86
Crown, West Street 75
Crown, Beerhouse, South
  Street 104
Crown and Sceptre, West
  Street 75
Dell Hole Beerhouse 195
Dog and Duck, Hornet 175
Dog and Partridge, North
  Street 84
Dolphin, Eastgate Square
  53, 168
Dolphin, West Street 14,
  53, 70, 90
Dolphin and Anchor, West
  Street 70, 125
Dragon, North Street 85
Duke of Richmond, West
  Street 73
Eagle, West Street 71, 116
Eastgate Brewery 176
Fighting Cocks 56, 118
Fleece, East Street 89, 99
Forresters Arms, North
  Street 83
Fountain, Southgate 177
George, East Street 38, 52,
  99
George, North Street 84
  ″   West Street 70,
  125
George and Dragon, North
  Street 84
Globe, Southgate 177
Golden Cross, Little London
  138

Golden Fleece 99
Green Dragon, Broyle Road 194
Green Dragon, North Street 85
Half Mooon and Seven Stars, Hornet 176
Heart in Hand, North Street 80, 82
Hole in the Wall, St Martin's Street 129
Hope, Broyle Road 195
" St Pancras 170
Jolly Sawyer, Orchard Street 189
Kings Arms, North Street 82, 84
Kings Arms, St Martin's 138
Kings Head, North Gate 84
" " South Street 102, 110
King of Prussia, Little London 138
Lion, East Gate 52-3, 167
Little Anchor, North Street 38, 80, 87
Little London Beerhouse 138
Market Tavern, Eastgate Square 168
Marquis of Granby, West Street 71
Mason's Arms, Little London 140
Mitre, West Gate 187
New Inn, Basin Road 181
Nursery Arms, Orchard Street 189
Old Carbiniere, Hornet 176
Old Cross, North Street 85
Olive Branch, Tower Street 116
Park Tavern, Priory Road 132
Plough, South Pallant 52, 152-3
Plough and Harrow, St Pancras 174
Prince Albert, Hornet 176
" " North Street 83
Prince Arthur 141
Prince of Wales, Tower Street 116
Punch House, East Street 68, 100
Queen Anne, North Street 80
Queen's Arms, North Street 80, 82
Queen's Head, Northgate 191

Railway, Southgate 177
Railway Arms, Basin Road 181
Railway Tavern, Basin Road 181
Rainbow, St Paul's Road 192
Red Lion, St Pancras 171
" " West Street 74
Red, White and Blue, East Street 92
Richmond Arms, Canal Basin 181
Ritz, Priory Road 132
Royal Arms, East Street 100
Royal Oak, West Street, north 71
Royal Oak, West Street, south 38, 75
Running Horse, Eastgate Square 167
St Martin's Brewery, St Martin's Street 129
Sawyer's Arms, Orchard Street 189
Ship, North Street 84
" Tower Street 116
" Westgate 187
" and Lighter, St Pancras 50, 174
Spread Eagle Inn, North Pallant 52, 147-8
Star, Broyle Road 193
" East Street 100
" North Street 53, 83
" West Street 75
" and Garter, St Pancras 172
Sun, West Street 75, 116
Swan, near East Gate 96
" East Street 14, 52, 70, 89, 100, 129
Swan, West Gate 187
" Tap, North Street 80
Taverns 52
Three Kings, West Street 73
Three Tuns, Chapel Street 57, 125
Three Tuns, Westgate 187
Trumpet, St Martin's 130
Unicorn, Eastgate Square 167
Victoria, St Pancras 170
Victoria Arms, Crane Street 126
Waggon and Lamb, Westgate 187
Wheatsheaf, North Street 38, 80, 85
White Hart, East Street 38, 99

White Hart, Orchard Street 189
White Horse, Near Eastgate 96
White Horse, Northgate 191
White Horse, South Street 52, 68, 102, 112, 144
White Horse, West Gate 53, 182-3
White Swan, Near Eastgate 96
Woodman Inn, Southgate 180
Woolpack, Chapel Street 121
John, King 75
Jumièges, Abbot and Convent 130
Land, named plots:
Bishop's Garden, St Pancras 171
Bishop's Palace Garden 164
Bowling Green 133, 138
Broyle 6, 41, 55, 188, 190, 191
Campis 189
Cherry Garden 83, 124
Choristers Garden 164
Common Hall Garden 181
Conduit Mead 195
Culverhouse Close 151
" Garden 118
Deanery Farm 179
Dell Hole 195
Dog Kennel Garden 189
East Breach 194
Great Oak, Old Broyle 55, 192
Greylingwell 191, 195
Guildenfield 3, 8, 165, 176
Head Acre 174
Hop Garden 171
Horsey Down 3, 191, 193
Joy's Croft 170
Little Scuttery Field 189
Longcroft 117
Michaelmas Fair Field 196
Millpost 194
Nursery – Newmans 177
" Silverlocks 189, 191
Our Lady's/Ladies Garden 181
Paradise 158, 160-161
Parsonage Garden, North Street (St Peter the Less) 85
Penny Acre 3, 194
Perrins Field 192-3
Portfield 3, 8, 10, 55, 165, 171, 176

Potter's Field 189
Priory Park 3, 80, 132-3
Realls 189
Scuttery 188
St Mary's Great Garden
    133, 138, 139
St Mary's Farm 133, 191
Saffron Plot 118
Sickleases 150, 153
Sloe Fair Field 194
Snedge Field 193
Spitalfields 171, 196
Stanney's Hill 194
Stubbers Garden 177
Subdeans Garden 117
Westhampnett Brick Kiln
    Farm 57
Land Usage:
    Arable 9, 179
    Barns 6, 67, 114, 117, 122,
        123, 126 179
    Barley 43, 55
    Cattle 1, 41, 51, 55-6
    Downs 1, 41
    Farms 6, 7, 41, 179
    Gardens 6, 114
    Grain and Granaries 1, 41,
        55, 67, 114
    Gravel working 9
    Hop gardens 179
    Land usage 6-8
    Open fields 8
    Pasture 9, 114
    Sheep 1, 41, 55-6
    Strip system 8, 9
    Water meadow 41
    Woodland 6, 41
Lavant, River 27, 49, 51, 165-8,
    172-4, 177, 181, 186, 189
London, Chancery Lane 5,
    160
Mills:
    Appuldram, 2 salt mills 55
    City Water Mill 55
    Dell Quay Post windmill
        55
    East Breach windmill 55
    Eastgate, Horse mill 55
    Great Oak windmill 193
    King's Watermill 55, 172
    Lavant Mill 172
    Portfield, Post windmill 55
    St James, Postmill 55
        "   "   Smock mill 55
    Westhampnett Watermill
        55
    Westhampnett Windmill
        55, 99
Montgomery, Roger Earl of
    132, 165
Nevill, Bishop 195

Owners of land and property:
    Arundel, Bishop 73, 82, 85
        112-3, 116, 118
    Augmentations, Court of 5
    Bishop 5, 41, 75, 104, 122,
        188, 191, 195
    Black Friars 2, 4-6, 97, 142,
        150, 154
    Boxgrove, Church 174
        "   Priors of 130,
        143
    Bracklesham, Prebend of 5,
        41, 180-81
    Canongate Manor 110, 158
    Canterbury, Archbishop's
        Peculiar 142
    Chantries 2, 4, 109
    City, 6, 8, 9, 72-4, 82, 85-6,
        89, 91, 94, 96, 102, 108,
        126, 129-30, 136, 139-40,
        167-8, 170, 172, 176, 179,
        181, 188, 191, 193-4
    Common Fields 41
    Dean 41, 179, 182-3, 188
    Dean and Chapter 5, 6, 61,
        64, 66-8, 71, 73-6, 78, 81,
        84-5, 91-2, 98-100, 102-4,
        106-111, 114, 116-8, 123-5,
        130, 138, 143-4, 146-7, 150,
        152-3, 158, 167, 175, 180,
        184, 189, 196
    Dissolution of Monastries
        5, 82, 89, 132, 139-40, 154
    Garrison, Paymaster 169
    Grey Friars 2, 4, 5, 133
    Halnaker, Manor of 165
    Hospital of St Mary
        Magdalen and St James
        the Apostle 141
    Jumièges, Abbot and
        Convent 130
    Pagham, Manor of 143
    Poor, Guardians of 183
    Public ownership in 1750 6
    St Augustine's Chantry
        109, 182
    St George, Guild of 3, 4, 5,
        74, 82, 86-7, 89, 94, 99,
        114, 125, 129, 140, 176,
        191, 193-4
    St John of Jerusalem 140
    St Mary's Hospital 4, 5,
        72, 87, 92, 94, 100, 102,
        104, 112-3, 117-8, 122,
        124-5, 131, 134-6, 138-9,
        168, 170, 174-5, 180, 191-4
    Shulbrede Priory 126
    Somerley, Prebend of 5, 41,
        181
    Vicars' Choral 6, 66, 73, 85,
        102, 104-5, 112-3, 116,
        132-3, 150, 164, 177, 181

Parliamentary Survey 1649
    67
Peckham, W.D. 113
Philpott 67
Poor:
    Poor 12-20
    Guardians of 183
    Rumboldswick 16
Population and Wealth:
    Census 1851 18-21
    Exeter 12
    Gloucester 12
    Inflation in 16th century 13
    Lodgers 20
    Norwich 12
    Population 12-24
    Salisbury 12
    Servants 13, 20
    Shrewsbury 12
    Socio-economic classes 18-9
Quarter Sessions 118
Richard, Bishop 116
Richmond, Duke of 5, 42,
    133, 141, 172, 198-199
Roger, Earl 124
Rumboldswick 10, 57
Schools:
    Central Girls 122
    Cloisters 158
    Dame's School, South Street
        109
    Elizabeth Johnson Girls
        School, St Pancras 170
    Lancastrian 56, 118, 140-41
    Middle Class School, South
        Gate 177
    National 118, 172
    New Park Road 171
    Oliver Whitby Free 71, 120,
        189
    Orchard Street 189
    Prebendal 74
    St Margaret's, North
        Pallant 148
    Vicars' Hall 104
    Young Gentlemens
        Preparatory, St Martin's
        Street 138
    Young Ladies Boarding,
        North Street 82
Ships, William and Mary ;
    Francis of Chichester 43
Spershott, James 23, 25, 55,
    67-8, 79, 139, 192, 202
Storey, Bishop 78
Streets:
    Adelaide Road 170
    Alexandra Terrace 170, 172
    Avenue de Chartres 7, 182
    Backeslane 115
    Baffins Lane 33, 97, 149
    Basin Road 7, 58, 181

Broyle Road 35, 193-5
Canal Basin 37, 58
Canal Road 58
Canon Lane 18, 68, 102, 162-3
Cartway to Old Deanery 182
Cavendish Street 191
Chapel Street (Upper West Lane, East Lane) 3, 13, 14, 22, 26, 55, 57-8, 66, 81, 83, 120-125
Clay Pit Lane 57
Cloisters 158
Close 14, 102, 158
College Lane 30, 195
Cooper Street 112-3, 147
Cow Lane 92
Crane Street 57, 80-1, 125-6
Crooked S Lane (Shamble Alley) 85, 130, 133
Cross Street, Northgate 191
  "   "   156
Custom House Lane 130
East Pallant 57, 60, 148-9, 151-2
East Row 16, 133, 140
East Street 3, 5, 13, 14, 16, 20, 33, 43, 48, 50-2, 55-6, 59-60, 68, 89-100, 102, 136
East Walls 22, 59, 89, 139, 141
Eastgate Square 53, 167-9
Elm Grove 118
Fishbourne Road 182, 189
Fore Street 177
Franklyn Place 30, 195
Friary Lane (Street) 156
George Street, Northgate 191
George Street, New Town 150, 156
Guildhall Street 84, 131
High Street 191
Hog Lane 129
Hornet 17, 30, 52, 59, 166, 175-6
Kingsham, footway to 179
Lion Street 14, 81, 130
Little London (Savory Lane, Saffron Lane, Petty London) 13, 14, 22-3, 60, 89, 94, 138-40, 168
Market Avenue 7, 166, 181
Market House Lane 130
Mellisher Court 122
Mount Lane 182, 184
New Broyle Road 35, 193
New Park Road 50, 171-2
New Town 3, 6, 98, 142, 154-6
Newick Street 166

North Gate 52, l26, 182, 188, 191
North Pallant 52, 60, 66, 99, 146-9
North Street 3, 13-4, 16,18, 22, 38, 44, 48, 50, 52-3, 55, 60, 67-8, 77-88, 102, 114, 122, 124-5, 130
North Walls 16, 126-7, 191
Orchard Street 7, 30, 176, 182, 188-9, 191
Orchard Terrace 189
Ox Street 92
Pallant 12, 22-3, 44, 48, 50-1, 55, 66, 89, 114, 143-56
Parchment Street 191
Paris Lane 120
Petars Terrace 172
Plough Lane 152
Pouke Lane 97, 153
Priory Road 132, 139, 141
Providence Place 122
Rose Court 118
Rumboldswick Twitten 166, 175
St Cyriac's Lane 80, 83
St James 36, 166, 171
St John's Street 3, 97-8, 156
St Martin's Court 134
  "   "   Square 68, 130-31, 134
St Martin's Street (Lane) 3, 4, 14, 31, 44, 48, 55, 58, 68, 89, 129, 136-8
St Pancras Place 174
  "   "   Street 17, 30, 49-50, 52, 55, 58-9, 66, 166, 169-75
St Paul's Road 191-2
St Richard's Walk 161
Scuttery Lane 188
Sicklease Street 150
Snag Lane 166
Somerstown 28, 30
Southgate 58, 66, 177-81
South Pallant 22, 52, 108-9, 152-3
South Street 3, 6, 13, 14, 20, 22, 48, 52, 60-1, 68, 77, 100-13, 153, 157, 164
South Street Court 110
Spitalfields Lane 30
Spring Gardens 118
Stockbridge Road 36, 51
Sweeps Lane 172
Tower Street (Lower West Lane) 13, 14, 16, 26, 51, 56, 58, 64, 66, 68, 115-20
Trumpet Lane 130

Vicars' Close 164
Walker's Alley 125
Washington Street 191
West Gate 7, 14, 23, 36, 53, 56, 59, 182-6
West Pallant 102, 144-6, 154
West Street 3, 6, 13-4, 20, 22, 24, 38, 44, 48, 51, 53, 58, 60-1, 66-8, 70-77, 114, 122, 157, 164, 182
West Walls 22
Whyke Lane/Road 33, 166, 176
Woolstaplers 118
Street Lighting 39
  "   Maintenance 37
Taxation:
  Church Rate 15
  Churchwardens Rate 15
  Guardians Rate 37
  Hearth Tax 13-4, 165
  Land Tax 165
  Lay Subsidy Rolls 12
  Overseers Rate 15
  Paving Commissioners Rate 37
  Poor Rate 15-6, 55, 165
Thomas, Dean 182
Trade, Business:
Exports, Imports
  Dartmouth 51
  Devon 85
  Dorset, pipe clay 57
  Emsworth 58
  London 55
  Port Books 43
  Portsmouth 55
  Port of Chichester – Dell Quay 1, 21, 36, 43-4, 58, 64
  Protectionism 42
  Plymouth 51
  Rye 51
Trades, occupations, etc.
  Agriculture 48, 59, 61
  Ale House keepers 47, 48, 52-4, 58
  Apothecaries 60, 82, 100, 110
  Attorney 137
  Bakers 47, 48, 73, 74, 75, 99, 103, 106, 113, 176
  Banking and investment 60
  Barbers 42, 100, 104, 137
  Bark, for tanning 51
  Basket makers 47, 104, 137
  Bellfounding 51, 118
  Bells, Amberley Church 51
  Blacksmiths 42, 47, 51-2, 61, 75, 83, 85, 111, 136-7, 167, 176, 180, 182, 195

Booksellers and stationers
  42, 47, 100, 103
Braziers 47, 100
Brewers and Brewhouses
  47, 54, 70, 83, 90, 106, 108,
  110, 129, 138, 147, 154,
  167, 170-71, 177, 180, 187-9
Bricklayers 47, 62, 66, 74,
  84, 104, 132, 146
Brickmaking 57, 65-6, 151,
  165, 196
Building 47, 59
Butchers 22, 47, 48, 59, 73,
  75, 92, 94, 100, 104, 106,
  113, 130-31, 137, 143, 146,
  167, 169
Cabinet Makers 92, 113,
  137
Candle makers 51, 122,
  131, 135
Carpenters 47, 61, 74, 84,
  132, 137, 167, 176, 178, 180
Carrier 60, 84
Cattle 47, 51, 55-6
Chandlers 47, 99, 104, 111,
  167
Chemists 82, 104
Chinamen 60, 100, 103
Chirurgeon 71
Cider making 112, 154
Clockmakers 47, 169
Clothiers and clothing 36,
  41-2, 47, 59, 85, 183
Clothiers Kent 41
Coachbuilding 59, 175
Coal imports 66
Collar and harness makers
  42, 47
Coopers 47, 132, 137
Cordwainers 42, 48, 51,
  103-4, 106, 116, 151, 169,
  180
Corkcutter 100
Corn dealer 108
Court Leet –
  alehousekeepers 52
Curriers 47, 51, 92, 140,
  153, 169
Cutlers 42, 47, 99
Distiller 85
Drapers 42, 104, 113
Dressmaker 132
Dyers, dye houses 42, 85,
  118
Entrepreneurs 60
Farriers 47
Fellmongers 47, 56, 117,
  177
Felt makers 47
Fishmongers 47, 99, 103-4,
  113
Fish Shambles 22, 102

Food and drink 47
Foundry, iron and brass
  147
Fullers 41
Fruiterer 103
Gardeners 122, 176
Glaziers 42, 47, 64, 74, 104,
  132, 137, 167
Glovers 42, 51, 99, 103,
  138, 177
Goldsmiths 42, 47, 71, 73,
  99
Grain and granaries 36, 41,
  43, 48, 55, 67, 113, 117,
  187
Grocers 47, 100, 104, 107,
  111, 113, 132, 137, 167
Gunsmiths 47, 82
Hat maker 104
Helyers 61
Hoop makers 47, 51, 169
Horse gelder 176
Hosier 136
Huxters 47, 52-4, 108, 143
Inn keepers 47, 48, 52-4,
  58, 86, 87, 89, 90, 99, 100,
  111-2, 167
Ironmongers 99, 169
Joiners 42, 61, 74
Leather cutter 107
Leisure and tourism 60
Licensing records 52
Lime house 132, 134
Locksmiths 47
Malting 36, 43-5, 47-8, 55,
  82-6, 91, 99, 108-9, 113,
  116-7, 122, 125, 129, 134,
  138, 140-41, 163, 168-70,
  174, 183, 187
Medical 48, 59, 72, 73, 75,
  76, 82, 100, 113, 153, 156
Mercers 42, 47, 59, 90, 100,
  104
Merchants 42-3, 47-8, 59-60,
  64, 74, 78, 84, 86, 90, 92-3,
  96, 100, 103-4, 139, 147,
  152
Metal working 47, 51, 59,
  165
Milling 41, 47, 55, 176
Mint 41
Needlemaking 8, 47, 48-50,
  165, 170, 172, 174
Painter (house) 74, 137
  ”   (landscape etc.) 75
Parchment making 47, 165,
  174
Patten maker 104
Peruke maker 42, 104, 138
Pewterers 47
Pin maker 96

Plumbers 61, 74, 94, 132,
  138
Poll books – occupations
  59
Printers 91, 103, 137
Processors 48, 59
Regrators 52
Ropemakers 42, 47
Sadlers 42, 47, 100, 104,
  169
Salt Storehouse 147
Sawyers 61
Service trades 47, 59
Sheep 41-2, 55-6
Shoemakers 48, 51, 91, 99,
  104, 108, 132, 137, 169
Silk weavers 47
Silversmith 99, 139
Soap boilers 47, 51
Spinners 41, 172
Stays dealer/maker 103,
  169, 176
Stone cutter 130
Stone mason 172
Surveyor 130
Tailors 42, 48, 83, 85, 104,
  106-8, 137, 144, 146
Tallow chandlers 47, 51,
  103, 122, 143, 177
Tanning 42, 47, 50-1, 56,
  74, 107, 143, 178, 185-6
Tanning Havant 51, 178
Tea dealers 104, 137
Thatcher 61
Tile maker 66
Tinplate worker 100
Tiplers 47, 48, 52-4, 106,
  143
Tobacco cutter 126
  ”   pipe makers 47,
  57-8, 124, 137, 169
Tobacco pipe making –
  Atkinson, D.R. 57
Tobacconists 47, 94, 137
Trade Directory 59
Turners 47
Upholsterers 47, 92, 180
Victuallers 47, 52, 54, 85,
  92, 116
Vintners 47, 52, 60, 70, 108,
  130
Watchmaker 100, 103, 110,
  113
Weavers 42, 47
Wheelwrights 47, 99, 122,
  167, 169, 177
Whitesmiths 92, 132
Wool, woolstapling 21, 36,
  41-2, 56, 99, 122, 152
Urban IV, Pope 157
Wickham 10